"What's God's role in suffering? As a theologian and as a father who knows what it feels like to put a child's stocking back in the box instead of hanging it above the chimney with care, I've wrestled with this question in all its painful complexities. And to be perfectly honest, every answer I've ever read has left me wanting, unfulfilled, and even at times more discouraged. That is, until I read this book. This book may very well be the missing link in your understanding of God's role in human suffering—it was mine."
—*Benjamin L. Corey, author of* Undiluted: Rediscovering the Radical Message of Jesus

"An alarming number of popular Christian personalities would have us believe that human suffering—even horrific tragedy—is ordained by God. Had Jessica Kelley followed this logic as she lived out the very real personal tragedy of her four-year-old son's brain cancer, she would have been left with a resigned, passionless faith—if any faith at all. But instead of drawing faint comfort from a God whose will cannot be thwarted, Kelley drew deep strength and hope from a God whose love cannot fail. Hers is a hard-won joy that only comes from realizing that no matter how great the darkness, love prevails."
—*Janel Kragt Bakker, assistant professor, Memphis Theological Seminary*

"Nothing forces us to consider life's most serious questions more urgently than great personal loss. And nothing I have read combines more effectively than *Lord Willing?* a moving account of life's greatest loss with a serious attempt to understand how such things could happen in God's world. Whether or not one shares Kelley's conclusions, her journey will touch the heart and challenge the mind of every reader."
—*Richard Rice, author of* Suffering and the Search for Meaning

"Few and far between are the books that both grow the mind and grip the heart at the very same time. But this is precisely the gift one receives in the reading of this book. Kelley explores both the unfathomably beautiful character of our triune God and the paradigm-shattering reality of spiritual war, all through the lens of a mother's heart. A powerful book that will leave no reader untouched."
—*Paul Rhodes Eddy, professor of biblical and theological studies,*
    Bethel University

"Jessica Kelley's perspective on God's role in human suffering is fresh, her writing style is gripping, and her ability to think theologically is sound. Somehow she manages to take her questions, her pain, and her knowledge of the Bible and walk through the valley of the shadow of death with her readers. An incredibly helpful companion on the journey for anyone who has been touched by suffering."
—*Amanda A. Yoder, associate pastor, Belmont Mennonite Church*

"Kelley looks past common responses to tragedy, which ultimately fail to give hope because they are locked into a 'perfect blueprint' view of God's interaction with creation. For those who have shared a similar path, Kelley offers hope from a loving God who battles evil with us. For those who have not faced such trials, her insight frees us to look carefully at our assumptions about God and gives us understanding about how to bring hope to those in grief."
—*David Woodruff, professor of philosophy, Azusa Pacific University*

Lord Willing?

Wrestling with God's Role in My Child's Death

Jessica Kelley

Herald Press
Harrisonburg, Virginia
Kitchener, Ontario

Library of Congress Cataloging-in-Publication Data
Names: Kelley, Jessica, 1978- author.
Title: Lord willing? : wrestling with God's role in my child's death /
   Jessica Kelley.
Description: Harrisonburg : Herald Press, 2016. | Includes bibliographical
   references.
Identifiers: LCCN 2015046094 (print) | LCCN 2016002238 (ebook) | ISBN
   9781513800196 (pbk. : alk. paper) | ISBN 9781513800202 (ebook)
Subjects: LCSH: Providence and government of God--Christianity. | Theodicy. |
   Suffering--Religious aspects--Christianity. | Children--Death--Religious
   aspects--Christianity.
Classification: LCC BT135 .K43 2016 (print) | LCC BT135 (ebook) | DDC
   231/.5--dc23
LC record available at http://lccn.loc.gov/2015046094

LORD WILLING?
© 2016 by Jessica Kelley. Released by Herald Press, Harrisonburg, Virginia
   22802 and Kitchener, Ontario N2G 3R1. All rights reserved.
Published in association with the literary agency of Daniel Literary Group,
Brentwood, TN 37027
Library of Congress Control Number: 2015046094
International Standard Book Number: 978-1-5138-0019-6 (paperback edition)
International Standard Book Number: 978-1-5138-0107-0 (hardcover edition)
Printed in United States of America
Cover and interior design by Merrill Miller
Cover photo by 1stphoto/iStockphoto/Thinkstock

For orders or information, call 800-245-7894 or visit HeraldPress.com.

20 19 18 17 16   10 9 8 7 6 5 4 3 2 1

To Ian

*The words in this book wouldn't exist
without your encouragement.*

*I love you for better or for worse, in
sickness and in health. We've said those
words . . . and we've lived those words.*

Here's to creating more words with you.

····

Contents

Foreword by Gregory A. Boyd 9

Author's Note 13

Introduction 17

PART I   What Is God Like?

1. Growing Up according to the Blueprint 27

2. Wrestling with the Jesus-Looking God 45

3. An Enemy Has Done This 57

PART II   Faith under Fire

4. Naming the Darkness 77

5. Love Always Hopes 99

6. Henry's Tiger 121

7. Henry the Snowman 133

8. The Sun Was Hot That Day 149

PART III   Triumph by Testimony

9. When Worldviews Collide 169

10. Passionless Hope 193

11. The Lord Gives ... and Takes? 209

12. A Beautiful Answer 227

13. If I Could Do It All Over.............................243

Common Questions about the Warfare Worldview 253

Reflection Questions 273

Acknowledgments 279

Notes 281

The Author 295

....

Foreword

In November 2012, I read one of the most touching emails I have ever received. A young mother named Jessica Kelley explained to me that her four-year-old son had an aggressive brain tumor. Despite his parents' and doctors' valiant attempts to find a cure, Henry was now quickly approaching death. I recall getting a lump in my throat when Jessica and her husband, Ian, wondered if I would be willing to videotape a short eulogy to be played at Henry's funeral. I was humbled when Jessica explained that my sermons and books had helped her to frame Henry's tragic illness and impending death in a way that made sense and brought much comfort. More than that, Jessica wanted people attending Henry's funeral to hear a way to picture God and understand tragedies that she expected most had never heard of before.

To say I was honored is a massive understatement. To prepare my eulogy, I called Jessica a short while later. I wanted to get to know her a little bit and to learn more about the story leading up to the email. Jessica informed me that, until about a year before Henry became ill, she had assumed that everything that came to pass, including the suffering of little children, happened by divine design. Most Christians do. Somehow, even the most nightmarishly painful events supposedly fit into God's mysterious plan, and somehow all these things "glorify" him. After a period of intensive study, however, she began to embrace a very different perspective. Jessica expressed to me the tremendous comfort she derived from knowing God was not in any sense behind her precious little boy's suffering during the last year of his tragically short life. In the midst of her grieving, she was hoping some people might catch a glimpse of the true God, who is always unequivocally on the side of life and is never in any sense involved in killing.

This liberating perspective on God and suffering is a gift that Jessica now hopes to share with you through the book you're presently reading. Even as I listened to Jessica tell her story over the phone during our first conversation, I had a strong sense that there was something very special about this young woman. I was not only profoundly moved by the poignancy of her story but also stunned by the almost lyrical way she spontaneously expressed it. Yet I was even more amazed by the depth and insight of her theological reflection and by how articulately she verbalized it—and this while death was closing in on her precious son! My appreciation for Jessica's communication skills only deepened as I got to know her and Ian over the following two years, which is why I began to encourage Jessica to consider putting her story, and her theological reflections, into a book. I am absolutely convinced multitudes are going to be tremendously blessed by the fact that Jessica decided that the time had come to put her story, and her thoughts, into print.

While I knew Jessica's book would be good, I couldn't have imagined it would be as remarkable as the book you're embarking on. I have spent a good portion of my life in books, and I honestly have never encountered anything like it. I'm quite certain that, once you've finished this book, you will agree. Never have I witnessed such profound theological insights woven together with such a masterfully written narrative—a narrative that frequently borders on poetry. Jessica possesses that rare ability to take us completely inside her moving story. You are right there with her in the doctor's office, hearing the gut-wrenching news that her son has a malignant brain tumor. You are right there in the tender, sacred moment as Jessica gives her fading Henry his last bath.

Jessica blends this remarkable skill with an equally remarkable ability to take readers inside her thought process as she reflects on her experience. Her theological arguments are as compelling as her narrative is heartrending. Never have I encountered a book that made me simultaneously weep and think the way this one has.

Maybe you are currently in the midst of a tragic ordeal like the one Jessica endured, or perhaps you know someone who is. Perhaps you are still trying to make sense of a similar ordeal you experienced years ago. Or it may be that you are one of those fortunate people who have thus far been spared the nightmarish pain that life sometimes throws our way, yet you wonder why an all-good God allows or ordains such things.

Whatever your situation, I assure you: this book is a gift to you! It will not leave you unchanged. In fact, even if you are perfectly comfortable believing all tragedies are part of a glorious plan, conceived by God before the world began, you will find that this book is a gift. Even if it doesn't change your beliefs, it will stretch you, deepen you, move you, and change you for the better.

Whatever motivated you to open this book, I encourage you to read this masterpiece slowly, thoughtfully, prayerfully . . . and to have a box of tissues by your side.

Thank you, Jessica, for being willing to so vulnerably share with us your powerful story and your compelling thoughts. And may God bless you readers who now have the privilege of getting to be on the inside of both.

—*Gregory A. Boyd*
senior pastor, Woodland Hills Church

····

Author's Note

It's a sacred honor to speak into the life of another. Perhaps this honor is most significant when speaking the language of pain. This book was birthed from my pain, and it emerges as an invitation.

You are invited in. You're invited into my faith journey, and into my deepest agony. In 2012, I witnessed my four-year-old son suffer and eventually die from a malignant brain tumor. If I've told this story well, you will experience the world as I found it then. You'll meet the fear, dread, and devastation. You'll encounter the moments of peace and the pockets of joy. You'll also feel the impact of the explanations that friends and loved ones offered: those that brought comfort and those that compounded the hurt.

This book will juxtapose the death of my child against the common notion that everything happens according to "God's perfect plan." It will offer a different explanation for why we suffer, one grounded in Scripture and the life of Jesus but one that too few

Christians even know exists. I believe this message has the potential to be paradigm shattering. Many who encounter it find it faith-saving. People across the world have written me to share that their lifelong "chains" have been broken and that, for the first time, they are beginning to experience God's love.

So if you are questioning the notion that God plans, orchestrates, or specifically allows radical suffering for mysterious higher purposes, then this book is for you. If you are wondering how God can be good while indescribable pain spans the globe, then this book is for you.

On the other hand, if you are in the midst of trauma, and the notion that life is operating according to God's perfect plan is holding you together, I invite you to set this book aside. I say this because I know how deeply we need our most treasured beliefs when the roof is caving in or the floor is bottoming out. This message will be here when the dust settles.

People sometimes ask me questions like "How do I correct my neighbor's theology? She says God gave her cancer for a reason."

I offer, "You don't!"

Please hear me on this: *the victim drives the theology car.* I'm not saying that we need to endorse the beliefs of every victim. But we should note that when a crisis hits, some devastated people find the strength to draw another breath by clinging to their long-held notions about God. This truth applies no matter how wrong one may think the victim's beliefs are. So, no matter how well-intentioned we may be, robbing those folks of a source of comfort is *not loving*, to say the least. I'd ask that no one give this book to victims in the midst of trauma in an attempt to "correct" their theology.

My personal approach is to not offer explanations unless the victim is asking for them. And even when hurting folks ask about

God's role in pain, it's wise to clarify by asking, "Would you like me to offer an alternative, or just listen and support you while you wrestle?" Remember: *the victim drives the theology car*. Even beautiful answers have the potential to do harm when recklessly applied.

For those of you who will continue reading, please note that this book will transition abruptly from the deep pain of a child's death to an intense, provocative dialogue with the traditional Christian view of God's role in suffering. The transition may feel jarring, and this is intentional. It's part of the invitation. It *was* jarring to watch my son suffer and slowly die while all around me Christian songs, books, and blogs were boasting about the goodness of an all-controlling God.

In chapter 9, I dialogue directly with the work of some of the most prominent leaders in American Christianity. My intention here is to critique the *messages* while honoring the *messengers*. Throughout the process of researching this book, I grew in my love and compassion for all the leaders I challenge. They all know deep pain. Several have lost children, siblings, their health, or their physical abilities. I honor their pain and pray blessings on them and their families. Yet as my love and compassion for these folks grew, so did my conviction that their messages must be challenged. All too often their answers leave traumatized Christians questioning God's goodness and doubting his love.

I should also mention that while I am indebted to the many people who have influenced my faith journey and theological development, the opinions I put forward in this book are my own and don't necessarily reflect anyone else's.

So if you are wrestling with the traditional explanations for God's role in suffering and are seeking a Scripture-based,

Calvary-centered alternative, this book is for you. And if you have been hurt, and your suffering has been compounded by what you've been taught about God's role in your pain, this book was written *specifically* for you.

I pray it brings freedom.

—*Jessica Kelley*

····

Introduction

*H*e was within hours of death, and he did not want a
bath. Convincing a healthy four-year-old to cooperate at
bath time can be challenging, but *this* was nearly impossible. Little
Henry's brain tumor, discovered just three months earlier, had
nearly destroyed him.

He didn't want to be moved. He wanted to sleep—except for
the moments he'd wake up and screech for microwave pizza . . .
only to fall asleep chewing it.

I stroked his baby-soft cheek and looked him over. His face was
puffy, maybe from the medications. His head, larger and more an-
gular due to the brain surgery, was nestled atop a Curious George
pillowcase. He wore soft gray sweats and a T-shirt that said "Captain
Awesome." A feeding tube, yellowed from formula and medication,
protruded from his warm, round abdomen. His hair was slightly
curly, overdue for a cut, and matted with ointment for the ten-inch
scar that stretched across the crown of his head, from temple to

temple. There was another scar above his right ear, a former drainage site for cerebrospinal fluids now trapped and building. He was the disheveled beauty of an angel dying.

He was my very heart. And I wanted to bathe him.

I wanted to bathe him one last time. I wanted to wash and nurture him and be his mother for one more moment. I wanted to ease him into the plastic bath chair that I thought we'd never need. I wanted its blue mesh material to cradle him while I gently scrubbed his limbs, tenderly shampooed his hair, and carefully cleaned around his feeding tube. I wanted to wrap him in a plush towel and to lift and cradle him, just as I'd done since he was a newborn. I wanted one last chance to stare into the mirror at the cozy, dripping manifestation of my lifelong dream.

I wanted to do anything other than pray more desperate prayers. They seemed to just ricochet off him. I wanted my Henry to die clean, smelling of affection and love and lavender baby lotion.

So despite his objections, I managed to coax him into the water. Soon he was drifting off to sleep, chest-deep in soapy warmth, and I was bathing my baby one last time. But in the slow blink of a tearful eye, he was clean, lathered in lotion, and settled into bed again. Then I waited.

The hours dragged by. Visitors came and left, and family reluctantly headed to bed. My husband, Ian, and I closed our bedroom door, sat on the floor with our backs against the wall, and waited. Our baby lay just a few feet from us, but he already seemed worlds away.

Our pale gray walls deepened to charcoal as night sank into the bedroom. We nervously nursed merlot and whispered to each other against the surreal backdrop of Henry's deafening, crackling breaths. We'd slept beside his "death rattle" for five nights. It was this violent melody that became the rhythm of our lives, conducted by the rise and fall of a small chest.

As death crept closer, I remembered that someone had once told me, "Jess, if things get too intense to pray, just say the name of Jesus over and over, and that will be enough."

That cold Sunday night, we sat and we waited until the world stopped spinning. At 10:19 p.m., the roaring breaths halted. The wait abruptly ended. And one sound pierced through the crashing silence. It was my cry, breathlessly repeated: *Jesus . . . Jesus . . . Jesus.*

The problem of evil

Why did God allow such unspeakable pain? The Bible teaches that God is love. Wouldn't healing Henry have been the loving thing to do? Scripture also says that God is all-powerful. Wasn't he able to heal Henry? Did God lack the *power* or the *desire* to spare my little boy?

It's easy to see God in the brilliance of creation. His glory is apparent in a sea of midnight stars or in the striking beauty of a sunset. But why do children starve under those same magnificent skies? Where is God when people suffocate in mudslides, drown in torrential rains, or are devastated by disease? How does any of this reflect a "loving" Creator? For many, these are the most important questions in the world.

Inadequate answers to these questions cause multitudes to reject God altogether. Others simply dismiss the questions with "His ways are higher than our ways." These folks are referencing the belief that God planned or preapproved every event that humanity would experience from before the foundations of this world. This means, then, that *everything* is part of a mysterious, loving plan that glorifies God. Some call this perspective the *blueprint worldview*.[1]

Yet if all things transpire according to God's divine blueprint, doesn't that mean that Henry's death was not a tragedy but rather a manifestation of God's glory? Doesn't that imply that the horror Henry experienced was simply a display of God's mysterious wisdom? Doesn't it mean that Henry's screams better demonstrated God's love than a healing intervention?

As his mother, I would have done anything within my loving power to save Henry. Any parent would have. Are we more merciful and compassionate than God?

Do we need to "cover" for God?

Despite the fact that the blueprint worldview permeates Christian culture, no one knelt beside Henry's bed and whispered this theology into his ear. No one ruffled the dirty-blond hair on his scarred skull and said, "Everything happens for a reason," or "He won't give you more than you can handle."

No one reminded Henry in his final weeks, "He gives and takes away, blessed be the name of the Lord." As his strong, healthy body fought against the disease-ravaged circuit breaker that was his brain, no one told him, "Sometimes we just can't see what God's doing when our eyes are filled with tears."

Why would no one whisper these words to a dying child? Aren't they the phrases we proclaim from pulpits, sing in worship, and affirm over coffee with friends? If we truly believe that these blueprint clichés represent the heart of God, why do we hesitate to share *God's very heart* with little children when the darkest moments come?

Perhaps it's because we sense the ugliness in this picture of God. Perhaps it's because we feel we must "cover" for God by refraining from sharing his will and character at inappropriate times.

Yet I'm compelled to ask: If we can't share the heart of God in life's darkest moments, when is the appropriate time?

What does God look like?

What do you think God looks like? When you read the word *God*, what image pops into your head? Does God look like a bridegroom, lovestruck with humanity? Or does God look cold and removed? Someone who never changes and is unaffected by human suffering?

Does God look like a harsh judge? Someone who holds impossibly high standards and is ruthless in doling out consequences? Does God look like the tribal warrior God of many Old Testament passages? A God who commands the destruction of entire people groups (Deut 7:1-2; 20:16-18)? Who causes pregnant women to be ripped open and their little ones dashed to the ground (Hos 13:16)? Who leads parents to cannibalize their own children (Jer 19:9; Lam 2:20; Ezek 5:10; Lev 26:29)?

Does God look like a checked-out parent—someone who doesn't notice when his kids are in pain? Or is God like the father in the parable of the prodigal son—someone who patiently waits, freely forgives, and gladly restores?

Does he resemble a stately king? Someone who wouldn't dirty his hands with the sinner peasants?

Or does God look like Jesus? Someone who went around healing every disease and sickness he encountered? A person who healed the ear of his arresting officer before he prayed for his assailants' forgiveness with his final breaths? Is he a Jesus-looking God of self-sacrificial love?

Is he a mysterious combination of all the above?

Or is it possible that the heart of God is more stunningly beautiful, more pure, and more loving than most of us have ever realized?

Let's wrestle

These are the questions I'll explore in the pages to come. In part 1, I'll share my past, including the painful experiences that informed my old understanding of God. Then I'll share my discovery of a beautiful, Calvary-centered, Scripture-based picture of God.

In part 2, I'll invite you to sit by the fire. It's the fire that refined my faith—the story of Henry's diagnosis and final months. I'll share the highs and lows and attest to the supernatural instances of God's love breaking into our darkest moments. I'll reveal here how my renewed picture of God radically changed my experience of suffering.

Part 3 will examine several popular examples of blueprint theology in recent chart-topping songs, bestselling books, popular blogs, and famous speeches. I'll then explore the notion that celebrating a God who always gets his way breeds an un-Christlike resignation to evil and compounds human suffering. Finally, I'll address several common questions related to the explanation of God's role in suffering put forth in this book.

I write this with the difficult knowledge that for each of us, pain comes. Loss comes. My hope is that when your calamity comes, it will not be compounded by a crisis of faith. I'm so thankful that I started wrestling with my picture of God *before* Henry's diagnosis. As a result, I had an assurance of God's goodness when I needed it most. For those of you already suffering, I believe these pages will bring hope, healing, and knowledge of the truth of God's good character.

The challenges that follow will be new for many. I walked this earth for more than three decades before honestly examining my beliefs about God's character and the use of his power. I know what it means to get security from believing that God controls everything. But as Christ-followers, if our security is rooted in a picture of God that doesn't look like Jesus, the one who healed, served, and laid down his life . . . then shouldn't we question it?

Let's take our cue from Jacob. In Genesis, we find Jacob wrestling with God all night long on the riverbank. He refused to let go until God blessed him. And because of his tenacity, God renamed him Israel. His descendants would become the Israelites. And like Jacob, they were known for their willingness to struggle with God. In fact, the Bible is filled with heroes and prophets who were unafraid to question God and unafraid to be honest.

So let's get honest. Let's plainly examine our beliefs about God. Let's meet Henry, the little boy who talked with God in the weeks preceding his death. Twice I had the privilege of listening in. Let's be honest about Scripture—about what we do know and about what we don't. Let's refuse to let go until God blesses us with a greater understanding of his heart. Let's hit the mat, friends.

Let's wrestle.

Part I

What Is God Like?

One

Growing Up according to the Blueprint

It was supposed to be my downtime, but I couldn't sit still. Ian was at work, and things were extra quiet. The only sounds that filled our house were the muffled chirps of birds beyond the windowpanes, the hum of air conditioning, and my footsteps. I was tiptoeing to the crib once again.

I peered over the railing at seven-week-old Henry. He was curled up on his belly, knees tucked under him, rump in the air. One plump cheek was smashed against the mattress. His tiny mouth was open, drinking in those sweet baby breaths as he bulldozed through the deepest dreams. My heart swelled as I studied him—the faint red birthmark between his eyes, his creamy skin, and the chub so thick it concealed any trace of ankles, wrists, or neck.

He wasn't due for a feeding yet, but I couldn't wait any longer to hold him. I scooped him up gingerly and settled his warm, soft weight upon my chest. Then I walked back to the living room and sank blissfully onto the couch. That was the moment, with tears building and spilling, that I balanced a pen and paper carefully at my side and wrote my first letter to Henry.

Dear Henry,   9/2/08

My precious baby boy, I love you so much. I want you to know that your dad and I are so grateful to be your parents. We hope to do a good job. We're excited over every new thing you learn. This week you smiled at us for the first time! One of those smiles came at 1:30 in the morning, and I completely forgot how tired I was. I hope you will always know that no matter what, you are a huge part of my heart. I know I'll worry about you (which may drive you nuts as a teenager), and we may have some rough days (like today you had your shots and I wanted to sob along with you at the doc-tor's), but the joy you bring by just being you outweighs any diffi-culty. I pray for you constantly and hope one day you'll experience personally Jesus' love for you. You are my answer to prayer, so I know how good he can be. So far we've survived your first seven weeks of life, and I pray I'll have many, many years to enjoy you and watch you grow. I know this letter is simple and short. Most of it was written while you slept soundly against my chest. I wish I could hold onto each precious moment forever but am storing the memories in my heart. Always remember that you are very loved. We are so proud of you and so thankful for you.

Love,

Mom

God's blueprint, his perfect plan for my life, never seemed clearer than at that moment. All my life I'd heard Jeremiah 29:11: "'For I know the plans I have for you,' declares the Lord, 'plans to prosper you and not to harm you, plans to give you hope and a future.'" It had been hard to believe that this verse actually applied to me.

But apparently, God was faithful after all. Now I could taste God's goodness in the sweet kisses of my newborn. Everything had been worth it. This was my "happily ever after," the fulfillment of my dreams. I had delighted myself in the Lord, as Psalm 37:4 instructed, and he'd given me the desires of my heart.

It seemed God had worked the pain in my past together for good, just as Romans 8:28 assured he would, because I loved God and had been called according to his purpose. As I rested in the glow of young motherhood on a quiet September afternoon, it seemed that everything I'd walked through had been leading to that moment. The God who numbered the hairs on my head (Luke 12:7) and recorded all of my days before a single one came to pass (Ps 139:16) knew what he was doing all along.

That was the first time as an adult that I could really picture God as loving or good. Most of my life, I hadn't been so sure. While preachers, teachers, counselors, and Bible verses had helped me create a rough sketch of God's image, a handful of pointed experiences filled in the details. And they seemed to cast God's character as one that ranged from kind to vicious, and from trustworthy to unpredictable.

Sometimes I thought he'd always be there. Sometimes I thought he was just looking for a reason to leave. Here are the moments that most vividly illustrated God's character to me.

A joyful introduction

On February 6, 1984, in a small townhouse in southwestern Virginia, I invited Jesus into my life. I was six years old. My dad introduced us. While my definition of salvation has deepened and evolved over the years, that night I just knew that *something* happened. I remember jumping around, bursting with joy. I wanted to stay up all night and sing worship songs.

Not long after, I was baptized. While I now better understand the symbolic reasons for baptism, that day I again just knew: *something* happened. As I emerged from the water, I was swept up in supernatural peace. I felt brand new.

My relationship with God was birthed through those experiences. They were so powerful that they inspired me to begin a lifelong journey with the Creator of the universe. And at first, it all seemed so simple.

Mysterious heart

I was between my parents, perched on a metal folding chair with a yellow padded seat. We had been worshiping with our church family for about an hour. Now one couple was walking toward the podium.

Even as a young child, I knew something was wrong before they reached the microphone. Typically, this would have been a time when excited whispers and giggles of anticipation rippled through the church. Often couples who had been giving each other doe eyes and shy smiles came to announce their engagement. Sometimes young married couples came, and we'd cheer at the news of a new pregnancy.

But this time was different. This couple was married. This couple had recently announced that they were expecting a baby. This time a hush replaced the giddy chatter.

With a hand linked to his wife's, the husband resolutely approached the microphone and said, "The Lord gives, and the Lord takes away." That's when his voice cracked, and he pressed through his tears with "Blessed be the name of the Lord."

I don't remember what he said next, but it became clear that their unborn baby had passed away. I felt sick. I hadn't realized that babies could die, especially before we'd even met them. More disturbing was the fact that God was supposedly behind it. *My* God was responsible—the One who'd flooded my heart with joy and washed my body in peace.

I couldn't understand why God would make those precious parents cry, or why he would take away their little baby. As hard as I tried, my heart just couldn't make sense of it. I would never wish this pain upon them. No one I knew would wish it either.

That was the day I learned God's heart was mysterious.

Saved, saved, and saved again

No single person—no parent or teacher or preacher—is responsible for the piecemeal theology that I formed growing up. I honestly don't know where all the parts came from, but they made a rather jagged puzzle of faith.

Somewhere along the way, I heard that if a person dies with unconfessed sin, he or she would not go to heaven. I also heard that I was born with a "sin nature." Combining that with the fact that I had an annoying little brother, I figured my sins came as naturally as breathing.

As a child, I thought about this many nights before sleep came. I'd rack my brain for all my sins: gossiping, being rude to my brother, rolling my eyes at my mom. When I finished confessing the sins I remembered, I'd pray a blanket confession for all the sins I couldn't recall. Then, just to be safe, I'd say the Sinner's Prayer again.

It was the prayer I'd said at six years old. I'd confessed that I was a sinner, and that Jesus was the Son of God, who had died a sinless death to pay for my sins before he rose again. I believed this and confessed this so I could go to heaven. Originally, that had been such a beautiful moment of joy and peace. I had found tremendous security in God's love . . . until I learned about this loophole of unconfessed sin.

I also gleaned somewhere that God doesn't hear the prayers of people who are "in sin." That meant if there was ongoing sin in my life, God couldn't or wouldn't hear my prayers. He was too holy to deal with that.

This tore at my heart, especially as a teenager, because I developed an addiction to cigarettes and entered into a sexual relationship. I remember lying alone on those painful nights, filled with guilt and shame, desperate for love and forgiveness. In the tortured moments before sleep came, I would confess my sins.

Even though I was sure that cosmic eyes were rolling, I would confess the sins I remembered and the ones I couldn't. I'd recite the Sinner's Prayer, but deep down I believed that God had turned a deaf ear to me. He knew I wasn't ready to break up with my boyfriend or swear off cigarettes.

Those were the nights I believed God was a rather harsh judge.

Ruthless grace

In my high school haze of breakups and break-outs, cliques and cattiness, it wasn't unusual to see a sixteen-year-old girl crying. Even my small Christian school had its drama, and I remember the day that girl was me.

We were arguing intensely when the warning bell rang. We fought through the tardy bell too, and my angry tears formed as our classes plowed ahead without us.

I remember him being kind but uncompromising. He was patient but absolutely resolved. And my heart was breaking.

"So God sends people in remote tribal villages to hell for all eternity," I said, "if we don't reach them with the gospel before they die?"

My Bible teacher calmly reaffirmed his position, citing verses and theology that I had no answers for. It was posed as absolute truth. He was so, so certain.

But I couldn't see how this was good or loving or praiseworthy. I knew God was strict, but at least if I jumped through all the right hoops I'd be saved by his grace. Those unreached folks didn't stand a chance!

But who was I to question God? I couldn't even sway a Bible teacher. And he insisted that *this* is what the Bible clearly taught. If I rejected this piece, I had to reject the whole puzzle. My sixteen-year-old options seemed to be either accept this ugly truth about God or reject God altogether and burn eternally with those poor unreached folks.

That day I took the coward's way out. I swallowed my objections, repressed my doubts, and headed to algebra class. But deep down, I was no longer certain . . . about God *or* his grace.

That was the day I learned that God was ruthless.

Finding God on the bathroom floor

"Is she okay?" I heard a friend call softly through the door.

Lying beside a dormitory toilet at two o'clock in the morning was a strange time to think about God's foreknowledge, but that was where I found myself. Physically drunk and emotionally wasted, I had been celebrating the end of a toxic relationship.

"Yeah," another friend loud-whispered back. "I think she just had too much to drink."

She was partly right. I had had too much to drink, but I also had too little to hold on to. In my drunken stupor, I'd been trying to explain the complexity of my pain.

Freshman year had been pretty rough so far. My world was spinning. Everything was changing. I'd gone from a small Christian high school to a large public university where I struggled to fit in. The stable family I had always known was reduced to a smoldering pile of collapsed dreams. I was devastated.

My parents' marriage was gone. My home was gone. My high school friendships were gone. Varsity sports and senior trips and Friday night pizza runs with my best friend were gone. It was a big, lonely, scary world, and I felt as if I didn't belong anywhere.

To cope, I had clung to an old high school boyfriend for far too long. That relationship was extremely unhealthy, to say the least. But now, like everything else, it was gone too. And I was completely untethered, drifting through the universe with one arm wrapped around puke-splattered porcelain.

"Nothing lasts," I sobbed. "Anyone, anything, at any time can just disappear. You can't count on anything. You're never really secure."

"You probably just need some sleep," my friend slurred wisely from outside the stall.

I did need sleep. But I knew that nothing would be waiting for me tomorrow that wasn't there tonight. Nothing would be there that I could truly, permanently count on.

I think that's the moment a lightbulb came on in my dark spirit. I realized that *God* was still there.

God was still with me. He might not be pleased with what he saw, but at least he was there to see it. In fact, apparently he wasn't even surprised by it. He'd always known that on this night I would be lying on a dirty bathroom floor, vomiting and crying and utterly lost. And despite my failures, he was there.

I think that's when a new resolution took root in my heart. I'd find a way to please him. After all, God was the only constant in a world where everything can break. It was so simple and yet so profound: God was there and he loved me.

That was the night I kinda loved him too.

Bloody hands

Not long after my toilet-side epiphany, I decided to give serious Christian living another try. I joined a Christian campus organization and discovered a whole bunch of other students who'd sworn off the ways of the world.

I traded beers for lattes and committed several evenings a week to small- and large-group Bible studies. I experienced some real healing during that time. This group provided structure, positive peer pressure, and the sympathetic ears of several kind leaders.

One of the main purposes of this organization was evangelism. That was also the part that made me the most uncomfortable. They stressed a particular form of witnessing, one in which I was trained to use a tract to reach out to unbelievers. This little pamphlet provided about two minutes of shared reading material before pointedly asking people to accept or reject Christ.

It felt unnatural to share God in this manner, but I thought I was pleasing him through courage and obedience. So that spring break I participated in a missions trip that involved approaching strangers on the beach with tracts. We worked under the guise of asking folks to complete a survey, but it ultimately led to a high-stakes sales job. We were offering eternal fire insurance: a get-out-of-hell policy signed on the dotted line with the Sinner's Prayer.

I remember being surprised when I realized that, deep down, I wanted folks to reject it. The truth was, I had grown into a new misery under a legalistic understanding of God's love and grace. It was an exhausting existence that I didn't wish on anyone.

Following God meant following rules—lots and *lots* of rules. I remember thinking that unsaved folks seemed a lot happier than those of us with clipboards and tracts. Anyway, for the most part, I could handle God's abundant rules. It was the heaping doses of guilt, shame, and desperate urgency that left me flattened.

I remember one large-group Bible study that closed with an admonition. If we encountered someone unsaved after the service, we were told that we *must* share the gospel. If we failed to witness to the unsaved person and then she died in an accident minutes after our encounter, her blood would be on our hands.

I left that meeting with my heart torn and my mind reeling. God's presence seemed so peaceful when the group worshiped together. But apparently God had rigged the universe such that if I didn't hard-sell salvation, I could face horrible consequences. If I didn't attempt to convince others to follow this God, then I would bear the weight of their tortured souls forever.

Those were the days I feared that I'd live for an eternity . . . with bloody hands.

Just trust

I was struck silent by her gentle spirit. She was so kind, disciplined, and devout. She prayed faithfully every day. I remember thinking she was a better Muslim than I'd ever been a Christian.

I met this friend during the summer before my senior year of college, on a two-month trip to North Africa. As I headed home, I agonized over my understanding of God. Would my new friend spend eternity burning with the people in remote villages who I'd agonized about in high school? Was I safe simply because I was born into a culture defined by Christianity, with multiple opportunities to say the Sinner's Prayer? Would God spare me and discard her? Could he really do that?

I poured out my despair to an older friend who was also a believer. I remember searching her face for answers. I prayed she'd have some insight, something obvious that I'd missed. But she simply shrugged, smiled sympathetically, and said, "We just have to trust him."

That was the day I knew I'd never understand God.

The perfect storm

I had always been a people-pleaser. But by my senior year in college, I'd become a stone-cold approval addict. Maybe it was because I was finally making friends again and was terrified to lose that sense of belonging. Maybe it was because I was struggling to form an adult identity and was attempting to piece it together on the basis of others' opinions. I don't really know all the reasons why I was in such an unhealthy state. But I do know that I based all my worth on the judgments of those around me. I gave friends, family members, teachers, and supervisors far too much power. Most didn't even realize that they could fuel me with a nod or break me with a frown.

I felt as if the worst thing *ever* would be for someone to be disappointed in me. I couldn't bear the thought of letting anyone down, including myself and my own perfectionist standards. So no matter the request or challenge, I said yes. No matter the time or energy it would involve, I said yes. No matter the emotional toll it would take, I said yes.

I said yes to a full course load and a part-time job. I said yes to church every Sunday and three Bible studies a week—one of which I agreed to lead. I said yes when family members—still reeling from my parents' divorce—needed me. I said yes when friends who, like me, struggled with anxiety and depression needed help. And when my childhood church fell apart with an emotional violence that still makes me shudder, I was in the middle of it all, saying yes to whatever I could do to ease the conflict.

Out of obligation, I kept saying yes. Out of guilt, I kept saying yes. Out of fear, I kept saying yes. I kept saying yes and I kept saying yes and I kept saying yes.

But one night, at the beginning of my senior year, something inside of me snapped. And for a moment, I couldn't say yes anymore. I just didn't care anymore.

It had been building all day. In math class, I found that I could hardly sit still. I barely contained the urge to throw the book across the room and run. I wanted to run until I couldn't stop. Was death the only escape? My life couldn't continue, not like this. I'd been carrying the world on my shoulders, and I was falling to my knees.

Sheer exhaustion had slammed into overextension. I couldn't keep up with the pace I'd set. I'd never meet the never-ending expectations. I'd made too many commitments, and I'd surrounded myself with too many people who were deeply hurting. My days were overly packed and streaked with depression, anxiety, shame, and failure.

Finally, I had reached the breaking point. And that night it all seemed eerily laughable. My job didn't matter, my Bible studies didn't matter, my classes didn't matter, and everyone else's problems just didn't matter. Yet, within the exhilarating freedom of numbness, a small voice deep inside warned of danger. I called a friend and told her I needed help. I knew I needed help. But first, I took a walk. It didn't even matter that it was pitch-black outside.

I thought I'd pass her car, and that she'd stop to pick me up. But somehow we missed each other. I learned later that she waited at my mom's apartment, wracked with worry for over an hour until I returned.

While she was waiting, I was walking. I walked through the apartment complex, showered in light by the occasional streetlamp, unafraid in the oddly euphoric darkness. The asphalt was smooth beneath me as I sailed upon the abandon of admitted defeat.

I needed the world to stop. I needed every self-imposed obligation and expectation to fall to the floor. My life had to change or it would end me. Deep down, under the numbness, I was rooting for change. I was rooting for freedom from my own unrealistic expectations. I was rooting for an end to overcommitment and unhealthy relationships. But I needed some serious help to get there.

Before long I was sitting face-to-face with an intake counselor at the psychiatric ward of a local hospital. I remember feeling fearless, determined to get the help that I needed to start over.

I said something like "I don't want to kill myself, but I'm afraid that I *will* want to if I don't get help. I'm just going kind of numb, and I have a feeling that's dangerous."

She looked bored. "What method would you use to commit suicide?"

I blinked. "I don't *have* a method. I don't *want* to commit suicide. That's why I'm here. I want some intense help, because I'm afraid I will become suicidal if my life doesn't change immediately."

"I need a method or I can't admit you," she said dryly.

"Um, okay. I guess I'd take too many pills," I said as she scribbled something down.

Minutes later I was obediently surrendering my shoelaces, presumably so I wouldn't hang myself. Then I followed a nurse through a pair of heavy doors and into the psychiatric ward. She showed me to a room and told me to put my things up high on a shelf so the other patients wouldn't rummage through them in the middle of the night. I was left with the final instruction to leave my door open at all times so I could be constantly supervised.

I did as directed and crawled triumphantly into the hospital bed. I contemplated how I had actually, for once in my life, taken charge of what I needed. Simultaneously, I'd sent an SOS to everyone who hadn't realized I'd been drowning. I had succeeded. Life was going to be different. Starting tomorrow. Now I just needed to sleep.

But the minutes ticked away and sleep didn't come. Before long my thoughts turned to the seriously psychotic patients on the ward. I thought about unstable people wandering through my open door and going through my things. I thought about how I wanted to go home.

It was probably a total of five minutes before my feet hit the cold tile. I approached the nurse's station and had a conversation that went something like:

"Hi, I know I just got here, and I'm sorry to be a bother, but this is not what I actually need. I'd like to go back home."

"We can't release you," the nurse said. "You have to take that up with a doctor tomorrow."

"But I'm here voluntarily," I explained. "I thought I needed some really intense help, but it turns out, I don't actually have to be *here*. I want to go home now."

"You provided a method of suicide," she said calmly, "so you have to stay until a doctor can decide tomorrow whether to release you."

"But someone *made* me make up a method at intake!" I objected. "She said I couldn't be admitted without it!"

We stared at each other for a beat. Finally she said, "I can give you something to help you sleep."

It was as far as I'd get. I took the paper cup, downed the sleeping pills, and slunk back to the hospital bed. I climbed under stiff sheets and laid my head on a cold pillow. Light was spilling through the door that I wasn't allowed to close. There was an eerie, rhythmic tapping coming from the hallway. An orderly was doing his rounds, pacing the halls and checking the beds.

What had I done? I was locked up with strangers, some of whom were suffering from serious mental illness. For now, my only escape from this terrifying realization would be to sleep. Yet the chilling fact was that when those pills kicked in, I'd be even more vulnerable.

I tried to pray, but I couldn't tell if God was snarling or smiling. So I just lay in the semidarkness with tears spilling, waiting to pass out. I thought of my family, and my friends, and my shoelaces outside that bolted door.

That was the night I was completely alone.

God's blueprint

Nine years later, on a September afternoon, I listened to baby breaths against my chest and knew that everything had been worth it. I could see that God had been in control all along. The twists and turns of his broken road had been part of his perfect plan. As I stroked my baby's cheek, I knew I'd do it all over again if I had to. My son had been worth every heartbreaking second.

Though I had wanted children right away after getting married, I impatiently waited for Ian to get established in his career. My greatest desire was to be a stay-at-home mom, but that meant waiting until Ian could support us completely. I kept expecting that moment to be just around the bend, but there were so many obstacles that we hadn't foreseen. I tried hard to trust God to fulfill my heart's longing, believing that "God is always on time," even when it seemed as if his watch was running slow.

For eight years my path from marriage to motherhood was filled with roadblocks and detours. That meant that for nearly a decade I witnessed friend after friend conceive and give birth to the babies I ached for. But in that moment, with Henry nestled against me, I could finally see that "God's timing" had been perfect. Ian had a great job, and though money was tight, I was able to fulfill my lifelong dream of being a stay-at-home mom.

Perhaps it had required a broken road to lead me to this moment. After all, I could see now how the sharp twists and angry potholes had served their purpose. The pain accompanying the dissolution of my parents' twenty-year marriage had served to make me a better wife. It had helped me understand that relationships are fragile, and so for the previous eight years I'd worked my tail off to make my marriage strong. Because of that, we'd brought Henry into a stable home.

My years of anxiety and depression had been agonizing and embarrassing, but I could see now God's hand had been in them. Surely God had reigned over my nervous breakdown at twenty years old, and he was present in the extensive counseling that followed.

Though I'd begged God to simply lift my burdens, in his silence I heeded the assurance of those who reminded me that he was always in control. I did my best to accept that unanswered prayers were sometimes God's greatest gifts. And in the end it seemed that my pain, birthed from genetics and compounded by poor decisions and damaging relationships, was something of a gift. I could see that now. The grueling work toward health and healing had been for a purpose. All of it led me into the counseling profession before Henry was born. Those experiences had made me a more empathetic elementary school counselor, a more compassionate coworker, wife, and friend, and an even more thankful mom.

There were days that God's broken road had broken me, but as they say, God doesn't make mistakes. That day I cradled the breathing evidence of his perfect plans. Though the path had been painful, he'd blessed me with an amazing marriage, sound emotional and physical health, and a beautiful baby boy.

It seemed God *was* just. I'd remained faithful through the fire, and now I could reap what I'd sown. It all seemed so clear. God hadn't given me more than I could handle. He'd known what he was doing. After all, it is the crushed grape that yields the wine.

Rainbows only come after the storm. Rain is required for blessings to bloom. And despite the storms in my past, God had showered me in blessings.

And yet . . . as I gently clutched my baby, I couldn't quite shake the knowledge that the God who gives also takes away. That day I prayed that my fragile happiness would last. I prayed that the broken road was behind me. I prayed for miles and miles of smooth, fresh asphalt.

Two

Wrestling with the Jesus-Looking God

A couple of years into happily ever after, Ian and I had moved into a beautiful house in a nice suburban Atlanta neighborhood. We had two children, a plush lawn, and granite countertops. I was living the dreams I had carried as a girl . . . and I found them lacking.

I adored my babies and loved my husband, but I was exhausted. I was discouraged and frazzled, worn out by motherhood. I was struggling to care for two rambunctious kids, manage a household, and caffeinate my way through an impressive lack of sleep. I often wondered if I'd ever truly find joy.

There were moments of peace, though; small pockets of quiet perfection. Most memorable were the nights after Miriam's birth. She and I would sleep hard, cocooned away from the world and nestled in the stillness of her nursery. When squeaks of hungry protest arose from my blue-eyed angel, I would ease her out of the crib and onto my breast.

In the deepness of night, soothed by the hum of a fan, we'd settle against chocolate-colored pillows. My baby would then quietly nurse, surrounded by shadowy walls of tranquil green and silhouettes of stuffed animals. When my exhaustion threatened to darken those moments, I'd slip in earbuds and turn on a podcast sermon.

"God's eyes are red and he's angry!"

I remember the night *that* exploded in my ears. My heart, pressed against my hungry baby, started to beat faster as my stomach turned. I had that cagey feeling of wanting to run, but I knew I couldn't escape an angry God. My hands felt shaky against Miriam's sturdy frame as I pictured cosmic, red eyes glowering at us.

The pastor—I'll call him Pastor Bob—had been talking about sexual immorality. Even though I, as a married woman, had a biblical green light to have sex, I couldn't shake that vivid image of an angry God. I couldn't rid myself of the anxiety ushered in by such a famous and powerful evangelical pastor. Surely he knew God better than I did. Surely that was an accurate portrayal of God's reaction to sin, right? And heaven knew I was far from perfect. Were God's eyes red with anger toward me?

When Pastor Bob's message concluded, I started another sermon by another preacher. I'll call him Pastor Gary. I'd been listening to both pastors in the months since Miriam's birth, logging well over a hundred hours of learning between them. As I settled back into the darkness, I pondered both preachers. It was becoming clear that there was a radical distinction between them. I just couldn't put my finger on what it was.

Nagging hope

"Pastor Bob serves an angrier God than Pastor Gary," I said the next morning. Bleary-eyed Ian was standing at the counter, baby in one hand, bagel in the other. I was talking over a rerun of *Curious George*, grabbing random bites of cereal, and hovering over two-year-old Henry. He was finger-painting at the kitchen table.

"Maybe you should stop listening to Pastor Bob," Ian said, glancing at the clock.

"I guess," I said, wrinkling my nose. The thing was, I *liked* Pastor Bob. He was funny and I liked his heartwarming stories about his house filled with kids. Plus, his fire-and-brimstone picture of God was one I recognized.

Pastor Gary's picture of God was a lot less familiar. And to be honest, I was kind of suspicious of Pastor Gary. I figured there was *no way* that God was as good as he proposed. In my experience, the only people who had rosy pictures of God were people who'd lived rosy lives. After all, if God's perfect plans for them included plenty of money and family stability—more *giving* and less *taking away*—it made sense that they'd have a Pollyanna optimism about God.

"Besides," Ian said, "I really want you to listen to Pastor Gary's series on imaginative prayer." He slipped on his watch, pocketed his wallet, and held out the baby. "That'll give us something to talk about on our date night."

"All right," I said, receiving little Miriam and a quick kiss. By this point, Henry was covered in finger paint and whining for a new project. Miriam was squirming and ready for another feeding. I watched Ian wistfully as he breezed over strewn-about toys and headed toward the door.

I thought about devising a plan. I wanted nothing more than for him to skip work. I wanted him to stay home with me and our precious, screeching monkeys and piles of housework. I had to eat. I had to pee. At some point that week I had to take a shower. But before I could concoct a brilliant scheme to keep Ian home, he was gone.

The frustrating reality of my fairy-tale ending had me yearning for more. It kindled the ember of hope that maybe God *was* as beautiful as Pastor Gary claimed. Maybe I could find joy in a God like that. I wanted that to be true. But, if experience was my guide, then I'd just be chasing another empty fairy tale.

So I made a decision. Before diving back into housework, feedings, and toddler entertainment, I decided to keep listening to Pastor Gary, at least until I could discount him. I figured that with such a loving, beautiful picture of God, he'd eventually say something unbiblical. Then I could write him off for good. I would keep listening, at least until I could stamp out my stubborn heart's nagging hope once and for all.

The Jesus-looking God of the Bible

That task proved difficult, because Pastor Gary's life had *not* been a piece of cake. In fact, he'd suffered substantial abuses and trials and yet seemed authentic in his joy. He believed that God's heart for humanity was fully revealed on Calvary. And as hard as I tried to catch him saying something unbiblical, he consistently preached a picture of God that was firmly rooted in Calvary and overwhelmingly supported by Scripture.

"Did you know about Hebrews 1:3?" I demanded one evening. Ian and I were driving around, downing hot tea and cake pops from Starbucks. At this point in our marriage, dates revolved more around finishing sentences and less around the quality of our dining experience.

That night, we were cramming in as much discussion as possible before relieving the babysitter and dressing two little wiggle-worms for bed. So with just minutes left on the sanity clock and only a couple of streets from our house, we were busy hashing out our new spiritual discoveries. Turns out, podcasts are good for a marriage that desperately needs conversation *not* centered on budgets, baby food, and the consistency of toddler poop.

"Did you even *know* that verse was in the Bible, Babe?" I repeated before he'd had time to answer.

"Not before now," Ian admitted.

"I know, right?" I said. "I keep checking to make sure it's still there!" I pulled Hebrews 1:3 up on my iPhone and sighed with relief, because it was still there. " 'The Son is the radiance of God's glory and the exact representation of his being,' " I read aloud. "That verse gives us written permission—heck, even the *instruction*—to believe that Jesus *exactly, fully* represents God's heart!"

"I know," Ian said, shaking his head. "It's crazy."

I twisted toward him as we edged closer to our chaotic house. "I always thought Jesus was just *part* of God's character. I didn't know we were supposed to think of Jesus as the *exact* representation of God's heart! Do you know what that means?" I asked him.

Ian glanced over, raised his eyebrows, and smiled slightly. "It changes everything."

Wrestling with mind-blowing love

In the months that followed, I threw all my assumptions about God onto the mat and invited the Creator of the universe to wrestle.

During midnight podcasts, drives around town, and the babies' naptime, I dove headfirst into reexamining my beliefs about God.

One of my first discoveries was that there were major differences in the way I viewed God the Father and the way I viewed Jesus. I'll explain using word association. Have you ever played that game? Someone says a word and then you spit out the first word that comes to mind.

I realized that for most of my life, if someone had used the prompt *Jesus* in this game, I would have said one of the following: *Son, Savior, Lamb, crucified, obedient, gentle, innocent, loving, miracle worker,* or *scapegoat.*

If someone said *God,* I would have said: *Father, all-powerful, all-knowing, jealous, mighty, holy, in control, ruler, wrathful,* or *judge.*

Do these descriptions sound like Jesus and God are two parts of a unified trinity? Does it sound like Jesus *exactly* represents God's character? Does it sound like they've ever even met? Regardless, I had positively known all those things about God. But once I began to wrestle . . . well, I seemed to know nothing.

The gap between my concept of God and my understanding of Jesus had been radically challenged. The initial skepticism and confusion I felt turned to joy as I realized that Jesus didn't represent part of God's character but *all* of it!

I'd always thought of Jesus as submissive and God as authoritative; Jesus as innocent and longsuffering and God as wrathful and vengeful. Once I'd even heard from the pulpit, "Isaiah 53 tells us that God delighted to crush his Son. If God delighted to crush his *own Son,* imagine what he'd do to us to get our attention!" It was a strong point, one that reinforced my long-held suspicion that God was indeed scary.

So when I was deep in the throes of wrestling with my picture of God, I couldn't get Isaiah's words out of my head. I'd hear them over and over like a chugging train: "Delighted to crush . . . delighted to crush . . . delighted to crush."

With no prayer of escaping this verse, I finally tackled it head-on. I attempted to reconcile a verse about a God who is "delighted to crush" with a Jesus-looking God. I thought about the outcome if the roles had been reversed. What if God the Father had become human and Jesus had stayed in heaven? Like every Christian teen of the nineties, I asked myself: WWJD? What would Jesus do?

Well, *crushing* someone didn't fit. Jesus had healed the sick, raised the dead, and showed compassion toward his enemies. Wouldn't a Jesus-looking God do the same? The moment I began to compare this verse against the love of the cross was the moment that love pinned me!

I caught a flash of insight in the stars circling my dizzy head. God wasn't delighted to *crush*; he was delighted to be *crushed*! After all, he turned over to destruction the One with whom he is one (John 10:30), his own image (Col 1:15), his own form (Phil 2:6), his own self-revelation (John 1:18). Jesus is God in flesh (John 1:14), and *all* of God's fullness resides in him (Col 2:9). Jesus is the One who created all things (John 1:1-3) and is the heir (ultimate point) of all things (Heb 1:2), and in him all things hold together (Col 1:16-17).

I finally realized that God didn't send down a more meek, mild, and submissive version of himself. He sent an exact representation of his being!

But why?

That's when thrilling questions began to explode inside my heart. What if God delighted in walking with humanity? In ruffling the hair of toddlers wrapped around his leg? In laughing with friends, sharing a meal, and bringing healing with a gentle touch? What if he was delighted to catch a glimpse of eternity, where he will again walk among us? What if he was delighted to replace desperation with joy, pain with peace, and hopelessness with hope? What if he was delighted to defeat evil no matter the cost to himself?

After all, Scripture teaches that God *is love* (1 John 4:8, 16) and that his love was defined through the self-sacrifice of Calvary (1 John 3:16), when Christ died and rose for his enemies (Rom 5:8-10).

So perhaps God was pleased to allow the crushing, because by becoming our sin, it became his pleasure to free us from sin's bondage. Perhaps he was pleased to deliver the deathblow to the kingdom of darkness with the gentle power of love. Maybe the God of love was delighted to pour out his love to save those he loves.[1]

That's when I began to ask myself: What if every description I have of Jesus is true of God?

Pink flamingo faith

Love pinned me once, but before long I challenged God to a rematch. After all, what was I supposed to do with the other portrayals of God, the ones that didn't look like Jesus? What was I to do with the faith that I'd clumsily cobbled together?

Until that moment, my faith could be compared to Ian's old poster of a pixilated, hot pink flamingo. That print was the bane of my newlywed existence, particularly when my darling husband insisted on hanging it in our *living room*. I can't tell you how many times I glared at that hot pink bird. Yet deep down (though he'd never hear me admit it), even I found that poster somewhat mesmerizing. The grainy flamingo was composed of thousands of pixels, and each pixel was actually a tiny photo of a nature scene. The scenes ranged from animals at play to vibrant sunrises to moonlit nights. Assembled together, they formed a portrait of a gaudy flamingo.

Much as an artist had done with that poster, I used to take all the biblical depictions of God and combine them with my varied experiences of God. I'd pieced them all together in a wild photomosaic of his character. Darker pixels were portraits of a harsh judge with a pointed finger, a stately king with his nose in the air, or a ruthless warrior with spear in hand. Brighter pixels portrayed a lovestruck bridegroom named Jesus healing the sick, washing the feet of the disciples, or laying his life down for mine. I thought each piece was supposed to contribute to a complex and mysterious whole.

But then I learned that Scripture didn't support this mixed-up picture of God! The New Testament says that although God spoke through the prophets (i.e., Old Testament pictures of God), God's final word was through his Son, Jesus (Heb 1:1-3). New Testament authors compare the relationship between Old Testament laws/ traditions and Jesus to the relationship between a "shadow" and "the reality" (Col 2:16-17; Heb 10:1). While a shadow offers evidence of someone's presence, it's not a perfect reflection of who that person is. So while the Old Testament testifies to God's presence, it's *Jesus* who shows us what God is really like. Jesus is the exact representation of God's essence!

All of God's promises are realized in Jesus (2 Cor 1:20). Jesus is the fulfillment of the law (Matt 5:17), and all things were reconciled to God through Jesus' death on the cross (Col 1:19-20). Amazingly, *all Scripture* points to Jesus (Luke 24:25-27; John 5:39, 46)!

Jesus implied that his testimony outweighed everything else written about God. This is evident when he said that there was no prophet greater than John the Baptist (Matt 11:11) and then claimed his testimony carried *more weight* than John's (John 5:36)!

Jesus said that he is *"the* way . . . *the* truth . . . *the* life" and *the only way* to get to the Father (John 14:6, emphasis added). To understand God's true nature, Jesus tells us to look nowhere else but to him (John 14:7-9). He alone knows the Father best (Matt 11:27; John 1:18). John says that "the law was given through Moses; grace and truth came through Jesus Christ" (John 1:17). Jesus is the *truth* about God's character. And the pinnacle of his ministry was the moment he gave his life for this world he so desperately loves (John 3:16).

And in the light of all this, there seemed only two options: either the love displayed on Calvary fully revealed God, or it didn't. God's character does not change (Heb 13:8). So either God had always been this other-oriented, Calvary-like love, or he never was. I couldn't qualify the beauty of the cross with ugly pixels any longer. Doing so robbed God's powerful self-revelation on the cross of purpose. It belittled his teaching, ministry, and love that sacrificed unto death and triumphed through resurrection.

This thrilling realization flew in the face of my photomosaic faith. As I wrestled and studied, something in my soul chanted *yes! yes! yes!* Sadly, I had viewed God as sometimes loving and sometimes not. He was the scary conductor of my life's broken symphony. I was supposed to trust that even his harmful actions were loving. I'd seen God as aloof, harsh, and ruthless, yet his Son was gentle, empathetic, and loving. This pixilated faith had created a lukewarm loyalty toward a seemingly confusing God. I had lived in fear of the God who loved me enough to slip on humble human form, share his heart in dirty sandals, and surrender to a shameful death . . . all out of his unsurpassable love for us.

I finally reached a crystal-clear understanding that Jesus is the supreme and final revelation of God. He is the very face of God (John 14:9; 2 Cor 4:6). He is the One believers are instructed to fix their eyes and hearts upon (Heb 12:2; Col 3:1-2). He is the *exact* representation of God—a God whose essence is Calvary-like love!

And when I began to embrace that, everything changed.

His proposal

Once again I was flattened by love. I began to trust that God the Father *is* the beautiful, self-sacrificial love displayed in his Son. As a result, my faith became less about rules and more about developing a relationship with Jesus, the One to whom all Scripture points. And in seeking to define that relationship, I rediscovered one of the most prominent biblical themes concerning God's desired relationship with us: *marriage.* Scripture often refers to God as the bridegroom and the church as his bride, one who will rule with him in eternity.

I realized that God was seeking a loving, covenantal relationship with me. He didn't want me to be a robotic follower who would profess that everything she'd endured was somehow *good.* He wanted to build an authentic, honest marriage on the basis of my confidence in his character.

It was as though I could see him extending a respectful hand and inviting me off the mat and into a covenant relationship. But as I reached for him, my anger surfaced. How could I enter into a covenant relationship with someone who had caused or specifically allowed the pain in my past? Everything happens according to God's quest for glory, right? So rather than rising, I pulled Jesus back to the mat.

Yet this time, something was different. This time I understood that love encircled me. This time I felt a little safer in his embrace as we began to wrestle once more.

THREE

An Enemy Has Done This

The year Miriam was born, several other women in my Bible study were expecting. My daughter was the first to be born, and consistent with tradition, we received many casseroles. When the other moms had their babies, I, in turn, delivered lots of takeout. I never could master the art of cooking for more than one family.

I remember one afternoon that Ian and I loaded the kids in our car, swung by our favorite Italian restaurant, and then headed off to make another delivery. When we arrived, I hopped out and carried bags filled with hot pasta, buttered bread, and fresh salad to the door. The new mom invited me in with a grateful smile. She and her baby were just getting back from an appointment at the hospital. Unfortunately, there would be many more in their future. My friend's daughter had been born with a serious medical disorder.

And as we made small talk and unpacked plastic utensils, the injustice began to weigh on me.

Why was it that I could walk back to my car, open the door, and slide back into life with a healthy infant? Why weren't hospitals and feeding tubes part of our daily lives? Why didn't my baby have seizures and need surgeries?

As much as I valued my new picture of God, I couldn't seem to reconcile it with the world's pain. I still had so many questions. For instance, if God is so beautiful, why wasn't every baby born healthy? Why did a child die from malaria every single minute? Why were millions of children starving or being sold into sex slavery? Why did God's perfect plan include a tsunami that wiped out 230,000 people in 2004? Or an earthquake that killed 159,000 Haitians in 2010? What about the six million Jews and five million others who died horrific deaths in the Holocaust? Was all of this God's will? How could a cosmic heart, so filled with love, devise a plan so filled with pain? I wanted to know *why*, for millions and millions of people, life felt like a war zone.

It was at about this time that I learned about the warfare worldview. Like Jesus and the New Testament authors, this view attributes evil as coming from *wills other than God's*. It's a view that boldly asserts that the world looks like a war zone because it *is* a war zone.

Reexamining the blueprint

I had never heard of the warfare worldview, despite its history and scriptural support. I thought that since God was all-powerful, he always got his way. I'd known he was all-good, and so I assumed that everything he caused or allowed must ultimately be for good. I believed that everything transpired according to God's perfect plan. Like many Christians today, I embraced a blueprint worldview.

As I began to examine this critically, I learned that this blueprint worldview comes packaged in two different forms. The "strong" form of the blueprint worldview is the belief that God *causes* everything (even bad things) to happen. The "weak" form asserts that bad things in life don't necessarily come from God, but suggests that God *specifically allows* them to happen for a mysterious greater good.

To illustrate the difference, consider a father who is standing by the family swimming pool, watching his toddler drown. In the strong form of the blueprint worldview, the father is the one who pushes the child in. In the weak form, the father never touches the child but also refuses to intervene as his baby creeps near the edge and reaches for a bobbing beach ball. In either form, the father won't rescue the child, and instead allows the trauma to unfold for his own mysterious purpose.

I was never clear on which view represented God best, so I'd toggled between the weak and strong forms of the blueprint worldview. In retrospect, neither option seems loving or praiseworthy.

I'd also unknowingly embraced a picture of God that was heavily influenced by ancient Greek philosophy. Those folks were big on the idea that God stands outside of time, is completely unchanging, and is affected by nothing. This view lends itself well to the idea that God unflinchingly runs the world according to a predetermined blueprint that's filled with good and evil. But how do we reconcile it with Scripture?

These ideas powerfully contradict the Bible's portrayal of a God who interacts with humans and is affected by them. Many passages show a relational God who experiences emotions such as regret, disappointment, and surprise. He even changes his mind depending on the circumstance (in fact, the Bible records God changing his mind forty times!).[1] Also, the Bible demonstrates that God was so deeply affected by human suffering that he underwent the most dramatic change in history. Namely, God became human.

Spirit became flesh. He left the heavens and lived among us. He died, and he was resurrected. While God's *character* remained unchanged, he was so moved by humanity's pain that he underwent massive changes to demonstrate his love.

As I studied Scripture in light of these realizations, it became clear that hideous pain and suffering were not God's ideal. Evil wasn't part of a mysterious blueprint. Instead, I learned that God's will is not the only will that accounts for the way things are. I learned about the warfare worldview, and it forever changed the way I looked at God. This view was a profound gift packaged in four little words: love, risk, rejection, and war.[2]

The warfare worldview

Love

I learned that God's very nature and character is love (1 John 4:8, 16). It is his foundational attribute.[3] And his "love" is not some mysterious label I had to slap on everything that he supposedly did. Rather, it's a love I could recognize! This love is defined by the cross (1 John 3:16). God's very essence is enemy-loving, self-sacrificing love (Rom 5:10).

The Bible also says this loving God exists in the form of a trinity. He exists as Father, Son, and Holy Spirit. These three distinct persons compose *God*, and they have eternally existed in a loving, giving, beautiful relationship. It's this love that God desired to expand when he embarked upon creation. He wanted to extend the love of the trinity to humanity (John 17:20-26), and to offer us the chance to participate in his divine nature (Eph 1:3-14; 2 Pet 1:4). We were created out of love, because God desired to expand his love.

Yet this desire required tremendous risk.

Risk

When Ian and I decided to have a baby, we knew there were risks. Like all parents, we knew it was possible that we could conceive a child with a devastating genetic disease. It was possible we'd suffer a miscarriage. It was possible that we'd have a healthy child who would be maimed in a tragic accident or would develop cancer. It was possible that we'd have a child who would one day harm others or reject our love altogether.

We could have gotten a doll instead. After all, dolls never experience pain and can't harm anyone. Dolls can be programmed to say "I love you," no matter what the circumstances. But we didn't want a doll. We wanted to expand our love. We wanted to birth a free person who could one day freely return our love. So we took a risk.

I learned that God also desired a loving relationship with his creation, so he took a risk. It was a huge risk because once he created free agents, there was no going back. Either we would be free to choose good *or* evil, or we wouldn't truly be free. And to whatever extent we are able to choose love, we must also, to that extent, be able to reject love. Without choice, we wouldn't be making free decisions but only following instructions. If God created beings who could only choose love, he would simply be making sophisticated dolls.

Love requires choice. Choice requires freedom. Freedom involves risk.

That risk doesn't just apply to the free choices of moral agents; it applies to the created universe itself. As I studied, I became convinced that when it comes to suffering which results from natural evil like tornados, earthquakes, and disease, I could be confident that someone or something other than the God revealed in Jesus was to blame. As with moral evil, God willed for the *possibility*, not the *actuality*, of natural evil.

There was more than one way for me to arrive at this conclusion. For instance, I could follow the lead of Christians who believe that the world once perfectly reflected God's love. When humans were created, God gave them the choice to continue in this Edenic state or to reject it. Angelic beings with free will may have also been entrusted with aspects of creation. Once sin was chosen, however, the very nature of the cosmos was adversely affected and destruction was woven into the fabric of existence.

On the other hand, I could embrace the view of Christians who account for natural evil by appealing to the conditions necessary to sustain biological life. These folks point out that in order for life to exist in this physical universe, we must have elements that contain certain risks. For instance, water is required for our survival. And while water is dense enough to quench our thirst, this density can also cause us to drown. Similarly, fire warms our hands and cooks our food, but it can also bring our buildings and bodies to ash. In the same way, the atmospheric conditions that enable us to live can also spawn deadly tornados and hurricanes. These phenomena aren't inherently evil or good. They arise from dynamic, free processes that are necessary yet contain unavoidable risks.

Regardless of whether I attributed natural evil to sin, or to the intrinsic risks of sustaining biological life (or some combination thereof), I arrived at the same place. I arrived *here*: in a majestic, chaotic universe where God's will is not the only will that determines what occurs.[4]

I came to realize that God wills *the* choice to sin but not *our* choice to sin. God wills the existence of biological life but not for a tornado to kill someone. In other words, when it comes to radical suffering, God willed the *possibility*, not the *actuality*. The possibility is necessary for freely chosen love. But when the possibility of evil is actualized, someone or something other than God is to blame. This is not to say that there's a demon behind every tumor or tornado, but simply that there are forces in the universe, other than God's will, that affect what comes to pass. In this way, I could always attribute moral and natural evil to *wills other than God's*.

Of course, an all-knowing God would have perfectly anticipated every possible instance of his will being thwarted and would have a plan in place should that occur. But God is love, and love always hopes (1 Cor 13:7). I began to believe that God took a hope-filled risk.

It was a risk he subjected himself to when he took on human form, experiencing firsthand the pain and vulnerability this life entails. It was a risk he deemed worth the cost. He began with a beautiful ending in mind. God created this world and filled it with free agents, desiring for them to know abundant life and to choose to walk in love.

His heart was like Ian's and mine when we decided to start a family. It was aligned with every parent who thoughtfully chooses to have a child. In the end, God felt that the opportunity to expand his love was worth even the risk of rejection.

Rejection

The rejection of God's love is powerfully present in Scripture. For example, there are verses about angels who rebelled (2 Pet 2:4; Jude 1:6; Rev 12:7-9) and there's the account of Adam and Eve's rebellion (Gen 3:6). Finally, one of the core beliefs of the Christian faith is that we've *all* sinned (Rom 3:23; 2 Chron 6:36) and turned away from God (Isa 53:6). To declare otherwise is to deceive ourselves (1 John 1:8).

When we reject God's love, we affect one another in countless ways. For instance, we've all been hurt by moral evil—someone lies to us, steals from us, or harms us physically. Yet sin influences natural processes as well. For instance, a corporation that dumps harmful chemicals into the water supply can produce results that come packaged in "natural" processes, such as sickness, cancer, and early death. In addition, the harm we've done to our environment can intensify and exacerbate the effects of natural disasters (for example, the Dust Bowl of the 1930s). Likewise, Hurricane Katrina highlights how inadequate preparation for and response to natural disasters can worsen the outcome, often causing the greatest harm to the poor and vulnerable. The bottom line is that, given the interrelatedness of humans and their environment, the boundary between natural and moral evil is hazy.[5]

As I reflected on our present state and considered the biblical passages above, I realized that life today isn't reflecting God's perfect plan for each of us. Everything about Eden pointed to God's good desires for humanity and his hope of expanding his love. In contrast, much of the world today points to a *rejection* of God's love. The world today points to war.

War

God is at war. I was surprised to find a warfare theme running throughout the entire Bible. God is continually battling forces of evil. Old Testament authors referenced these evil forces as hostile waters or cosmic creatures (Job 3:8; 9:13; 26:12; Ps 87:4; 89:10; Isa 27:1; 51:9). And the biblical authors praised God's power to defeat them (Job 26:12-13; Ps 74:13-14).[6]

Jesus and the New Testament authors speak explicitly about struggling against cosmic powers and spiritual forces of evil (Eph 6:12). Depending on which Bible translation I picked up, I could find Jesus referring to Satan as the "ruler" or "prince" or "chief" of this world (John 12:31; 14:30; 16:11). Satan is also described as "the god of this age" and "the ruler of the kingdom of the air" (2 Cor 4:4; Eph 2:2). In fact, Scripture warns that "the whole world is under the control of the evil one" (1 John 5:19).

Jesus seemed well aware of this dynamic during his ministry. We're told that Satan once offered Jesus all the kingdoms of the world. And Jesus never denied that they were Satan's to give (Luke 4:5-8)!

When it comes to natural processes that cause harm, Jesus never taught his followers that mechanisms like disease and deadly weather were God's ideal. Instead, Jesus *battled* against them. The New Testament repeatedly demonstrates Jesus rebuking sickness and disease (Mark 9:25; Luke 11:14, 13:11-16; Acts 10:38) and even rebuking a violent storm at sea (Luke 8:24). By doing this he demonstrated that when nature is destroying God's beloved creatures, we are not witnessing God's perfect plan in action.

Scripture portrays again and again the truth that God is not sending or even specifically allowing evil; instead, God is battling against it. Whenever we experience radical suffering, we're not experiencing God's best for us. Rather, we're experiencing something he opposes! Our unique suffering results from any number of infinite variables in this complex universe, many of which lie outside of our awareness.[7]

This insight is beautifully exemplified in the book of Daniel. In chapter 10, Daniel has a vision of a war that is coming. He goes into mourning and fasts for three weeks. During that time, his prayers receive no response from God.

I'd love to know what Daniel thought about during those three weeks of silence. Maybe he thought that God was turning a deaf ear because it somehow served a higher purpose. Or perhaps Daniel thought that it was God's will to watch him suffer. Maybe he thought God was putting him through a spiritual growth exercise. Or perhaps this was a test of his loyalty or punishment for his sins.

Yet this passage doesn't support any of those options. Instead, it provides a very different explanation. Three weeks into Daniel's fasting, he got a visit from an angel who said, "From the moment you decided to humble yourself to receive understanding, your prayer was heard, and I set out to come to you" (Dan 10:12 *The Message*). God answered Daniel's prayer *the moment* he began praying! So what happened?

The angel goes on to explain that his mission was thwarted by an opposing angel. It wasn't until his angelic buddy Michael came to help that he was able to come answer Daniel's prayer.

The silence Daniel experienced for three weeks had nothing to do with God's timing or his perfect plans. God didn't leave Daniel high and dry to teach, test, or punish him. This passage shows that God didn't automatically get his way in this situation. God's answer was delayed, and it was due to *wills other than his own*. It was due to war.

God doesn't orchestrate evil. God battles against it. The Bible takes care to make this distinction. It calls Satan a "murderer from the beginning" who has "no truth in him" and is "the father of lies" (John 8:44). He "prowls around like a roaring lion looking for someone to devour" (1 Pet 5:8). And he's the cosmic "thief" who comes "only to steal and kill and destroy" (John 10:10).

Jesus, on the other hand, came to bring *life* that's more beautiful than our wildest dreams (see John 10:10). God's very essence is love. He doesn't desire to harm anyone (Lam 3:33). He is light, and in him there is no darkness at all (1 John 1:5). He cannot be tempted by evil, and he doesn't tempt anyone (James 1:13). He is not a God of confusion but of peace (1 Cor 14:33). With him, evil may not dwell (Ps 5:4). He is righteous in all his ways and kind in all his works (Ps 145:17). His plans are to prosper us and not to harm us (Jer 29:11). Every good and perfect gift comes from him, the "Father of heavenly lights" (James 1:16-17).

And so my understanding became remarkably clear. It was as simple as good versus evil. Light versus darkness. Love versus hate.

God is good. God battles evil with love. That's what the cross was all about.

Calvary: The love story

Growing up, I had seen the cross as a scary symbol. It reminded me of a vicious God who was furious about my sins. It was where this angry God unleashed his wrath onto gentle Jesus so he wouldn't have to unleash it on me. I believed this act meant my sins were cancelled out. All I needed to do was accept Jesus' punishment as a gift, and then I could escape the eternal torment that I deserved. That was supposed to be beautiful and praiseworthy and a reminder of God's love. It seemed more like an act of divine child abuse to me.

But as I wrestled with a warfare understanding of the world, the beauty of the cross began to shine through my confusion. I'd already accepted that God hadn't sent a weaker, more submissive version of himself to earth but rather had sent an exact representation of his being. I added to this knowledge my new understanding that this world is in bondage to sin. And in order to free its captives (Luke 4:18; Eph 4:8; Heb 2:14-15), Jesus gave his own life as ransom (Matt 20:28; Mark 10:45; 1 Tim 2:6; Heb 9:15). Why would he do that? Because he loves us (John 3:16)!

I started to see Calvary as the climax of a gripping love story. I once even heard it expressed as the story of a groom fighting to rescue his bride.[8] The bride of this particular groom was cheating on him. What she didn't realize was that her new lover was a madman, and before long she was in grave danger. One day the bride's lover tied her to the bed, set her house on fire, and left. Stranded and terrified, the bride cried for help.

Minutes later, her groom arrived on the scene. He'd just learned about her adulterous relationship and had raced home to see her. But his fresh anguish was replaced with terror when he realized that his house was consumed in flames and filled with the screams of his bride.

And though he knew it would likely cost him his life, the groom couldn't stop himself. He charged through the thick, black smoke and wove through superheated rooms before he finally reached her bed. That's when he knelt beside her and set to work upon the ropes. He moved fast, with a fierce focus. Despite her unfaithfulness, his eyes blazed with deep, passionate love. It was that very love that he hoped would win back his bride.

Within the choking smoke, the process grew long and tedious for the groom. As the room grew darker, he tore off his shirt and placed it over his bride's nose and mouth, giving her a barrier against the toxic air.

Finally, the last rope fell to the floor and the groom scooped up his bride in his arms. He barreled toward the doorway, which was now encased in flames. Just as they reached the threshold, it collapsed, blocking their only exit.

Without hesitation, the groom gritted his teeth and lifted a thick, fiery beam a few feet off the ground. Seconds before the roof came crashing down, the bride escaped. Her groom died in the center of her disaster.

It was the sacrifice of his life, given to save her, that most poignantly demonstrated the groom's love. Despite a full awareness of her betrayal, he was compelled by love to complete the fatal rescue mission.

And that's when I finally understood the beauty of the cross. It's a love so outrageous that we need the Spirit of God to help us understand it (2 Cor 4:4-6; Eph 3:16-19). It's a love that can't be reduced to a formula, a specific prayer, or a transfer of punishment. It's the deep, abiding love of that groom for his unfaithful bride. God's love goes to any length and faces the greatest evil to save his beloved.

An enemy did this

As I considered again the evil in the world, it seemed clear that God didn't nod in approval when children drowned or when women were sold into sex slavery. God wasn't folding his powerful arms when young men were gunned down or when the elderly were neglected. He was battling, always battling, to bring good out of evil. In this world that breathes anguish and births heartbreak, I began to see how important Jesus' words were in the parable of the weeds.

In that parable, a farmer sowed good seed in his field. But while everyone was asleep, an enemy came and sowed weeds among his crop. When the seeds began to sprout, the weeds appeared also. The farmer's servants asked him, "Sir, didn't you sow good seed in your field? Where then did the weeds come from?" The farmer said, "An enemy did this" (Matt 13:24-28).

Notice that he didn't say, "I have allowed an enemy to do this for a higher purpose."

I realized that this distinction was key, because just as a farmer would have no desire for weeds to devastate his crop, so also God doesn't desire evil and horrific suffering to devastate humans.

I imagined a young couple grieving over the baby they lost, and it was as though the words of Jesus sprang to life: "An enemy did this." I thought of the pain that surrounded my parents' broken marriage, my damaging relationships, and my destructive choices. And I recognized that the one who delights in broken roads is not God.

I considered all kinds of radical suffering, from tsunamis to tornados, from human trafficking to deadly disease, and I realized: "An enemy did this." The farmer sows good seed; so whenever I encountered evil, I wasn't witnessing the work of God. And I could stop blaming the farmer.

Burning my blueprint

"Isn't it amazing?" Ian asked one afternoon. We were home with our healthy and energetic toddlers, trying to discuss a podcast over the clamor of riding toys and happy squeals. "Isn't it incredible to know that God loves you so much that, if you were the only human on this planet, he'd die *just for you*?"

I wanted to agree, but I just couldn't. Despite my growing understanding of God's love, I wasn't ready to accept this. "I feel like God has a more collective love for all humanity, you know?" I finally confessed. "It's hard to believe that he actually loves *me* that much."

Ian's eyes softened with sadness. He tried to reiterate what we'd learned from the sermon—that because God's love is infinite, it can be divided billions of times and he still has the same infinite amount of love for each and every one of us. And so God loves us as if *each* person were the *only* person.

While I understood the logic in my head, that beautiful truth just couldn't reach my wounded heart. I wasn't ready to accept that God's love was poured out for *me* specifically. Not after everything I'd experienced.

"Jess," Ian said softly, "I think you need to pray about this. Why don't you try using imaginative prayer to help you accept God's love for you specifically?" We'd been learning recently about how using our God-given imaginations can invigorate our relationships with God and usher in a deeper intimacy.[9]

So somewhat reluctantly, I stole a moment away, put on some classical music, and imagined myself talking face-to-face with Jesus. I closed my eyes and scrolled swiftly through my painful past, trying to sort truth from lies, facts from fiction.

After a few moments, I felt the tears start. "Where were you?" I demanded of Jesus. "Where were you in all that pain?"

Truth be told, I expected to control the imaginative prayer experience. I expected to place Jesus in the various scenes of my early years. I thought I'd imagine him comforting me during times of brokenness, stroking my hair on the nights I'd cried. But what actually happened still steals my breath.

Deep in prayer, I was hit with the clearest vision of a night I'd long ago suppressed. It was my darkest night, surrounded by walls of white. I was passed out on sleeping pills. I was completely alone: no family, no friends, and no shoelaces. I was lying motionless on a hospital bed. In my vision, standing beside me, was Jesus. His head was bowed, and he was weeping.

He wasn't snarling, and he wasn't smiling. He wasn't nodding stoically because everything was happening in accordance with his divine, mysterious blueprint. He was overcome with compassion. His shoulders were shaking from quiet sobs. It was as if he looked upon his broken daughter and ached from the knowledge that an enemy had done this.

I blinked back to the present, opening my teary eyes to the realization that God loved *me* with the love portrayed on Calvary. Everything I'd experienced that didn't reflect his love did not reflect his ideal will for me. God's love was raw, personal, and stunningly perfect. He had persistently pursued me, even in my worst moments, longing for me to know and embrace his unfailing love.

I lay back on my pillows. I could finally rest from all the wrestling. It was time to recover safely in God's powerful arms. I had discovered a breathtaking, life-changing, mind-blowing picture of God, and I couldn't wait to share it with the world!

I had no way of knowing that I'd soon have the chance. My new-found faith was about to be refined by a fire so fierce it would draw a crowd. I had yet to face the moment that every parent fears.

In just a few short months, I would look upon my son's small body and my heart would whisper, "An enemy did this."

Part II

Faith under Fire

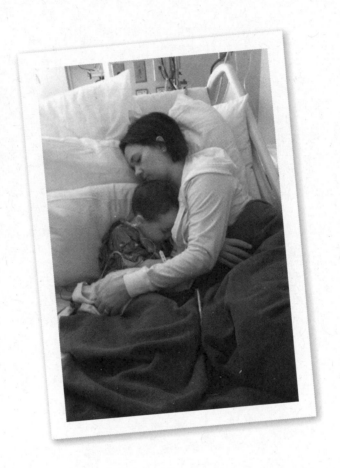

Four

Naming the Darkness

I an posted the following to Facebook on Sunday, September 23, 2012:

> For everyone who has not heard, we found out Friday night that Henry has a large brain tumor. He is in the pediatric intensive care unit. . . . Brain surgery is scheduled for Tuesday . . . we'll take all the prayers we can get.

That's where our public story began. But our private story started much earlier. The year preceding Henry's diagnosis was extraordinary. Yet in some ways, it was rather ordinary. Much of it mirrors the daily happenings of families all over the world. Much of it resembles the simple joys and challenges that generations of people have faced, dating back to our earliest ancestors. And much like the Bible's portrayal of humanity's very first couple, there was a tree in the center of it all.

Winter

Henry and I had assembled our special "tree" on a chilly afternoon while Miriam napped. We collected small branches from the woods behind our house. Then we assembled them in a glazed pottery vase the color of ruddy earth. The branches cast a web of twigs, fanning three feet in all directions. Henry and I placed the tree in the center of our great room. It sat atop a four-foot ledge that divided our kitchen and living room, defining the spaces and reflecting the season of our life.

In January of that year, Henry and I dressed the naked branches with glittery icicles and dangling, crystal clear beads. He pursed his lips together while working, his analytical eye always assessing our progress. It was tedious work for tiny hands. He was captivated by the task and engrossed in his productivity.

That was on a healthy day. When Henry felt good, he was productive. He tackled important projects like finger-painting, coloring, sculpting play dough, fizzling mountains of baking soda with vinegar, and crunching through winter leaves in the backyard. He'd spend time with his special friend, Grandpa. They'd venture out to the neighborhood playground, gather armfuls of sticks, search for butterflies, or swing high on a large porch swing. Whenever Grandpa left, Henry would run to the window and wave vigorously as the car pulled out of sight. Then Henry would dive immediately into his next adventure. Healthy days were busy days.

But the winter of 2012 brought challenges. Germ season ushered in a slew of ear infections for Henry and various cold and sinus problems for Miriam. On sick days, one-year-old Miri and three-year-old Henry camped out a few feet from our family's tree and watched *Curious George* in their matching Elmo pajamas.

In February, the tree got a fresh spattering of sparkly red hearts, hung gently with the dedication of Henry's whole heart. While his recurring ear infections seemed to make him more agitated and moody, they didn't dampen his overall warmth and constant desire for affection.

Night after chilly night, I'd snuggle beside him to read him stories and say our prayers. Then Ian would come in for a hug and kiss. Afterward I'd ask Henry, "Before I go, would you like *four* kisses or *five* kisses?"

Henry would ponder this for a moment. Then his sapphire eyes would sparkle, his tiny teeth would flash a giant smile, and he'd proclaim, "Ten!"

"*Ten*?!" I'd repeat, pretending to be shocked. Then I'd cover his face and head with a least a dozen loud kisses while he squealed and laughed.

I lived for that laugh. When Henry laughed, every cell in his body participated. He'd throw his head back, burst into a massive smile, and cackle from his gut. Waves of joy would emanate from his delighted little body and flood the atmosphere. That laugh was positively magnetic. It captured the attention of everyone around him, family and strangers alike. Hundreds of passersby had laughed with Henry over the years. No one could be sad around little Henry's mighty laugh.

So with his mighty laugh and my tired smile, our family marched into March. We were starting to grow weary from winter viruses and were hopeful that spring would bring relief.

As wooden leprechauns and four-leaf clovers replaced Valentine ornaments, our beloved family tree bore witness to our caginess and crankiness. Sicknesses persisted, and the cold winter days dragged on. That tree stood solidly while our patience thinned and our relationships struggled.

One afternoon, Henry was coloring but quickly growing bored. Usually, when I left a room, my three-year-old shadow would drop whatever he was doing and plod along. But that day, he stayed behind. Instead, bored from sickness and stir-crazy from winter's dreariness, he decided to stir up some mischief.

When I returned to the kitchen where I'd been working, I realized that Henry had scribbled all over our new stainless steel refrigerator. My jaw dropped. I began trying to frantically scrub away his marks, with no success. Frustrated, I tried to explain that he'd actually done permanent damage. "Henry!" I exclaimed. "You hurt the refrigerator!"

That's when my tenderhearted boy's eyes filled with tears. "Oh!" he cried and pointed empathetically to the fridge. "He wants his mommy!"

I sighed, mad at myself for the bad choice of words. Then I gently scooped him up and tried to explain that the refrigerator didn't have feelings and that what he'd done was mischievous but not malicious. The truth was, Henry didn't have a mean bone in his little body.

Though he was growing increasingly cranky, restless, and sick of being sick, his little heart was always swollen with love. Love for his family, love for his friends, and love for his special projects, especially our family's tree.

Spring

By the time delicate little Easter eggs dangled from our tree, spring had brightened our days with outside play. My tiny tots and I spent hours on our back patio. Sometimes they'd splash around on their water table or spill sand from their sand table. Other times they'd dot the warm breezes with giant bubbles drifting from thick plastic wands.

The world was never more perfect than when they played chase. There was no object to their homemade game. They just ran around and chased each other, giggling and squealing and not knowing what to do when they caught each other. That's when they'd start again.

Henry loved having a little sister. He also loved to boss her around. He loved to stretch his arms around her gently as she woke from a nap. He also loved to take her best toys and steal her pacifier. He loved to teach Miri important toddler things through his broken, toddler speech. He would often proclaim that she was his "best fwiend Miwi," the "cutiest girl!" He genuinely adored her.

And she thought he hung the moon.

Those spring days were filled with their budding love and laughter. Healthy days were happy days. But sick days were becoming worrisome. We had hoped that spring would bring steady health and rejuvenate our spirits. Yet while I was experiencing beautiful changes in my relationship with God, my family was still struggling with the discouragement of frequent illness.

Little Henry was having more and more sick days—days when he'd breathe through his mouth because colds clogged his sinuses. Days when his little cheeks would flush from fever. Days when he'd nap more than usual. And with an increase in ear infections came the use of antibiotics, which seemed to alter his moods dramatically. When he was on an antibiotic, he'd have little patience for others and no tolerance for transitions. Tantrums were frequent.

Sleep was heavily disrupted. He'd often lose his appetite. When he felt really bad, he'd refuse food, and then sometimes his hands would get slightly shaky from low blood sugar.

We thought it was from low blood sugar.

On the days that Henry was feeling well, however, he was back to his happy, busy self. I remember the afternoon I convinced him and Miri to eat mixed vegetables for a snack. I told them it was their "power source" for good playing. One-year-old Miri looked up at me with a mouth full of peas and said, "Tasty!"

Henry popped a carrot in his little mouth, looked down his button nose, and said, "No Miwi, it is not *tasty*, it is just . . . *wummy*!" When he used that authoritative tone, I had a flash into his future. I saw a teacher, training a young student.

I often saw "Future Henry" so vividly. When he started music school, I saw the concert pianist. When he sometimes preferred listening to opera singer Andrea Bocelli to watching cartoons, I saw the brilliant vocalist. When he was gleefully surrounded by splashes of paint, ink, glitter, glue, and beads, I saw the artist.

When he demanded to know where the water went when it disappeared down the drain, I saw the scientist. When he drew a schematic of a wastewater treatment system with markers and computer paper, I saw the engineer. When his sharp mind and gentle touch met his little sister, I saw the pediatrician.

When he went silent and wide-eyed when our pretty neighbor came by, I saw flashes of the appreciative husband. When he playfully nicknamed his plump baby cousin "Baby Katato" (after Mr. Potato Head), I saw the tender father and grandfather.

When his arms were spread wide and his heart overflowing with love, I saw the pastor, the counselor, and the friend. When we snuggled together and read the books we'd enjoyed a thousand times, I saw the son who would help care for his mother in her old age, patiently reading to this fragile old friend.

I saw a thousand possible futures for my son. He was fearfully and wonderfully made, a stockpile of potential. And so even though the times were tough and sick days frequent, I knew the seasons would change. We *needed* the seasons to change.

Ian and I banked on that pretty heavily. We believed the sicknesses would pass. Our tired eyes and fraying patience would surely find rejuvenation.

Summer

By the time colorful tissue-paper flowers dressed our beloved tree, we'd found our lazy, hazy summer rhythm. I took Henry and Miriam outside during the humid mornings and evenings. We spent midday in air conditioning at home, at the gym, or wandering the toy aisles at Target.

Ian picked up a few overtime shifts so I was able to purchase Henry's homeschooling supplies. By his fourth birthday in July, I'd planned his entire upcoming kindergarten year. It was early, but I figured that whatever we actually accomplished would be gravy.

We had tried sending Henry to preschool the previous year, but it didn't work out that well. I used to say that Henry collected "germs like matchbox cars," so paying tuition for him to be absent so frequently seemed like a waste. Plus my dream had always been to homeschool once my kids reached kindergarten age, so I decided we'd just get an early start.

By this point Henry could sound out all the letters, read small words, and count to twenty like a champ. His only issue was fine motor coordination, which affected working with a pencil and scissors. We employed his former teacher's advice of working with play dough and sorting small beads for fun. I figured that fine motor skills were something he'd grow into. I assumed it was simply because every child develops differently.

I thought that it was a harmless delay.

Ian and I had high hopes for a healthy fall. After all, at home Henry would be exposed to fewer germs, and we had scheduled an ear tube surgery for him. That meant no more antibiotics and no more extended sickness. That meant an increase in appetite and weight gain.

Henry saw two pediatricians at the same practice. Both kept an eye on his stagnating weight. One ran a full blood panel. Everything came back normal. It always seemed as if he just had another bug. And even despite the multiple sicknesses, his weight stayed in an acceptable range. He just wasn't gaining well. He also wasn't eating much. I did everything I could to keep the calories coming until the next virus came. Health *had* to be around the corner.

But by this point, he was starting to get stomach viruses too. The fevers, the weakness, the vomiting cycled in and out of his life. He just couldn't catch a break. We couldn't catch a break. And I was breaking.

Summer storms

I was exhausted from the sleeplessness. Henry was waking up constantly. He would crawl into our bed during the night and then toss and turn, which kept me awake. Ian would retreat to Henry's room to garner enough sleep to perform well at work. I just staggered through a blur of days and nights, an endless cycle of toddler tantrums and sickness, with ever-increasing worry and isolation.

I dropped out of my summer Bible study. I dropped out of church. Ian was working Sundays and Henry was always sick, so it wasn't that hard. But it wasn't just for health reasons.

I was coming to the isolating realization that my picture of God wasn't popular. The belief that God always gets his way is pervasive. The local Christians I knew believed that God either causes our pain or specifically allows our pain to transpire for a mysterious, higher purpose. These views didn't match my renewed picture of God. But I didn't have the confidence or ability to articulate the differences well.

And there was no time to learn. Our family was increasingly in crisis mode, responding to another sickness and to the increasing agitation, impatience, and tantrums Henry displayed.

I went inward. I tunneled deep into our hard realities and hoped that if I threw myself completely into my family's care we would emerge soon enough, healthy and strong again. But inward is a lonely place. It's easier to hear the accuser's voice when there's no one to drown him out.

On the hardest days—when both kids were screeching and I hadn't showered in forty-eight hours, when we were weary from sickness and stress, when the house was a disaster, when the laundry was piled up and dinner not yet started, when I felt completely alone—I could visualize a finger pointing in my face, reminding me of my failure.

Being a mom had been my life's ambition. I wanted the twenty-nine-year wait to be worth it. I wanted everything to be perfect. I wanted to be the perfect mom. I wanted to prove to myself that my life was fulfilled and that I was blissfully living out my dreams. But life just wasn't working out that way, and rather than recognize my flawed expectations, I internalized the defeat.

On those days, I breathed failure. I ate and drank failure. I saw failure reflected in the eyes of my tots when I was too quick to discipline and too slow to ask for help.

Some days I wondered secretly if my kids would be better off without me. I wanted them to have a Mary Poppins mom. I wanted them to have a Carol Brady mom. I wanted them to have anyone other than a real, human mom who was reaching the end of her human limits. I was just desperate for sleep and support, believing and begging that these storms would pass.

On the darkest days, I felt victorious when I simply *stayed*. I stayed and was a mom again for one more day. I'd confess my failures, put an action plan in place for the next crisis, then put both feet on the floor and try again.

And with that persistence came moments of sweet relief. I tried to accept that my kids didn't want perfection or a television character. They wanted *me*. And it seemed that the more grace I accepted, the more graceful I became.

I even tried to employ an "attitude of gratitude." I started to thank God, night after sleepless night, for two beautiful children, even if they kept me awake. And with that gratitude came some increased hopefulness on my part. I truly believed everything would get better. I just had to be patient and get past all these viruses. I was confident the ear tubes would help.

The day of Henry's ear surgery came and went quickly. He was in and out of the procedure like a flash. I remember sitting in a vinyl rocker in post-op, cradling my sleepy angel, thinking about the bright future ahead. I was so thankful, so hopeful, and so ready for health.

Several hours later I tucked my little man into bed. After he had received at least a dozen kisses, he asked, "Mommy, where did I come from?"

I raised my eyebrows and said, "From my tummy, Baby!"

Henry closed his eyes, tucked his head down toward my stomach, and declared, "It's time to go back!"

I laughed and squeezed him close. Then I promised that he'd start to feel better now that the tubes were in place. He was such a little kidder, and I loved his sweet jokes.

That night I was sure that he was just joking. Now I think that somehow . . . he knew.

Free fall

Exactly one week before Ian posted that heartbreaking update to Facebook, I was baking. It was a new recipe: pumpkin muffins with maple icing. The sweet smell of cinnamon and nutmeg filled our home. It wafted past the kitchen and past our special tree, which was draped in the jewel tones of autumn leaves. Flashes of crimson, fiery orange, and canary yellow dangled from the delicate branches.

It was Sunday, and on Ian's current schedule, his weekends began on Sunday. He had recently arrived home from work, and our weekend had begun. We'd survived another long week! But I wasn't baking to celebrate.

I was trying to distract myself. I was scrambling to create warmth and goodness. I was attempting to ignore the fear that had started to crawl around my gut and claw at my heart.

The ear tubes weren't doing what we'd hoped. Henry was growing more irritable, more fatigued, and less interested in eating. The slight trembling was becoming more pronounced. Over the past few days, we'd started to research potential causes. We decided that if he didn't improve by Monday morning, we'd head back to the doctor.

So that Sunday evening, I baked. And I counted the hours until a pediatrician could assure us, or refer us, or do something to fix everything. Normally, my little kitchen buddy would be by my side, mixing and spilling ingredients. Whenever I cooked, he liked to make a "special soup for Daddy." That meant he'd dump a little of every spice I owned into a bowl, mix it with various liquids, and concoct the most foul-smelling "soup" one can imagine.

But on this terrible, cozy day, he was snuggled in the corner of our living room sofa. He had grown territorial over my iPhone, wanting to curl up with a puzzle app for hours. He was content, and I was afraid, so I left him alone and baked.

I soaked in the swirling smells of pumpkin muffins, and then I choked one down. It had a rich and bitter taste. It was warmth and fear, coziness and dread.

I kept on like that for hours—moving, mixing, baking, and scrubbing away at the darkness. It was a darkness that had wormed its way into our lives slowly, but it was gaining momentum. It was a mysterious presence: intense, invasive, and elusive. But soon it would have a name.

Monday

On Monday, Henry was worse. He'd slept beside me and trembled during the night whenever he tossed or turned. I called the pediatrician early, and they worked us in immediately. I'd never seen any doctor's office scramble so quickly to accommodate.

In a blink, our family was clustered in a small room with fluorescent lights, staring at posters about the flu and ADHD. Eventually the doctor came in with a quizzical look.

Henry looked so ordinary. He was just sitting sweetly upon the white paper. He wasn't trembling or shaking. He wasn't pale. There was no fever. No dehydration. No apparent crisis.

I gently lifted Henry off the table and asked him to step up on a stool for us. He tried. When his legs began to wobble, my stomach twisted. When we had to clutch him as support, a lump formed in my throat. It would remain for days.

The doctor ordered blood work. It could be an autoimmune disorder. That meant there could be a cure. He also scheduled a spinal MRI for later in the month. Perhaps Henry had a pinched nerve? Finally, he arranged for us to see a neurologist the following week—just to be safe. We left with a growing sense of dread.

Before long the blood work was back. It was normal . . . again. We'd never make it to the other appointments.

Tuesday afternoon

Music school was a special Mommy-Henry time, an increasing rarity since Miriam's birth. Henry loved it because we got to march and dance and sing with the other parents and kids. I loved it for a different reason.

Henry hadn't spoken much in his first few years of life. He could communicate pretty well, but it was largely nonverbal. He did gain full language rather suddenly at three years of age, but it was always the sweet, broken speech of a toddler.

Since the spoken word had never come easily for him, hearing Henry sing was akin to watching a miracle unfold, over and over. Like a flower that closes at night and spreads open each morning, every song was a magnificent wonder of off-key simplicity. Each note that sailed past his lips was a victorious celebration, a blossoming of little Henry's growth and development.

So even though life was falling in pieces around us, I took Henry to his music school that Tuesday afternoon. We were just stumbling through what we knew. After all, the road ahead seemed long—for all we knew, he could be battling multiple sclerosis, or Parkinson's, or something equally taxing. I didn't want Henry to stop participating in everything he loved while we waited to find out. And though a little weak, Henry was willing. So we went . . . and it was a mistake.

For the first time, Henry wasn't cooperative, sweet, and obliging with his teacher. He couldn't climb onto his music bench like the other four-year-olds. He didn't want to try, even with the collapsible step stool I'd brought. He just wanted to sit on my lap. As the class progressed, he became increasingly impatient and frustrated.

He eventually melted into a tantrum and we left early, both of us in tears.

Tuesday evening

There's a shimmering lake at the center of town and a wooded path that surrounds it. Ian and I headed there on Tuesday evening. It had been hard to leave Henry and go on our weekly date night, but our babysitter was like family. And she had two grown children of her own. I trusted her judgment completely. We'd filled her in on everything, and she agreed that we needed a chance to breathe. Ian was eager to strategize with me. I just wanted the space to break down.

Ian took my hand as we walked beneath a bright September sky and breathed in the scent of thick forest. We were surrounded by a rainbow of foliage—deep emeralds and bright jades mingled with the arrival of early autumn blush. I was with the love of my life on a spectacular fall day, but I couldn't appreciate any of it. I couldn't even catch my breath. My composure came and went. Ian kept begging me to work with him.

"I'm going to throw up," I sobbed through a fresh wave of tears. "I can't focus. I can't think!"

"Jess, we can let fear cripple us, or we can focus on what we *can* control," Ian insisted. He knew our opportunities to have a discussion without interruption were limited. He would head back to work the next day, and our week would be a blur of toddler-filled days and sleep-disrupted nights.

"We have an appointment with a neurologist on Monday," he continued, "and we need to make the most of that opportunity. We should tell the doctor *anything* that could help with a diagnosis. We have to think of everything that could possibly be relevant. Let's go over Henry's entire medical history, from your pregnancy to today."

I nodded and tried to swallow against my nausea. But it would take more than the hot mint tea in my Starbucks cup to settle my stomach.

"I'll keep researching on my own," Ian continued, "but in the meantime you can make a list of every symptom that could possibly point to . . . *whatever* this is. So let's brainstorm now and you can compile it when we get home."

It was all so dreamlike. I walked and stared blankly ahead. Was this real? Was this life? *Our* life? The wind was lifting and tousling my hair, the trees were gently swaying, and a passing wisp of clouds was listening for my response.

"I had hypertension in my third trimester," I offered weakly. Deep down I knew that Ian was right. It would be worse if we failed to do our part. We'd never forgive ourselves if a specialist lacked some bit of critical information that we'd failed to provide. It would be worse if the doctor wrongly dismissed us.

"You're right!" Ian affirmed. "And Henry was small when he was born, under six pounds, but otherwise he was perfectly healthy."

I cleared my throat and focused. "He had a little jaundice, but it resolved quickly."

And so it went. From sensory sensitivities to the occasional head or backache, from sleep problems to chronic ear infections, from picky eating to speech delays, we brainstormed. We brainstormed every major or minor or just plain *odd* symptom we could recall.

When we got home, I dutifully compiled the symptoms, creating a thorough, bulleted list for the neurologist.

But we would never see a neurologist. Soon we would see a neurosurgeon. Then a neuro-oncologist.

By then, our list would be irrelevant.

Wednesday

Ian went back to work Wednesday evening. I had previously scheduled a hair appointment that morning, and Ian insisted that I keep it. I obsessed about Henry while rushing there and back. As hard as it was to witness his symptoms, it was harder to have him out of arm's reach.

It took every effort to make small talk with the stylist. I did manage to brag about my babies, even with a smock snapped around the lump in my throat. I didn't, however, mention the fear that had recently moved into our home. I just made it through and made it home.

Ian left for work that afternoon and I stayed busy. I did routine stuff with the kids. We played, we ran errands, and we watched cartoons. When they were settled into bed, I cleaned out closets and bedrooms.

I was as sane as I was productive. I kept telling myself that I just had to hang on until Monday, when an expert could offer some answers. So I doggedly burned off the excess anxiety by cleaning, clearing, and creating space within our home.

I didn't know then that we'd soon *need* that extra room. Our quiet house was about to be filled with extended family members wanting to help. In fact, over the next three months, our front entrance would become a revolving door for folks offering care and comfort.

As I toiled into the night, I had no idea that every space I emptied would soon be filled to overflowing. We were about to be inundated with gifts and casseroles from family and friends. We would receive thousands of cards and numerous gift cards from acquaintances and strangers all over the world. Our family was about to receive an unprecedented outpouring of love.

It would all be for the precious little boy, sleeping soundly down the hall, nestled in his parents' big bed.

Thursday

The one sweet relief I experienced during this horrible week was this: I didn't rush. I didn't rush the kids out the door. I didn't rush them through errands. I didn't rush us off to the gym. I was busy, but I wasn't rushed. I played when the kids were playful. I worked around the house when they were napping. I took the time to enjoy the quiet fullness of being a mom.

Yet our gentle, steady pace was laced with worry. Henry was gradually getting worse. He was napping by this point—something he hadn't done in two years. This was in addition to his full nights of sleep. He was running slower, and the trembling had persisted.

Ian had another evening shift that Thursday. After I had tucked my babies into bed, I tried to launch into cleaning with the companionship of a podcast sermon, but I needed more.

I called my brother, Joe. I wanted him to pray, to offer support. So when he answered, I tried to explain what was going on . . . but mostly what came out was hysterical sobbing.

Eventually he was able to piece the story together. Then he prayed. He listened. And he stayed on the phone with me until Ian got home.

Friday morning

Henry's defeated groan was something I'll never forget. It was the groan of someone who had triumphed over one hundred obstacles only to find one thousand more waiting. Friday morning was bathed in warm autumn sunlight, and I had taken the kids to a playground.

Henry wanted to climb the play equipment as he always did. But while his mind was alive with creative possibilities, his wobbling legs were cursing his efforts. I had gently helped him up the first several steps, swallowing against my terror as I watched his body struggle. Then we crossed a mercifully flat bridge, only to encounter a larger, steeper set of steps.

That's when I heard his pitiful groan, and my heart ripped in two. To hear him acknowledge the defeat of his sudden disability, to have it smack us both so cruelly in the face, was nearly more than my heart could take.

That's when two-year-old Miriam breezed by, tackling the stairs with perfect coordination. Her abilities seemed so extraordinary. They were so average.

We made it home and I drew a bath for little Miri. Henry wanted no part of a bath, and I didn't want the battle. I did insist that he try to use the bathroom; I *knew* he had to go. He refused. He threw a tantrum. He eventually went along with my insistence, gritting his teeth and straining while standing in front of the toilet.

"I don't haff to go!" he yelled.

"Fine!" I snapped, my nerves shot from the persistent terror and compounded by tantrums. I helped him into my bed, which was a few feet from Miri's bath. I gave him my phone to play his puzzles. Minutes later I realized he'd wet himself . . . all over the bed.

"Henry!" I yelled, "what is *wrong* with you?!" I moved him to the bathroom tile and started to angrily strip the bed. "I just *asked you* to use the potty!!"

Henry started crying. I threw the sheets in the laundry and started sobbing. I came back and wrapped my arms around him, then apologized to both of my kids.

I wish someone could have told me, "You want to know what's wrong with him? He has a bilateral tumor growing in his frontal lobe that makes him anxious, clingy, sleepless, irrational, and kills his appetite. He also has fluid that's trapped and building within his skull. It has finally led to urinary incontinence. He really tried to go potty when you asked, and he didn't mean to wet your bed." But there were no explanations that day, just tears, fears, and forgiveness.

Answers would come soon enough.

Friday afternoon

I was supposed to meet a friend at the gym for our weekly walk. When I texted her that I couldn't leave Henry, she called.

"Hey," she said kindly. "So what's going on?"

I gave her more details and was surprised when she urged me to head to the children's hospital. She's an ICU nurse, and I've never known her to overreact to health issues.

"You don't think they'll just send us home?" I asked. "I mean, since he already has an appointment with a neurologist on Monday? His symptoms are only slightly worse than when his doctor saw him a few days ago."

"No, they won't necessarily send you home," she said. "They can do things there right away, like a CT scan, just for peace of mind."

It didn't take much convincing. Ian was scheduled to be off in a couple of hours, and by the time he got home, the sitter was on her way. My dad was also driving down from Virginia to stay as long as needed. I packed an emergency overnight bag for Henry, and before I knew it, the three of us were heading to the emergency room.

"I get all da candy!" Henry exclaimed from the backseat. Ian and I smiled weakly at him. Dried fruit strips were one of his favorite snacks, and I had brought a box. "I don't haff to share with Miwi!"

That was only part of his fun. "Dis is amazing!" he said appreciatively when he got to sit in a shiny red chair and receive new hospital bracelets at the intake desk.

"Wow, wook at dis!" he exclaimed while exploring the waiting room. It was decked out in kid-friendly sculptures and primary colors. Ian and I took turns following him and choking down coffee.

And as we waited, we noticed. We noticed that he was starting to shake while walking, not just while climbing. We noticed that his right leg was beginning to drag.

By the time a nurse ushered us to an exam room, Henry was wobbling through a heavy limp, snapping pictures on my iPhone, and joyfully exclaiming, "Dis is amazing!"

That was one way to look at it.

Just after midnight

"He has a tumor . . . on his brain," I repeated slowly, with Zen-like calm. "And you're going to do surgery. On his *brain*. To remove it." I stared at the surgeon, blinked, and then added, "I think I'm in shock."

His misty eyes reflected the gentle warmth of a wise father. "I know you are."

We had been in the ER for over six hours, making a tense home in a tiny room with a little boy whose patience had run out. I could hear his shrill screams past the door as the nurses desperately tried to give us a minute alone with the surgeon.

They knew we were receiving devastating news. They probably wanted to spare Henry our response, which, ironically, turned out to be quiet shock. Ian was trembling, as shaky as his son. I was dumbfounded.

I knew this was big. It was life changing and terribly serious. But I also had a sense of relief because we weren't alone anymore. We weren't the only ones afraid anymore. Concern for our son had shot across a team of medical professionals—people who could *do* something to stop the escalating madness.

Tests had always come back negative, and diagnoses had always been frustratingly simple in the face of what had become increasingly complex. Now finally, *finally* the world had halted to make priority of the trials our precious boy faced.

We no longer had to spearhead an effort to make people understand, to gather and compile and convince. There was a tumor on a CT image, and we were no longer alone.

A brain tumor wasn't good news. But now the darkness had a name. And that meant there was hope.

The surgeon patted my knee and looked at Ian. "We need to get him well, folks."

Yes, that's what we needed. We needed to get Henry well. Then we needed to go home and celebrate. We needed to celebrate Halloween and Thanksgiving and Christmas. We needed to continue our homeschooling and return to music school. We needed to live a happy life, busy and bustling and beautifully reflected in the changing seasons of our family's tree.

That tree had been birthed from a simple pile of sticks, but it had become so much more. It paired the old with the new and the subdued with the colorful. It had evolved into a tender reflection of our life together.

I had no idea that in a few short months I'd strip our family tree of its decorations and pack away the dreams we'd shared. Then I'd lift the sticks from their vase and return them to the earth, leaving them scattered across the woods and lost in a tangle of memories.

FIVE

Love Always Hopes

*M*inutes *after* we talked to the neurosurgeon, Henry was admitted as a patient in the pediatric intensive care unit (PICU). He was wheeled to the third floor where his favorite orange sweatshirt was replaced with a gown that matched his tired blue eyes.

As a nurse bustled around us to help him settle in, I thought about how grateful I was that Henry was calmer at that point. He was tolerating the wires attached to his chest, as well as the many plastic bracelets that circled his small wrist. But he didn't want me to leave his side. He didn't want me to collapse on the cot beside him.

"Will you sweep wiff me, Mommy?" Henry asked. He looked so little in that big hospital bed.

In those early hours of dark morning, I climbed into bed beside him. I draped an arm over his little body and pulled him close. He tucked his head into my chest and nestled his small warm hands against my neck. I leaned against a hospital pillow and rested my cheek atop his soft hair. Surrounded by the random, shrill beeping of strange machines and the brisk shuffling of hospital employees, we closed our weary eyes. And somehow, cocooned together within the freeway of activity that defines a PICU, we finally found sleep.

Through little eyes

The following morning Henry was whisked off for his first surgery, coupled with an MRI, while under sedation. The surgical procedure, a ventriculostomy, would provide some temporary and immediate relief from the pressure building inside his head. A small hole was to be drilled into his skull and an external ventricular drain inserted. This drain would allow cerebrospinal fluids, trapped by the tumor, to begin slowly exiting his body.

Ian was home spending some time with Miriam. We lived about an hour from the hospital, and he planned to arrive late morning. So while Henry was in surgery, I restlessly occupied a patient waiting room in the radiation department. There I sipped coffee and absently flipped through my phone.

That was when I came across Henry's photography from the night before, when he had played with my iPhone while we waited. Those blurry, off-centered shots painted a striking picture. One glance delivered a massive dose of perspective.

From his angle, the room looked so much bigger. The heavy, closed door seemed larger and the supply cabinets extended higher into the air. I paused on a photo of a twelve-eyed, alien-looking creature staring down from the ceiling. Would a four-year-old know it was just a surgical light?

Then I noticed that he'd captured Mommy and Daddy talking. I studied the photo of Ian. His posture was rigid, his mouth turned downward, and his eyes were hyperalert. The next one was of me. I was perched in a plastic chair, knees toward my chest. My shoulders were hunched a bit, my lips were tight, and my eyes were wide with alarm.

I closed my eyes against a tidal wave of truth. My little boy was in a radically strange environment, watching his parents react to something. And from what his photos captured, it must be something scary.

That was the moment that I resolved to rise above my own reactions, no matter what lay ahead. I would strive to focus on positive thoughts and feelings when I was near Henry. He didn't know what was happening or what would come next. He didn't understand words like *hydrocephalus, tumor,* or *craniotomy.* But the world must have seemed like a scary place when Mommy looked so afraid and Daddy looked so serious.

Struggling for air

Moments later, it was Henry's neurosurgeon who looked serious. He approached me just outside the hospital entrance. I was taking a break from the windowless cave of a waiting room. The radiology nurse had assured me there was plenty of time for a breath of fresh air. But before I could fill my lungs, the surgeon began to deliver the bad news. The initial findings from Henry's MRI showed that the tumor was extremely large and vascular (fed by major sources of blood supply to the brain) and extended into both hemispheres.

I had no idea what to do with this information other than to blame myself. After all, I'd always believed that anything Henry endured or experienced could be traced back to my success or failure as a mother. And as the surgeon sailed away, waves of blame began to swell. *Where did this tumor come from? Was it that super-stressful day at work when I was pregnant? Was it some sneaky toxin that I ate or touched or breathed while he'd gestated? Could I have caught this sooner? How had I missed something so massive?*

But before I was completely submerged in an ocean of shame, I received a text from my brother, Joe. It simply said: "Jesus wanted me to tell you this isn't your fault."

That's when I paused to inhale, exhale, and weep. I was amazed at how much God cared for me, even my overburdened conscience. His brilliant truth had broken through the guilt piled upon my vulnerable spirit. It left me free to focus solely on the task at hand.

And as it turned out, I'd need all the focus I could get.

Henry has a germ

My mission was to keep a four-year-old on forced bedrest for the three days preceding his craniotomy. The drain in his head required that a nurse be paged every time he moved up or down in bed, even by a few inches. Any sudden shifts would cause fluid to drain too quickly or too slowly, which would result in terrible head pain. There was little to do, and Henry's patience was paper-thin. So we relied heavily upon an old friend to help us pass the time: Curious George.

"George has a germ," Henry said, pointing to the dancing, amoeba-looking germ on his screen. We were curled up together on crisp white sheets, staring at his tablet.

"Yes, and you have a germ too," I said, smoothing the soft hair jutting from his cowlick. "Your germ is in your head. It's called a tumor. That's why we're here at the hospital, so the doctors can take it out." I squeezed him gently and kissed his temple. "Soon you'll take a long nap while the doctors get that germ out. Then we can go home."

Henry just listened. He didn't seem surprised or concerned about this. When I was close, he could handle anything.

But while he was content in my arms, I was growing increasingly distraught. I was worried about Tuesday's craniotomy for many reasons. But one in particular was the fact that he'd have to face it alone. I kept imagining him screaming and reaching for me as he was wheeled back into an operating room. I didn't want to leave him sobbing and surrounded by strangers while being taken into such a traumatic procedure.

So I did what I could do. I held him tight and prayed hard for his peace.

Game day

"Are you ready?" a nurse asked.

It was Tuesday morning, and the moment had arrived. Henry's craniotomy was scheduled to last between six and twelve hours. The surgeon assured us that the mortality rate for this type of surgery was "relatively low." His goal was to remove as much of the tumor as possible and to biopsy the removed pieces. A quick, intraoperative analysis would tell us whether the tumor was malignant or benign. It would be days or even weeks before the biopsy results came back, providing an exact diagnosis.

"We're ready," I lied with a brave smile.

"You can ride with him," the nurse offered. So I pulled Henry close as our bed was wheeled out of our PICU home. Ian walked behind us. We put on our best and brightest performance, making silly jokes and keeping our little man giggling all the way down to the surgical area.

After a few long minutes of winding hallways and tight elevators, we were ushered into the bowels of the hospital—a large, windowless gathering area outside of the operating room. It was filled with dozens of medical professionals sporting various scrubs, masks, and surgical caps.

All heads turned toward us as we were wheeled into a small exam room just off the gathering area. There was an intense focus behind the polite smiles and courteous nods. I could sense the anticipation in the air. It was "game day," and when we passed, all the players paused. Each stole a glance at the small head that housed their opponent.

Despite the surreal nature of the situation, I was immediately struck by the magnificence of this assembled team of professionals. In some ways, they were just ordinary people, gathered from various walks of life, dealing with their own heartbreaks and challenges. But this particular group had power, knowledge, and skills that I lacked. They could charge into areas I couldn't touch. They were strangers to Henry, yet they were gathered to save him.

I fought the urge to kneel before them in deep gratitude. I knew they received paychecks and that they likely enjoyed their work. But I got the impression that this was more than just a job to them. The stark sense that they were fighting for a child's life filled the air.

And though these medical pros sported scrubs of various colors, in this mama's eyes, they all wore gleaming white. They radiated the exquisite beauty of elite warriors rallied together, pooling and pouring out their extraordinary resources, all in the tender attempt to save a child.

Perhaps Henry shared my sense of this staff's competence and heroism, because when the moment came for us to leave, miraculously, he didn't protest. He simply accepted a warm blanket and a gentle smile from a stranger in a surgical cap. And with his plush seahorse beside him, Henry left us peacefully.

But before he was wheeled into that ominous operating room, his nurse paused and invited us to kiss him one final time. Ian and I walked confidently toward our son. We delivered kisses and hugs with brave smiles and dry eyes. Then we waved goodbye to Henry and silently prayed that we'd see him again.

Silence

A few hours later, a friend posted the following update to Henry's growing base of supporters:

> Hey gang . . . Got a voicemail from Ian. . . . They are getting an update from a nurse every hour. The surgeon has made it to the tumor and is beginning to remove pieces of it. Henry is getting some blood transfusions. Things look to be progressing well. Thank you for continuing to pray as there are many more hours to go.

We staggered through that day, doused by waves of shock, fear, and supernatural peace. There were lots of quips and jokes, nervous laughter, and countless moments of staring blankly into space.

Several friends and family members came to encourage us, and a small group stayed all day. We were increasingly covered in prayer by loved ones, friends, and strangers. And we developed a growing sense of optimism. Our prayers were specific and strong.

We prayed that 100 percent of Henry's tumor would be removed. This would increase his chances of survival. The more tumor removed, the better. We also prayed that the doctors would report that the tumor was benign. His fate was obviously far better if the tumor was a benign nuisance rather than malignant cancer. We prayed that all of this would soon be a memory—just a testament to God's healing love and the power of prayer. Those confident prayers helped ease the reality that Henry's skull was open and sharp instruments were invading his brain.

Every hour a nurse from the operating room called to update us. Each time I nearly dropped my phone and threw up on it. But each call was positive in tone, assuring us that Henry was stable. Finally, six hours into the procedure, we got the call that they were closing him up. We were instructed to head to the PICU waiting room, where the surgeon would come up to meet with us.

Our small group marched resolutely into the elevators. Ian and I stood in the hallway to wait for the good report while everyone else took seats in the waiting room. They could see us through the interior windows, but the closed door kept them from hearing what transpired.

They watched as we huddled with the surgeon and his assistant. They studied our faces as we nodded, listened, and offered short responses. They saw us hug the medical professionals before we were left to stand alone. Then they watched us embrace. After a long pause, they witnessed us pull apart and walk toward them. Ian placed his hand on the waiting room doorknob, and they held their collective breath as sight met sound.

We found seats within the square configuration that the group had assumed. We sat while avoiding their faces, avoiding their hope. My hand gripped Ian's. My eyes created a laser-beam lock on the floor.

Everyone waited in absolute silence, but their thoughts were nearly audible. *They got it all! It's benign!* they seemed to chant in unison. *They got it all! It's benign!* was what they needed to hear. *They got it all! It's benign!*

"It's malignant," Ian finally said.

Silence.

"They only got fifty percent of the tumor."

Silence.

"They had to stop the surgery because Henry started bleeding fast and needed a transfusion," Ian said, continuing with the cold, hard facts. "He ended up getting three liters of blood."

I didn't see the white knuckles that gripped one another. I didn't see our family's pale faces or their eyes filled with tears. I kept my vision on the white, speckled floor tile directly in front of me. Its boundaries were straight and firm, a fortress against the violent reality barreling toward us.

"He'll probably be on the ventilator for a couple of days," Ian explained, "And it will be a while before we get the exact diagnosis."

Silence. Nothing but echoing, deafening, pregnant silence.

And in silence, I focused on my tile. That piece of linoleum didn't know that my baby had almost died on that table. It didn't know that the odds that he would die soon were significant. My tile and I shared the silence, communed in silence, and denied in silence. We sat for decades in silence until one chair creaked.

One pair of tennis shoes squeaked across the floor.

They stopped on top of my square, speckled friend. Then knees clad in faded jeans dropped into sight. My brother's arms wrapped around me.

He gripped me with such force that the spell was shattered. Love and hideous pain met and merged and wrapped around me.

I shook like a wounded child, reeling from the insistent, persistent reality that refused to back down.

I shut my eyes and surrendered to the arms that rocked me like a baby. Encircled in strength, I faced the doom with heavy sobs and a heart that screamed, *God, help me. This is real!*

Looking good

The nurses were amazed at how good Henry looked, considering the blood loss. The three liters of blood that he received were enough to fill his entire body. For this reason, the nurses were expecting a pretty bleak-looking patient. But when he arrived, they kept marveling at how good he looked.

Yet as I studied the "good"-looking child wheeled into our PICU room, I struggled to see what they saw. I even struggled to see my son. This child's body was the same size, but his face was so bloated that his features were nearly flat. His skin was so pale and stretched from swelling, he seemed almost plastic.

This child's head was wider and more square. A long line of severed flesh across his crown had been stapled, dozens and dozens of times, to hold it together. Those gleaming staples were lined up like angry soldiers, marching right through his playful cowlick. I was terrified to touch this little boy's face, afraid that his entire head could crack open like an egg.

His puffy lips had been forced open, and a clear tube ran from a monstrously loud machine down into his throat. The loud, rhythmic pump beside the bed breathed for him, causing his exposed, wire-clad chest to rise and fall.

I knew my son was in there, but I couldn't quite see him. He was deep, deep within there, under the heavy surgical sedation and trauma of brain surgery. He was present somewhere under heavily swollen features and machines that invaded his sweet little mouth.

I wanted so badly to connect with him again. And it was terrifying to know that there were no guarantees that I ever would. He might not wake up. Even if he did wake up, he might be drastically different from the Henry we had known. We knew it was possible that he'd have significant emotional, mental, language, or physical impairments.

I wondered, *Will he be able to move? Will he be able to communicate? Will he know me? Will his personality be intact?* He'd lost three liters of blood during a six-hour brain surgery, and half of that massive tumor was still snaking through his healthy brain tissue. Anything was possible.

All I could do was wait and pray. So as the doctor recommended, I prayed that Henry's internal bleeding would stop. I prayed that his lung function would improve. And I prayed that the precious, pitiful creature before me would be made whole again.

"He looks so good," a nurse said, stopping to reset a beeping machine.

I wiped my eyes, touched his soft, puffy hand, and tried to see what she saw.

Giving thanks

My PICU cot was shoved far into the corner to make room for additional medical equipment. During those first critical days of recovery, Henry was surrounded by an astounding amount of machinery. A massive instrument behind his bed snaked out in various directions like a metal octopus, each steel arm extending toward my baby's body with a different purpose.

During the first twenty-four hours, I spent a large part of the time just staring at him. I gazed at him thoroughly and intentionally, trying to force my eyes to drink in enough of him to last a lifetime. But I knew it would never be enough.

Often I'd shift my gaze to his monitors, and I soon learned how to read his heart rate, oxygen level, and blood pressure. I spent time staring at the tube that drained red fluid from his skull and watched for it to run clear. That would mean his internal bleeding had stopped.

When I wasn't staring at Henry or his medical equipment, I was camped out on my cot, staring at my iPhone. I'd try to watch TV or offer the occasional update to our growing group of prayer warriors. The day after Henry's surgery, I posted the following:

> "Rejoice always, pray continually, give thanks in all circumstances; for this is God's will for you in Christ Jesus" (1 Thess 5:16-18). Today I am thankful for Henry's stability through the night and for his responsiveness through the sedation (a sign he'll recover well from the procedure). I'm thankful for an outstanding surgeon and excellent medical staff. . . . I'm thankful for . . . each of you taking time to pray for & encourage us. I'm thankful to serve a God whose heart is FOR us, and I'm thankful for all the ways He's already using this journey. I'm thankful and confident that we'll see Henry's smile again . . .

Despite the pain, I was thankful. In terms of his immediate recovery from brain surgery, there were signs of hope. For instance, though we'd been instructed not to stimulate Henry, my mom had slipped her hand in his just hours after surgery and said softly, "Henry, it's Nana." That's when he shocked us by trying to open his eyes and sit up! That was definitely a positive sign. And when the nurses occasionally tickled Henry's arm, he'd flinch. That was an indicator of good responsiveness. So I was growing more confident that once his heavy sedation wore off and the swelling in his brain subsided, we'd be able to connect with him once again.

That night, twenty-four hours after we'd received the horrible news of his cancer, I kissed my baby's hand once again and then stretched out on my cot. In the semidarkness, I listened to the soft melody of classical Christmas carols that played on Henry's tablet. It was music that made the nurses pause and smile, and hopefully it was reminding my little boy of the season he loved.

It was a quiet moment to stop and offer thanks. It was the peace I needed to close my eyes and draw a breath. Before long I had drifted off to sleep.

The loudest pain

I awoke quickly to the most intense and hideous night of my life. Henry was still intubated, and his heavy surgical sedation had started to wear off. He awoke suddenly with wild eyes and muffled screams, stifled by the tube in his throat.

I jumped from my cot and rushed to his side. I stroked his arms and face and managed to soothe him. I assured him that he was okay, that Mommy was here. I promised that the tube would be gone soon. And within minutes, he mercifully passed out, until the process repeated, again . . . and again . . . and again.

Henry's nurse spent most of her midnight shift in our room, striving to keep him calm. Apparently Henry couldn't be extubated—have the breathing tube removed—during the night shift, because the hospital was not staffed as fully as during the day. That meant they'd be less able to respond adequately if a problem arose during the procedure. So Henry was kept under only mild sedation until morning, when a full medical staff would be available to extubate him. The staff was afraid that heavy sedation would cause him to sleep through another day, thus causing him to repeat the torturous experience another night.

So Henry was trapped, intubated, and terrified, in and out of consciousness the entire night. Hour after hour I soothed my precious, strange-looking baby. All of it ripped my heart in half—his pain, his fear, the fact that he looked so foreign to me. I could only watch as the devastating impact of a vicious tumor was compounded by the effects of a surgery that nearly took his life.

In my darkest moments of anguish and exhaustion, I began to wonder if we'd ever leave the PICU together. I felt so helpless as I watched his shocked little body struggle and fight, unsure he'd survive, and afraid of what lay ahead.

At one point that night, my prayers changed. *Just take him now if his life is going to be nothing but agony*, I began to pray. *Please just spare him this hideous existence. If he's not going to be healed, just take him now and spare him this torture.* But then I paused, wondering if I'd taught Henry enough about Jesus.

Would Henry know who Jesus was? Would he recognize him? Or would he arrive in heaven feeling all alone? I closed my eyes and begged Jesus to begin visiting Henry in his sleep. I didn't know *how* to prepare Henry, or if I'd have time to prepare him for meeting Jesus face-to-face. *I* was supposed to go first. Moms are supposed to die before their kids. But I was healthy, and I wouldn't be there to meet him. And I couldn't go with him. I so desperately didn't want him to feel alone.

Please, I began to pray again, *just come visit him right now and let him meet you, Jesus. Let him get to know you, so if he's heading to heaven he won't be afraid or feel alone when he gets there.*

I utilized the skills I'd learned in practicing imaginative prayer. I visualized, as vividly as possible, the outcome that I was praying would transpire. Draped over Henry's bedrail, I cried and prayed and imagined that Jesus was entering the dreams of my trauma-tized boy. I imagined the two of them building a tender relation-ship. And while I was in this concentrated state, my mind went somewhere unexpected.

Suddenly, I saw a misty image of Henry in heaven. He was standing with a small crowd. When he turned around, he laid eyes on Jesus for the first time. Jesus, several paces away, knelt down and opened his arms wide. His divine face was beaming with brilliance and love. To my surprise, Henry's eyes lit up with recognition just before he raced into those open arms.

I blinked back to the darkened PICU and realized what God was communicating to me: *Henry will know me, because he will rec-ognize the love you gave him when he was yours.*

And suddenly my loudest pain was hushed with hope. I realized that, just by loving him, we had already prepared Henry to meet Jesus. From that moment, I trusted that Henry would be okay even if he left my earthly arms.

Anguish and hope

The following day I posted this update:

> "Are not five sparrows sold for two pennies? Yet not one of them
> is forgotten by God. Indeed, the very hairs of your head are all

numbered. Don't be afraid; you are worth more than many sparrows" (Luke 12:6, 7). Today we are thankful for:

1) Henry is OFF the ventilator and breathing well. The surgeon's look of happy shock was priceless upon learning this. He marveled at this "little Hercules," and we marvel at the answered prayers of thousands of kind souls.

2) We can snuggle beside him now in the bed. This morning I laid my hand on his warm, soft face as we drifted into a nap. We can watch him nod or [we can] listen to a few whispered words. Ian was able to hold him in a rocker for twenty minutes, and we got our first smile!!

3) Our two-year-old daughter is thriving under the care of my parents and sitters at times when we are both away; this gives tremendous peace.

4) God is present and doing powerful work. You all, His body, have lifted us with each kind word, each prayer, and every act of service. Specifics on Henry's diagnosis will come to us down the road, but we know that in the face of any prognosis, our Father remains faithful, powerful, and evident.

You all have made our hearts burst with gratitude. God bless you and your families.

My updates were genuine and my gratitude sincere. But I always waited until quiet, hopeful moments to write them. They were written before I'd found my public voice, before I'd found the courage to be vulnerable. They were written when I was in perpetual "work mode," resolving to be strong and thankful for Henry's sake, coasting on the prayers of thousands.

What I didn't share publicly were the moments of weakness, the darkest realities. I endured those privately, behind thick hospital walls.

Mercifully, Henry had been extubated that morning. This allowed me to interact with him more freely. I quickly climbed into bed beside him and listened to his hoarse whisper. The most he could manage at first was just a weak yes or no.

At one point he wanted his favorite puzzle game on my iPhone. But every time he tried to touch a puzzle piece, his finger hit exactly a half inch outside the target. My heart broke as he stabbed fruitlessly at the game that had previously brought him so much comfort.

When Ian arrived late morning, I was reading Henry a Llama Llama book, the only one that had elicited a laugh since we arrived at the PICU. Henry was too weak, too sick to laugh that day, but he smiled. And when he smiled, one corner of his sweet little lips turned upward; the other remained still.

I seethed inside. When my dad discretely brought Henry's broken grin to my attention, I gave him a dirty look. I hated the cancer for stealing everything, including my baby's joyful expression. I hated that anyone could easily notice it. I hated my rudeness toward my loving dad and my own embarrassment of my baby's lopsided smile. I hated myself for feeling anything but joy in those first responsive moments. But mostly I hated the disease that had robbed us of Henry's smile, tempering even fleeting moments of joy with the abrupt reminder that cancer was ravaging his brain.

Not long after Ian arrived, a nurse offered to change Henry's sheets. The drainage from his head had wept diluted blood onto his pillowcase and the upper part of his bedding. So we gingerly moved Henry to his dad's lap while the bed was stripped and redressed.

Roughly a week earlier, Ian and I had sat together on our back porch. In the coolest part of a late summer day, we had watched Miri toddle and tried to coax Henry to eat. Eventually Ian and Henry developed a game out of it. Every time Henry took a bite of toast, Ian would throw a foam football into the yard. Henry, with gleeful giggles, would trample barefoot on freshly cut grass, scoop up his football, and run back to his daddy's arms. Then he'd take another bite of toast and they'd repeat the process.

"He's running around great," Ian had remarked. "He seems like he's getting stronger, healthier."

Now, about a week later, Ian was sitting in a vinyl rocker instead of a patio chair. Rather than inhaling a moist summer evening, he breathed stale hospital air, tinged with the scent of commercial laundry soap. The magical glow of a fading sun had been swapped for oppressive florescent lighting. And Ian's athletic son was replaced with a rigid, weak, and traumatized child.

Henry screeched as we scooped him from the bed and placed him in Ian's lap. Just last week our boy had thrown his head back in carefree laughter; now he needed his dad's throwing arm to hold it upright. Henry's eyes had so recently reflected joy and innocence in the warm Georgia twilight. Now they were glazed, bruised from swelling, and weary from pain.

So while the nurse changed Henry's sheets, we sat in horrified awareness of our son's trauma. And love pursued us. While we reeled from the chaos and heartbreak, people around us responded with astounding generosity. Gas cards, gift cards, checks, meals, toys, and letters poured in from family, friends, and a growing number of strangers. Toiletries and groceries were delivered to the hospital. There were offers for housecleaning and childcare for Miriam. We were added to prayer chains across the United States and around the world.

All of this generosity was extremely humbling for us. Ian and I had always prided ourselves on being strong, hardworking, and independent. We'd understood the importance of *giving*, but we were instantly thrown into the art of gracious *receiving*. We did our best to bumble through it.

It was a lesson in humility that we needed to learn. We began to allow people to participate in alleviating our pain through their service and generosity. We wanted to hold up our hands and say, "No thanks! We're fine! We don't need any help!" But we began to realize that this was coming from a place of deep-rooted pride.

We learned that graciously receiving the generosity of others blessed them. There were people who yearned to accompany the brokenhearted, and there was a sacredness to this. It wasn't our place to deny them. So we opened our hearts to receive the deep encouragement intended by others.

In time, we were able to pass along extra funds and toys to others, but in the moment we did our best to receive well the tremendous outpouring of support. We learned to just be thankful for the breathtaking love shown to one bright-eyed boy with a cowlick swirl of dirty-blond hair and a giant, contagious smile.

So in that bleak PICU, we ached and we thanked. Our hearts bled out and were infused by God through others. Where anguish waited, love persisted. When we were weary it was others, sometimes even strangers, who brought the hope.

Hell week

The next seven days were a blur of hellish recovery. It was common for me to pass out around midnight, after Henry had gotten his final dose of meds. Then I'd wake five hours later to the abruptness of medical staff in work mode. I'd jump up, fully clothed, then slip on shoes and scramble to Henry's side.

I'd have to keep pace beside his rolling bed, walking briskly down cold, bright hallways. My head was always half in a disappearing dream as I forced a smile and cooed, "It's okay, Baby. Mommy's right here. We're just going to take a picture. It won't hurt, I promise."

We'd crowd into an elevator and I'd wonder, *Will I get a shower today? Will Henry go back to sleep after this? Oh, I'm so, so exhausted. Why does he have to get a CT scan at five a.m.?* But I knew why. His doctors wanted to monitor his healing and the tumor's growth. Five a.m. worked well for the doctors, because they could have the results before morning rounds. It made sense for them, but it was hard on us.

Bleary-eyed and weary-hearted, we'd eventually arrive at the cavernous room where CT scans were conducted. We were always met by the kind smiles of perky techs, who seemed unaffected by the dreary lack of sunlight. Whoever was present would slip on blue lead vests and then circle around our little patient. Henry was usually pretty calm and sleepy at this point, but everything changed when we had to move him from his bed to the CT table.

As a team, we'd do our best to scoop his rigid, weak, and uncooperative body from its warm nest and place it awkwardly onto to the cold, hard surface. He would respond with the pitiful screams of a tortured animal.

The kid who had sensory issues and hated loud noises was then inserted into a noisy machine that hummed and whirled around his head while he cried out. Sometimes the techs would turn on a projector that cast cartoon images onto the ceiling of that monstrous doughnut. And I'd wonder, *Does that soothe any kid, ever?*

Once Henry was inside the CT machine, I could stand behind him and lean as close as possible to his face. I would have crawled inside if they'd let me. While the machine moaned, I'd recite Henry's favorite books. I lured him into the stories that we'd read hundreds of times since his infancy, so frequently that I'd memorized every page. I recited them clearly and gently, determined to keep my speech steady while blinking back the tears that he couldn't see.

I poured out every stitch of energy, every ounce of hope, every molecule of strength that I possessed during those scans. I did the only thing I knew to do: be his mommy, his cheerleader, his teacher, his coach, his advocate, and the one who nestled him close and made him feel safe in a horribly scary world. Most often, the soothing sound of my voice, reciting his favorite books, brought him just enough comfort, just enough sanity, to stop crying. And soon enough, the imaging was done.

Then we'd all cheer for little Henry and proclaim, "You're all done! Good job, Buddy!" And he'd give a weak smile as the noise of the machine quieted. But then it was time to move him back to his hospital bed, and the tortured screams would start again.

And so went our week. Often a 5:00 a.m. CT scan would kick off a day straight from Hades. Henry's neurological trauma, combined with living in a busy PICU and being tethered to a bed by IV wires, began producing in him anxiety that rocketed off the charts. I did everything I could think of in response. I kept his favorite classical Christmas carols playing softly in his PICU room. I also kept the lights down and made sure my phone was off, because he couldn't tolerate any sudden sounds.

But that was about all I could control in his environment, and it was just a drop of calm in a bucket of chaos. I couldn't prevent the frequent, shrill beeping from the hospital equipment that would grate on my baby's frazzled nerves. And I couldn't stop the constant employee foot traffic that kept us both on the brink of insanity. Throughout the day a barrage of strangers entered the room, including nurses, pharmacy techs, doctors, custodians, physical therapists, occupational therapists, speech therapists, nutritionists, nurse assistants, and the very rare visitor that I'd approved. Every time the doors swooshed open, Henry cringed. He never knew what to expect, nor how badly it would hurt.

He hated the constant stimulation. All he desperately wanted was my quiet, undivided attention. He yearned for it so badly that he'd melt down when I spoke to his doctors, and he'd scream inconsolably when I raced to the bathroom.

Yet if there was one great blessing in that horrific week, it was the fact that my constantly engaged, taxed, and stressed mind could not stop for too long to face reality. Deep down, I knew that if I stayed focused enough on the relentless demands of my neurologically devastated child, I could avoid thinking critically about the future. I could shove aside the realization that Ian's tone had darkened as he kept researching. I could keep avoiding the conversations that he wanted to have.

As long as I kept my focus on Henry's care, I could hold out hope.

Six

Henry's Tiger

*C*ome *with me, guys,"* she said warmly. But I didn't want to.

It was the moment we'd been anticipating since Henry's hospital admission. The biopsy results were back. The neuro-oncologist had an exact diagnosis. But by this point I knew enough to know that I didn't want to know what we were working with.

I didn't want to hear from the nice lady in business casual wear. I didn't want to see the stats, hear the odds, or face the truth. But what *I* wanted was ruthlessly disregarded by necessity. So while my dad stayed with Henry, I took Ian's hand, and we followed the friendly clicking of the doctor's heels.

As we threaded through the PICU, I relied heavily on my now skill of practicing the presence of God.[1] I had learned during Henry's hospitalization to associate everyday things, like sunlight streaming through the window or encounters with living, breathing people, with reminders of God's love. I knew from Scripture that Jesus holds all things together (Col 1:17), so I drew comfort from the miracle of breath being drawn and released all around me. I recognized reflections of God's love through hearts beating and pulses pumping. Light, life, and even the nature of gravity became a reminder of God's love.

So as I sat in a bland room with neutral décor, I envisioned God's hand taking the form of the couch and cradling me in perfect, powerful love. And as love embraced me, I breathed.

For a long time, I just breathed. I breathed while the doctor's lips were moving. I breathed as reality wrapped its icy hands around my neck. I breathed as logic jerked my chin upward and demanded that I look it in the eyes. I breathed through imagined flashes of ripping down watercolor paintings, overturning end tables, and smashing an empty flower vase against the door. I breathed through the twisted torture of a diplomatic discussion about my child's fate.

When it was over, we all agreed to meet again the next day. Then I returned to my cancer-ridden baby, and Ian posted the following:

> Henry has a very aggressive malignant tumor called a Supratentorial Primitive Neuroectodermal Tumor (PNET). It is very large and vascular. It's also rare (only ten to forty children in the United States per year are diagnosed). Unfortunately, because of his age and the nature of the tumor, treatment options are limited. . . . Treatment protocols are still being discussed, and it might be several weeks before a decision is made.

The breaking point

After seventeen days in the PICU, Henry was transferred to the neurology unit of the children's hospital. It was a move I hoped would lift his spirits, but as we weaved through more cookie-cutter hospital hallways, sometimes passing the scary cries of other neurological patients, and into an older, dim room, his disposition got worse.

He desperately wanted to go home. He wanted his baby sister and his toys and his family all around him. He wanted to be far from beeping machines and wires that restricted his movements. He wanted to be four. He wanted to go *home.*

It was after ten that evening when I finally got all of our stuff moved into his new room. After I finished the essential unpacking and ensured that Henry got his nightly meds, I tucked him in.

I kissed his sweet, scarred head and said softly, "I love you." But for the first time ever, my baby turned away from me.

He looked at the wall and said quietly, "No, you don't."

And on that cold October night, it took every ounce of self-control I had not to rip off all his wires, scoop up his ravaged body, and run all the way home.

Lazy laughs

The next morning, a child life specialist stopped by. I had learned in the PICU that part of what these specialists do is provide age-appropriate coping strategies for the hospitalized children. So I told her about Henry's dark mood, and she miraculously returned with play dough and foam paint. Then, for a few minutes, my little engineer was able to create.

His smile reappeared, and I noticed that it was stronger than before. Physical therapy was helping. I'd been offering him drinks through a straw on the left side of his lips, and slowly the grin I'd loved so much was coming back.

But with play dough spread across the table in front of him, I noticed that Henry only played with his right hand and kept the left hand tucked into his lap. Remembering his smile's progress, I lifted his left hand and teased, "Henry, you have to say to this hand: '*Lefty*! Don't be *lazy*!'"

Henry's eyes lit up and he yelled, "*Wefty*! Don't be *wazy*!"

And we both *waughed* our butts off.

Taming the tiger

As Ian and I poured ourselves into caring for Henry and Miri, we used what was left of our dwindling physical, mental, and emotional resources to focus on the most critical decision of our lives. Like stumbling upon a wild tiger and teaching it to sit, Ian and I had to face Henry's unthinkable diagnosis, analyze our options, and plan a response.

Taming that tiger was an extensive, messy, and terrifying process. There were countless hours of research and numerous discussions with elite medical professionals. We explored and evaluated standard, experimental, and even alternative treatment options. Tragically, we learned that even with the most aggressive treatments, the survival rate was very low, and the treatment process would be extremely grueling for Henry. Our task was to weigh the devastating nature of treatments that could possibly extend Henry's life against the value of ensuring him the highest quality of life in the days that remained.

Trying to determine what to do was excruciating, because there was no clear-cut "right" answer. We knew that no matter what we decided, someone else would make an entirely different choice under the same circumstances. It was a subjective decision, left completely in our shaking hands. The fear of making a mistake was nearly crippling. How could we be sure about what was best for

Henry? What would we want if we were in his position? Would we look back one day and have regrets?

That beast roared loudest one afternoon when Ian and I were walking in the hospital garden. Surrounded by rare urban greenery and the rumble of traffic behind an iron fence, we sat and stared straight into its yellow eyes.

"We have to make a decision," Ian said quietly.

"I know."

So in the sunny chill of that noisy oasis, we breathed life and discussed death. We ran our hands over that tiger's fur, and we marveled at its fierceness.

Henry's body wasn't fighting his cancer. That was one reason it was so powerful. The original cell mutation had been so slight that, rather than discarding it, his body had allowed it to multiply. His system had fueled the budding tumor, causing it to grow staggeringly large even as it destroyed good brain tissue around it. That greedy beast had then siphoned off the blood supply to healthy cells and had grown mighty from their nutrients.

Before Henry's hospital admission, the tumor had become so enormous that it blocked circulating cerebrospinal fluids from leaving his brain. This caused pressure to build as the fluid accumulated. That violent animal was so belligerently aggressive that despite the fact that the surgeon had removed half its mass, it was rapidly growing again. Its cells were multiplying even then, as we sat in devastated reverence on a cold stone bench.

Henry's tiger was ferocious, and he was helpless against it. He needed us to face his monster and decide what to do. So again we prayed, we talked, and we cried. Then we made a decision.

After sharing it with our family and Henry's medical professionals, Ian posted the following update:

> Well, it's been a week of discussion, prayer, and reaching the most agonizing decision of our lives. All treatment options for Henry's brain cancer were weighed and researched, and in the end we felt peace with only one path.
>
> We [will] proceed with inpatient rehab therapy only, for the purpose of reaching peak motor skill/mobility before bringing our precious boy home with hospice care for these final months.
>
> The neurosurgeon said he wished he had a reason to disagree, or to encourage us to keep fighting, but admitted that he couldn't, and that he would choose the same path in our position. He spoke of the dignity we can give little Henry—taking him home to security & familiarity, surrounded by family.
>
> Today we are thankful for the care he has received and will receive. We're thankful for his giggles this week while playing with play dough and paints, and his wide-eyed joy as we explored the hospital from the view of his Radio Flyer wagon.
>
> We're thankful that for the past few years we've been studying the heart of God, especially in the face of evil. We've gained tremendous perspective from a book titled: *Is God to Blame?* by Greg Boyd. Having that knowledge before tragedy hit our home has framed this whole experience with the assurance that our Father's heart is FOR us, and for little Henry, regardless of the outcome.
>
> Please pray our days at home will be filled with joy, peace, and the making of precious memories. And please know that as long as his heart beats, we continue to pray for a miracle. We ask that

you join us. Thank you again for the tremendous outpouring of support. Love and blessings.

Bright mornings

They say it gets darkest before the dawn. After we opted for hospice care, Henry was transferred to the daybreak of rehab. The rehab unit was bright, new, and cheerful. Aside from the medical equipment, Henry's new space felt like a modern hotel suite.

It was an ideal atmosphere for motivated labor, which was good, because Henry was sent there to work. He was better able to handle stimulation at this point, and so he cycled through speech, occupational, and physical therapies from dawn until dusk. Thankfully, his therapists were highly creative and flexible. They struck the right balance between being pushy and being patient.

After four surgeries and three weeks in bed, Henry's physical therapist stood him upright on his rigid legs and led him through the motions of walking. He screamed bloody murder from discomfort and anxiety during those early efforts. But with her gentle persistence, he progressed. In fact, in just three days Henry achieved all the physical therapy goals set for his entire stay! And by the following week, he was walking without assistance.

He continued to thrive with therapies that incorporated all his favorite activities, including painting, doing puzzles, playing with play dough, riding elevators, climbing stairs, and even attending a Halloween party in the downstairs game room.

One of his favorite therapies was riding the specialized tricycle. His feet and chest were secured with Velcro straps while his legs relearned their responsibilities. Once Henry got the hang of it, he found freedom. He peddled around like a wild man, circling the rehab unit, grinning and shouting "Hewwo!" to the nurses, all of whom paused to laugh and wave.

It was amazing to watch him regain strength and mobility. It was so encouraging to see him conquer challenges. And it was sheer joy to watch him giggle, play, and just be *four*.

Sweet dreams

After an intense day of therapy, Henry and I always made video calls to family members who were thrilled to see his sweet chipmunk cheeks squished into a smile. Then I'd help Henry brush his teeth before reading him stories. And after his nightly meds were administered, I tucked him in with *ten* giggling kisses.

Then I'd retreat to my makeshift bed about eight feet away. But after a few quiet minutes, I'd hear, "Mommy?"

"Yes, Baby?"

Then my little man, who never mastered consonant blends, would ask sweetly, "Should we *suggle*?"

No matter how exhausted, I could never resist him. I'd say, "Yes, we should snuggle." And I'd cross the room, slide into bed beside him, and gently scoop him close.

After another minute I'd hear again, "Mommy?"

"Yes, Baby?"

"Should we hold hands?"

"Yes, we should hold hands," I'd say. And we did.

With Henry's world a little safer and his mommy much closer, his breathing would soon grow heavy and his body would relax. But I could never get comfortable there, smashed against his bedrail. So once he drifted off to sleep, I'd gingerly crawl out of his bed and head back to mine.

But no matter how desperately I longed for sleep, it wouldn't come. That had been different when we were in the PICU. There I'd always passed out easily, because I knew the nurses were monitoring Henry's vitals. They knew instantly if the slightest problem arose. But after we opted for hospice care, most of Henry's monitors were removed.

The lack of wires meant that Henry could move more freely and sleep more easily. But I couldn't. I couldn't sleep because the nature of his tumor meant that it was possible that he could die suddenly from an "event" such as a seizure.

So as he lay across the room, unmonitored, I struggled to fall asleep. I was afraid he'd die alone. I was scared that I'd wake up in the morning and he'd be gone.

Eventually it occurred to me that I should slip in my earbuds and turn on a podcast. And without fail, hearing about God's perfect love provided enough peace for me to relax. And once I relaxed, sleep came barreling in.

Sour candy

After our first long week of therapy, Henry took me on a date. Our reservation was at the bench outside of the hospital gift shop. There we had an elite view of the glistening, sapphire ocean—featured on interactive screens against the hospital wall.

My dashing companion ordered for both of us—gummy bears. And as we dove into the vibrant rainbow assortment, we enjoyed light and sophisticated discussion.

"Mommy, watch dis!" Henry said and bit off one of the bear's heads.

"Oh, Henry!" I shrieked in mock horror. "That poor bear! How could you do that?!" He started giggling incessantly, pausing only to repeat the process. And so went our highbrow conversation: bite, horrified shriek, incessant giggles, repeat. It was a perfectly lovely date.

But there were pauses . . . moments when the words ran out. Moments when my thoughts rushed in. Moments when I heard the echoing advice of kind supporters instructing me to savor every minute. And on a whim, I decided to heed their instruction.

I opened my heart and studied my date. I soaked in his essence, as bright and varied as a painter's palate. I really *looked* at the peachy richness in his cherub face. I stared into his country blue eyes, framed with thick, onyx lashes. I ran my hand through his slight curls, the color of late-summer straw, and soaked in the amber glow of his warm, loving presence.

But as my heart opened, the pain invaded. The crushing reality that this was one of our *last* dates swooped upon me. My eyes began to burn, and my lower lip began to tremble. So I pulled away, turned away, and tried to shut it all out again.

After a few hard swallows, I did my best to transition back to carefree gummy dismemberment. I tried to pretend that Henry didn't have cancer. I tried to pretend that he was going to grow up. I tried to laugh loudly while discretely wiping tears. I wanted *so badly* to enjoy the simplicity of sharing candy with my four-year-old.

But those tears kept falling, like rain on wet canvas, blurring and streaking our perfectly lovely date.

Reunited

"Bo-Bo!" Miri shrieked behind her turquoise pacifier. After three weeks apart, she'd spotted her big brother. He was on a couch in his rehab room. We watched her curly ribbons bounce as she padded across the room in scuffed pink Crocs.

Henry lit up like a Christmas tree, grinning from ear to ear now that his face had regained full muscle strength. And for an instant, cancer and feeding tubes and impending death faded into the background while two little friends hugged.

They giggled and snuggled and played with "Get Well" balloons as we blinked back our tears and watched with quiet admiration. At two and four years old, they depended on someone else for almost everything in their little worlds. But it was obvious that the love between them transcended anything that anyone could orchestrate.

We quietly bore witness to the tender, innocent affection between siblings, two little friends skipping arm in arm through the crazy maze of childhood. They didn't understand the chaos invading their family. They just knew that, for a moment, they were together. And their joy was radiant.

After a few minutes, Henry grew tired and needed to lie back down. And without a thought, Miriam crawled into bed beside him. They shared his covers and stared up at us through matching sets of bright blue eyes and thick dark lashes. Ian and I wrapped our arms around each other and gazed back at our babies. We stood broken and thankful, sad and full, and ready to go home.

And on October 18, after twenty-eight days, four surgeries, and three patient rooms, we did just that. We brought Henry home.

We brought Henry home . . . to die. On some level I knew that. But I couldn't accept it. I was his mama. I loved him like the breath in my lungs. I couldn't stop dreaming. I couldn't stop wishing. I couldn't stop praying for a miracle.

Even in the face of impossible odds, I couldn't abandon hope.

SEVEN

Henry the Snowman

Henry's grandparents were waiting at the window when we pulled into the drive. Before the car even rolled to a stop, they had burst out of the front door. Balloons were dancing atop the mailbox behind us as we hugged, smiled, and tenderly transferred Henry from the car.

It all felt deeply familiar and yet strangely foreign. I kept having flashes of bringing baby Henry home from the hospital to begin his life. Four years later we were unloading a feeding machine instead of a baby carrier and a wheelchair instead of a stroller. I never dreamed we'd bring Henry home to die.

But home was where he longed to be. Home to his baby sister's giggles and her adoring gazes. Home to a soft sofa and fuzzy blankets. Home to his art supplies and favorite books. Home to an oversized bathtub filled with mountains of bubbles and drops of food coloring in assorted cups. Home to Mommy and Daddy's king-sized bed with extra-soft sheets. Home to spacious rooms and a big backyard that tumbled off the patio. Home to privacy and peace.

We were home, and we had a mission. We were going to celebrate, savor, and infuse every moment left with the joy of a lifetime. So despite the October warmth, we launched into Henry's favorite holiday.

We made gingerbread houses. We lit cinnamon candles. We decorated our ten-foot Christmas tree, set the fireplace ablaze, and played Christmas classics on TV. We celebrated with gifts and giggles and giant meals with extended family.

Our house was filled with love and the evidence of God working. At times, the quiet undercurrent of dread was almost imperceptible. We were all distracted by the priceless relief of being home together.

One evening, overcome with this great love, I shared the following with Henry's online supporters and prayer warriors:

> I have often wondered what it would look like to wander through the "valley of the shadow of death" with someone so close to me. And now home with a terminally ill child, I believe we've entered the valley. Some of my assumptions were correct—there are pockets of darkness, fear, dread, and a deep sadness. But I was mistaken about one thing. This valley is not desolate. By God's grace, our valley is flooded with your prayers and tears, your support and cheers. Most of all it is flooded with the light of our Father's love. This valley may be many things, but it is not a lonely place. Thank you for flooding this valley with love.

We were loved, and Henry was happy. My button-nosed boy was home, and that made the world good in some fairy-tale way. Maybe that's why I couldn't accept that he was going to die.

I had told our supporters that I *believed* we had entered the valley of the shadow of death. I couldn't say that I was certain. I *wouldn't* say I was certain. Not when I was surrounded by so much love. Not when Henry was so alive. And not when I had one last hope of finding our happily ever after.

I just needed the phone to ring.

Magical formula

When it finally rang, I sprang off the couch and sprinted for the bedroom. Fifteen minutes later, that's where Ian found me, a quiet phone in my hand, a blank look on my face.

"What did he say?" Ian asked.

I bit my lip. "He said it's possible that 'unconfessed sin' is blocking our prayers for healing."

"What?!"

I glanced at our bedroom door. My parents were down the hall, no doubt wondering about the mysterious call that had me racing for privacy. How was I going to tell them this?

"He said it probably wasn't Henry's sin, since he's four," I clarified while biting my nails. "But he said that according to some verse in the Old Testament it could be *our* sin, or the sin of our parents or grandparents. It could be something done decades ago that we don't even know about. He said they're willing to pray with our family, to help us root it out."

"Like a group confessional?!" Ian asked.

"I guess . . ." I trailed off.

"You're serious right now?"

I knew it all sounded strange, but for some reason I felt slightly defensive of the pastor. Maybe it was because *I* had called *him*. I'd heard that his church had experienced miraculous healings, and I was desperate for a miracle. Perhaps I was defensive because he'd been so kind and so obviously sincere. He didn't pressure me to set up a meeting and had prayed such a pure, heartfelt prayer for Henry before we'd hung up.

"Could he be right?" I whispered through tears. "What if this is somehow our fault?"

"Jess," Ian sighed. He'd been hesitant about this from the start, and my playback of the conversation wasn't helping. "We confess our sins to God and each other. Even if we forget some, would God let Henry die of brain cancer on a technicality? We don't have to publicly rummage through every failure. Besides, are you going to put your parents through that? They've dropped everything to come help us."

"I know," I said. I knew they'd be willing to do anything for Henry. But was this necessary? Was this the magical formula that could vaporize Henry's tumor?

Ian sank to the edge of our bed, and I began pacing. "This guy says he's seen miracles! And he told me about a guy who wasn't willing to do this because his family practiced a different religion . . . and the guy died!"

"Does this approach look like Jesus?" Ian asked wearily. "Were the disciples taught to heal in the name of Jesus? Or were they instructed to conduct a scavenger hunt of past sins first?"

I stopped pacing and inhaled slowly. That verse in 2 Corinthians came to mind: the one that says that in Christ, I am a new creation, the old is gone and the new has come. I figured that meant that our sins, and even the sins of our lineage, couldn't supernaturally curse Henry. I realized that no matter how sincere the pastor had been, I couldn't reconcile his method with the restorative work of Calvary. So while we were willing to do anything to pursue healing from the God we'd grown to love, this activity seemed to presuppose a picture of God as a bean-counting, grudge-holding God of technicalities.

Ian stood and wrapped his strong arms around me. "Why don't you and I pray right now?" he murmured in my ear. "And remember, thousands of people, all over the world, are praying for Henry."

So we prayed, we held each other, and then we got back to Henry. And amazingly, at the end of the day, I could honestly say that Henry didn't seem worse. In fact, he'd shown improvement every day that followed his brain surgery. The trembling had long ceased. He was getting increasingly mobile, thanks to his desire to keep up with Miri. So even though we'd passed on that particular group prayer experience, I couldn't help but hope that maybe, *just maybe*, the thousands of prayers still being offered were taking effect. Maybe Henry would be healed. Maybe we'd get our happily ever after, after all.

Made of snow

Of all the holiday classics we watched that season, *Frosty the Snowman* was a definite favorite. Perhaps that's because in our house, Henry was so much like that dancing snowman.

He was the life of the party. He was the playful one everyone else gathered around. Instead of the skinny kid he'd been in years past, he'd become a plump little beefcake due to lots of time in bed, steroids, and high-calorie formula. He bumbled around in snowman-like fashion on legs that were striving to remember their function. He knocked over lamps and bumped into furniture, always a bit loopy from the pain meds. But he did it all with a mischievous twinkle in his eye and a laugh on his lips.

On Halloween, our little snowman was happy to dress up and dance through another candy-filled holiday. So we all followed his jolly lead, and celebrated like we always had . . . with a few exceptions.

Like every year, Henry was in costume, but this year his getup had to be roomy enough for the gastrostomy tube jutting from his abdomen and snaking down his leg.

Like every year, we ate dinner before going trick-or-treating. This year Henry's meal was formula dripped directly into his stomach. His chaser was a cocktail of hospice meds to help his digestion and manage his pain.

Like every year, we took pictures. This year we couldn't seem to get enough pictures.

Like every year, we went door-to-door soliciting candy. This year we brought along the wagon, because Henry couldn't walk very far.

Like every year, we were just another family wandering from house to house. This year we were also *that* family, the one everyone had been talking about. This year Henry was *that* little boy, the one with the brain tumor. The one who'd just come home from the hospital. The one on hospice care.

Like every year, we passed our neighbors on the sidewalks. This year several stopped and introduced themselves, many with tears in their eyes.

Like every year, Ian and I tucked our dumplings into bed after trick-or-treating, collapsed on the couch, and turned on the TV. This year we turned on the local news, and we watched a story about Henry.

The piece had been put together with our blessing, using footage we'd provided during our hospital stay. It was beautifully and reverently done, but oh, so tragic. It was titled "Henry's Last Holidays," and I remember gasping when I saw those words.[1] Obviously, those kind reporters didn't know that our little snowman was getting stronger every day. They didn't know how full of life he was. They didn't know that thousands were praying for a miracle. They didn't realize that Henry still had no trace of trembling. Trembling was the big red flag that had placed us in the ER and ultimately revealed that fluids were building in his skull. They didn't know that his trembling was long gone.

That night I went to bed with one thought in my head. Like every year, the news station would run another story the following Halloween. But next year they'd present their most amazing personal interest piece yet. It would be a story about the little boy named Henry who miraculously defied all the odds.

I went to bed hopeful that everything would be fine and the celebrations would last forever. I snuggled beside my little angel and placed a hand on his small chest. It rose and fell in perfect rhythm, his heart thumping gently. I placed a hand under his nose, and felt his breath, steady and warm. Everything about him was so vivid and bright and completely alive. I yawned and closed my eyes. Despite what the doctors or the reporters or the holiday classics said, I was more convinced than ever that our little Frosty wasn't made of snow.

Magic hats

There was something magical about that helmet. It looked like an ordinary firefighter's helmet, but somehow it transformed Henry into the goofiest, cutest little firefighter our neighborhood had ever seen. And it brought out the best in everyone around him.

A few days after Halloween, I opened our front door and found our county's fire chief and deputy standing on our porch. "Would Henry like to see a fire truck?" they asked. They'd seen the news story and had jumped to do what heroes do: help.

"Yeah!" Henry said, bumbling past them into the yard.

Minutes later *two* fire trucks were parked out front, and several of the firefighters were circled around Henry. They squatted down to his level, answering all his giddy, rapid-fire questions about their mighty vehicles. My eyes filled with tears as I watched strong, smart men—warriors and heroes—kneel in tender patience, offering gentle dignity to the little man before them.

After a few minutes, one of the firefighters crouched behind Henry and wrapped his arms around him to keep him steady. Together, they turned on the fire hose. Henry shouted with laughter as the powerful propulsion knocked him back. He held tight, though, and managed to give our lawn a nice watering. After that, Henry accepted the hand of another firefighter. Together they slowly circled one of the trucks to inspect its ladders and gadgets.

Finally, to Henry's delight, he and his daddy were invited to climb inside. No sooner had they sat down when the rest of us threw our hands over our aching ears. The truck's siren had suddenly sprung to life, and it kept screaming, and screaming, and screaming. I looked at the firefighter beside me in bewilderment.

"Your husband's stepping on the alarm!" he shouted with a grin. About that time, Ian sheepishly lifted his foot, and we all sighed with relief. Then we waved as Henry, Ian, and one of the firefighters drove off to cruise the neighborhood.

In the days that followed, police officers started visiting too. They'd arrive with gifts and smiles, piling extra joy onto our holidays. Other days, neighbors I'd barely met showed up on the doorstep, arms filled with toys, meals, or cards with checks.

The grace-filled days started to race by in a blur. While Ian and I got somewhat lost in those exceptional moments, we remained acutely aware that he had only five weeks of paid leave from work. Much of that time had already been spent. But thanks to the diligent efforts of some folks at his job, Ian was enrolled in a leave donation program, and the sick days began flooding in. Coworkers across the nation gave up days with their families so Ian could have more time with his son.

Mountains were moving, and everyone was scrambling to accommodate our little boy. Petty competitiveness and flimsy walls of societal separation were stripped away. I witnessed the deepest kindness in the eyes of the toughest folks. I saw powerful men shed silent tears because their brute strength was no match for Henry's tumor. In our direst circumstances, the best of humanity was revealed.

While we were immeasurably thankful and deeply touched, I kept wanting to clarify that everyone needn't be so sad. I wanted them to lift their chins and return to work with a smile, because Henry didn't seem worse. In fact, he seemed a little better. Every day he seemed better.

On the day that the firefighters came, I eventually handed that magical helmet back to the chief. I managed to simply smile and say thank you. What I really wanted to do was meet his sad gaze and assure him, *You don't have to worry about us. I think maybe he's getting better.*

Having some fun

We dumped a collection of gift shop loot onto the front counter. "Um, I fink I want the udder one," Henry said thoughtfully. His focus was on the moderately sized stuffed panda.

"You want me to get the big one instead?" I asked.

Henry nodded. I smiled apologetically at the cashier and promised to be right back. It was the third day of our whirlwind Make-A-Wish weekend. The first day we had visited an aquarium. The second day was a limo ride to Cirque du Soleil, and on this final day we were enjoying a trip to the zoo.

Within seconds I was hoisting a massive stuffed panda onto the counter. As soon as I met the cashier's gaze, I saw the smirk. I saw the judgment. Her eyebrows rose, her nose lifted a bit, and her lips pursed more tightly.

Perhaps I was paranoid. Maybe I was just sensitive about my lavish actions. Either way, a wave of shame washed over me. That stuffed toy probably cost what she earned in a day.

Her judgment was understandable. She didn't know. She didn't know why the little boy dancing around was wearing a cap. She didn't know that under that cap was a ten-inch scar. She didn't know that under that scar was a giant brain tumor.

She didn't know that the only reason we were at the zoo was because the doctors were convinced that he was going to die. She didn't know we were trying to cram a lifetime's worth of fun into a matter of months. She didn't know this panda might be the last toy I ever bought him.

She didn't know that this day might be Henry's last chance to hear the chirps of exotic birds or breathe in the smell of mud-caked animals. Between our VIP experiences of petting African elephants and feeding giant pandas, she hadn't seen us step off the sunlit trail and slide into the shade. We had paused near the reptile exhibit so I could discretely retrieve the G-tube from Henry's sweatpants and push narcotics and neuropathy meds directly into his stomach. She didn't know the emotional and logistical lengths that Ian and I endured so that Henry could enjoy a carefree zoo adventure.

She didn't know that I felt impulsive, conflicted, and confused about every purchase I made for him now. My pragmatic, frugal side battled with this new Sporadic Santa side. When Henry was born, we lived on a fraying shoestring budget. I'd prided myself on buying all his clothes, books, and toys secondhand or gladly accepting hand-me-downs. In fact, two months earlier I would never have *dreamed* of buying either of my children a seventy-dollar stuffed animal. But the thought of losing Henry had me doing things I'd never done. I'd have bought a *real* panda if I could have . . . if it would have brought him one more smile. But she didn't know any of that.

It wasn't obvious that one day soon, I might not be able to hug Henry. I knew that if that day ever came, I could wrap my arms around that giant panda. And just for a second, I would be able to close my eyes and remember this day.

Alive as he could be

My brother, Joe, posted the following on Sunday, November 11.

> We are preparing to storm the gates of hell and declare heaven on earth for my nephew Henry. The enemy would love to bring death, but our king is the author of LIFE. Today we stand and fight with the one who makes all things new, whose promises are YES and amen . . . Jesus, thank you for healing my nephew!

He was coordinating with a local church to organize a prayer meeting, and he was inviting everyone to join us. My brother was like me—holding out hope for a miracle. Others were just desperate to do *something* to ease our pain.

For example, just the previous day I'd run into a neighbor who was also a Christian. He really wanted to help. "What can we do for you guys?" he had asked again. We were standing side by side at the park, watching our sons play. His was agile and quick. Mine was lumbering around, loopy and erratic, acting much younger than his age.

My neighbor watched Henry with brokenness in his eyes. "Can my wife take you out for some girl time? Can I take Ian out for a break? We just really want to minister to you guys. What can we do?"

"Well," I said, "There *is* a group coming over to pray tomorrow. They want to surround our house and ask God for a miracle. You guys could come to join them if you want."

That's when he looked away and his eager eyes sobered a bit. "Well, prayer is good and all," he said with quiet conviction, "but ultimately God is sovereign over whether he chooses to heal."

I guess in his view, prayer wasn't really that important. After all, an all-powerful God could do whatever he wants whenever he wants. He could heal Henry or let him die. It was all in his hands. Minutes later I watched his son bound off while I gathered my bumbling snowman. We all headed for our homes.

My neighbor didn't make it to the prayer time. Ian and I weren't sure if *anyone* would make it to the prayer time. The date and time had been posted, but apart from my brother and a few friends, we had no idea who would actually show up.

So that Sunday afternoon, Ian and I camped out in our bedroom, occasionally peeking outside. At first the street was bare. But finally one car pulled up and parked. It was followed by another . . . and then another . . . and then another. Soon tears were filling my eyes as cars filled the street. Friends, family, and people I'd never met walked past our windows and gathered in the backyard. They arranged themselves in a circle and started sharing, each in turn.

"I don't get it," Ian said softly, peering through our blinds. Henry was nestled in our bed sleeping soundly, just a few feet away. I'd closed our bedroom blinds because I didn't want Henry to wake from his nap and find a bunch of people outside. I didn't know how to explain what was happening. I didn't want to him to feel uncomfortable.

"What don't you get?" I whispered back.

"Why does it matter whether people *gather* to pray or just pray separately in their homes? I don't want you to get your hopes up about this," he said.

I looked at him incredulously. "It matters because there's something *special* about God's children gathered in prayer! They fuel one another's passion! They join their hearts and focus on bringing the kingdom together. Remember the verse that says if two or more are gathered then God hears their prayer? I mean, I know God hears individual prayers, but there's power in numbers!"

"I guess," Ian said.

It was about that time that the group stopped their sharing and grew quiet. We continued to spy through the window as they then joined hands, bowed heads, and from what I was later told, presented bold and powerful prayers for miraculous healing.

Inside, Ian and I placed our hands on our sleeping son and whispered prayers of agreement. I launched into imaginative prayer. I envisioned the tumor shriveling cell by cell. I imagined new, healthy cells growing in their place. I pictured the look of be-wildered joy on the neuro-oncologist's face as she reported a clean MRI scan.

Before long Henry stirred awake from his nap and quickly bounded out of bed. When he realized there were people outside, he begged to go play with them. Seconds later he was bursting into the yard, as alive as he could be!

He ran past most of the curious and hopeful gazes, but paused in the middle of a small cluster of adults. He'd spotted his uncle Joe. Joe knelt beside him and asked if he could touch Henry's forehead with some oil.

"Okay," Henry said lightly.

Joe touched Henry's head gently and prayed a simple prayer with a giant smile and soft tone. The group murmured their agree-ment just before Henry giggled and ran away.

Soon several women surrounded *me* and began praying. They poured blessings over me, poured their faith into me, and asked God to infuse me with supernatural peace and strength. As I left their embrace to chase Henry, I was struck by how many precious souls from various walks of life, many of whom had never met, had united as siblings in Christ.

Much as the team of medical professionals gathered on the day of Henry's craniotomy, this group had assembled with purpose, united in mission, and ushered in a fresh wave of hope. The posts that followed reflected the rising sense of optimism.

One woman shared on Facebook: "I can't begin to tell you how the filling of the Holy Spirit empowered us to pray, anoint, and walk around Henry's home today. Great things will happen as a re-sult of the prayer on 11/11." Another posted: "So thankful for such an amazing time of prayer for Henry today. Thank you to all who were there with us and to so many others who were with us in spirit praying. We could definitely feel the Holy Spirit moving."

In the days that followed, Henry continued to thrive. Besides the fact that he was still free of trembling, he was quickly regaining his ability to run well. He was eating a higher quantity and larger variety of food than I'd seen in months, and his body began growing at a rapid rate. Every day he seemed bigger, stronger, better.

Even Ian finally admitted, "Who knows? Maybe he *was* healed."

EIGHT

The Sun Was Hot That Day

artoons were playing. The Christmas tree was twinkling. Steamy coffee was filling the air with the aroma of productivity. And Henry's hand was shaking as he reached for the sippy cup.

I was barely awake enough to process it. Ian and I had just stumbled into the living room after a night of restless sleep. As I sat, staring at the jittering plastic cylinder, I thought back to Henry's last doctor's visit. I'd told the physician's assistant that I thought I'd seen a slight tremble earlier that day. But by the time Henry was examined, there was no trace of it. Even so, she dutifully checked his pupils and his balance.

"It's not hydrocephalus," she said, dismissing my concerns that Henry's cerebrospinal fluids were again trapped and building inside his skull. We all knew he wouldn't survive hydrocephalus again.

"I didn't see it," Ian had volunteered. So that day I'd shoved the gnawing fear downward. After all, even if I *had* seen a slight trembling, it could just be medication. He was on lots of medication. It was probably just the medication.

But that bright morning the shaking was more pronounced. The little blue cup clearly vibrated by its bright green handles. I looked over at Ian and our eyes locked.

"I see it," he said softly.

Cartoons were playing. The Christmas tree was twinkling. Steamy coffee was filling the air with the aroma of productivity. And we were reeling as we watched him.

He was sipping and swallowing.

He was sipping and swallowing and the plastic was shaking.

He was sipping and swallowing and the plastic was shaking and the whole world was crashing.

Henry was going to die.

Living in the moment

It was all so big, much bigger than us. We were zigzagging through a network of piers jutting over a nearby lake. Ian and I were on a special playdate with Henry, and when we reached the farthest edge, we all stopped to rest.

Henry settled onto my lap. Ian stood silently beside us. We gazed at the massive expanse of cobalt blue framed by tall, thick evergreens. Together and alone with our thoughts, we sat silent in the uncontainable, untamable landscape. We were just a freckle on nature's body. A comma in her story. We were no more in charge than the brown leaf drifting past, bobbing over ripples.

I'd never felt so small . . . though I sensed that we mattered to someone big. I knew we were loved in that holy moment. And Henry knew I was crying, but he didn't ask why.

I was flashing back to the news story from Halloween night. In it I'd praised Henry for teaching me to live in the moment. I'd told the reporter about how Henry had used one simple word to cut through my rushing thoughts and make time stand still. We'd been in the hospital garden, tossing pennies into a fountain.

"You're supposed to make a wish," I'd said as we watched a coin splash into the water. I was trying to figure out if I could make him happier somehow. "What do you wish for?" I asked. "If you could do anything in the world right now, what would it be?"

Henry had paused for an instant and stared at the gleaming coin in his hand. Then he said "This" as he tossed it into the fountain, sending shimmering ripples across the water's surface. In the midday sunlight, those tiny waves sparkled like a thousand Christmas lights. It was all he wanted in the world, that moment with me and a glittery pond.

So that afternoon as I stared across the sunlit lake, I tried to exist as simply as my child. I attempted to live in the moment. I filled my lungs with piney breezes and wrapped my arms tightly around Henry. I stared appreciatively at God's creation, consuming a visual feast and drinking in the tranquility.

I truly *lived in that moment* . . . and that moment sucked. The promised joy of living in *that* moment turned out to be a mirage. The reality was a mixture of deep sadness and dread. And it was quickly compounded by guilt because, although I'd lived in the moment, I failed to discover happiness in that cross section of time and space.

That day, pain was prevailing as the dock swayed. Hot tears were mixing with cold water, and all of it was slipping through my fingers. Tangible and elusive, it kept tickling my palms but leaving me with empty fists.

There was nothing I could do. Even the solid planks beneath us were resting on a spinning world, and I'd never been so dizzy from the earth's rotation. So as I sat and savored that moment, I tasted the bitter truth that there would never be, *could never be*, enough moments.

Dancing around

I'd never seen Henry dance, at least not like that. He was grooving in front of a crowd and didn't care who was watching.

A local ranch, known for their hayrides, paddleboats, and a pumpkin patch, had opened exclusively for Henry just after Thanksgiving. So we all headed out on that clear, perfect November day to cram in some fun.

We gathered under a pavilion for lunch, and after downing a hot dog, Henry wandered over to big speakers that were playing beach music. He started jamming while everyone else was eating. The conversations quieted, and all eyes followed the bobbing, goofy cowboy hat. Giggles floated across our small crowd, and eventually my mom got up to join him.

At one point I noticed that some in our group were watching me watch Henry. Maybe they'd noticed I wasn't laughing. Instead I was swallowing against the rock in my throat. I was trying to blink back the tears discretely.

We were all watching the same thing, but I didn't see what they saw. I saw my son, who had always been shy and reserved. He'd never been the carefree type. I saw something I had once longed for—my baby freed from his inhibitions. The irony was that he was only free because his pain was increasing, so his meds were increasing, which sent his inhibitions flying out the window. This version of him only existed because his brain was being destroyed by a tumor.

To the backdrop of happy, groovy beach music, I realized that the son I'd always known was gone. And watching my angel dance like a drunk guest at the wedding's end was too painful for me to enjoy. Despite the sunshine, despite his cuteness, and even despite that goofy cowboy hat.

Abnormal routines

The sun kept rising and setting. Our bodies continued to function, and our needs never ceased. There were still errands to run, dishes to wash, and things to do. Despite the circumstances, Ian and I still had a household to manage and two toddlers to raise.

Our little snowman, though more shaky, was still chock-full of energy. So we both put one weary foot in front of the other, and proceeded with life. Eventually, though, the emotions that raged against life's routines began to take their toll.

Once they came spilling to the surface in Walmart, next to a pungent wall of air fresheners. That's where I had slipped away, leaving Ian to keep an eye on our tots.

The kids were giggling at the fish tanks. And at first I'd laughed because they were so cute together, jumping up and down and pointing at ugly fish with googly eyes. Miri was spontaneously kissing the tank because she was always overflowing with love. And I had the thought that life couldn't be any sweeter, but then I remembered: *our son was dying.*

My eyes had darted around frantically. The people around us were shopping because Christmas was coming. They were passing us quickly, their faces wearing the frustrations of life. None of them realized that our son was dying. And the utter lunacy and cruelty of it all was too much to handle.

So I slipped away to sob discreetly, because I was finally accepting that our son was dying. And after a few seconds I swallowed my heartache, squared my shoulders, and dove back into parenting, because our son was dying. Because his need for normalcy trumped my need to fall apart.

That's how we lived. We washed dishes, took showers, and answered emails while knowing that our son was dying. We snuggled Henry on lazy mornings and diapered our baby girl while contemplating the horror that our son was dying. We made love and made lunch and smiled politely at guests while trying to grasp and simultaneously forget that our son was dying. We ran errands and paid bills and grabbed food on the go in a whirlwind of normalcy with the surreal backdrop of reality that our son was dying.

Then Ian and I began to listen for the perfect songs. We started to set aside our favorite photos. And one night after we read Henry stories and tucked him into bed, we contacted a preacher to officiate his funeral. Because despite the routines, the errands, the dishes, the entertaining, the laundry, the meals, the bath time, the stories we'd read for years, and the innocent good-night prayers, the truth never escaped our thoughts. *Our son was dying.*

Running here and there

"So why did you bring him?" our out-of-town friend asked gently.

We were out enjoying the last part of our Make-A-Wish package: a trip to the city's botanical garden. The garden had been transformed into a glowing wonderland of holiday lights and was added to our package because of Henry's love of Christmas lights.

Weeks earlier, the Make-A-Wish Foundation had even transformed our home into a life-sized, gleaming gingerbread house of lights. A professional lighting company had turned our lawn into gumdrop colored magic and lined our house's edges and roof lines with white lights reminiscent of sugary icing. Each night our yard transformed into Henry's private sparkling playground. He and his grandpa spent hours out there, jogging up and down our winding walk or just sitting, surrounded by the glow, staring up at the stars.

But there wasn't much sitting that evening, as our crazy day bled into night. We'd been winding wildly through the botanical garden, chasing Henry as he raced. Ian had been trying to explain to our friend that this wasn't how our son acted normally.

Henry wasn't spoiled and impulsive, he'd explained. He understood limits. He didn't normally try to barrel into chilly ponds on winter evenings. He usually stayed with us instead of charging ahead of us at full speed. But since the tumor he'd developed only two settings: racing or asleep. He was different now . . . vastly different now.

So why did you bring him? It was a reasonable question. An obvious question. But I didn't have an answer. So I left Ian to string together a response while I bolted after our son. I chased him just as I'd done for weeks now.

One of these times when I'd chased Henry through our sunlit backyard, I'd called out on a whim, "I love you!"

"I wuv you," he said back. *And I needed to hear it again.*

"I love you," I repeated.

"I wuv you," he'd replied without a pause in his steps.

"I love you," I said, my eyes filling with tears and my throat tightening.

"I wuv you," he sang without looking back.

"I love you," I said, because I could never hear his response enough.

"I wuv you," he said. So sweet, so simple, so vital to helping me catch my next breath.

As I chased Henry that cold, sparkly evening, I stumbled upon the answer to my friend's question, so why did you bring him?

We brought him because we loved him. And our love had blinded us to the truth. We'd brought him because we had over-estimated what he could handle. We couldn't accept that we could barely contain our own child, the one who'd always been so cautious and obedient. We'd brought him because we wanted to cram as much life and fun into the minutes that remained. We'd brought him because soon there would be no more fun together. No more "I love yous." No more adventures.

After all, how could we deny his appetite for life at just four years old? How could we keep him home when all he wanted to do was run and explore? On the other hand, how long could we keep going like this? Running and chasing all day, desperately trying to keep him safe until the tumor killed him?

We wouldn't have to agonize over those questions much longer. Soon the choices wouldn't be ours to make.

Down the streets of town

He awoke with a shrill scream, grabbing the right side of his head. I bolted upright in bed, then raced to the mini fridge we'd set up in our bedroom. Ian came and crouched beside Henry, trying to soothe him while I scoured my medication journal, trying to determine how much of which meds I could administer.

Then I dosed various liquids with hands that shook with terror and frustration. Up until that point, we'd been able to manage Henry's pain. But as he progressed toward his end, we seemed to simply chase it. With hospice's collaboration, I'd started bumping up dosages as his pain increased. But just when we seemed to find the right cocktail, Henry's pain would shoot through the threshold of medical relief.

It became a routine throughout the night, Henry awaking with a shrill scream, me striving to find that perfect cocktail to answer his pain without depressing his vital signs. Too much could kill him. Just enough would ease the pain.

Within minutes he'd drift off again and I'd crawl back to bed beside him. I'd stare at his chest, rising and falling. I'd put my finger under his nose and check for breath. Then I'd finally pass out until my alarm went off or he'd scream again. Either way, I'd jump up again to administer more meds.

As we plowed through December, his pain wasn't the only symptom that intensified. His voice began to get weak and raspy. He started to stumble around more, and the slight facial tick that had developed with his tumor became more pronounced.

One evening a friend visited who hadn't seen Henry in several years. She smiled at our little snowman as he stumbled into the kitchen with bloodshot eyes. He was slurring and screeching about microwave pizza. He soon fell asleep at the table while chewing, sauce on his face. I gathered him up calmly and took him back to bed.

After making sure Henry was settled and fast asleep, I slipped into my Civic and drove quietly out of the neighborhood. Then I unleashed everything pent up inside of me.

I released the rage of a mother watching a gunman take aim at her child. The devastation of a mother watching her son stagger around, a bloody, dying mess after being attacked by a rabid dog. The hysteria of a mother whose little boy had fallen on train tracks while she was on the train barreling toward him. She kept being offered another sip of tea, a few more cookies, and the instruction to savor these moments before he was obliterated.

For some reason, the diagnosis of cancer, the structure provided by healthcare, and the availability of medications to answer Henry's screams seemed to set an expectation of socially appropriate responses. I was supposed to smile and shower and speak and breathe. I was expected to give baths and read stories and make small talk. I was supposed to keep my composure while remnants of Henry's personhood clung to life and longed for death.

But my Honda didn't know any of that.

So I screamed down the streets of town. I screamed until my throat ached and my voice became raspy. In the blackness of night and the insulation of my car, I mocked God and cursed at him. Then I begged and pleaded and sobbed for God to heal my baby and stop this insanity. I drove and parked and drove and parked and drove again. Passing headlights became obscure streaks in my blur of existence.

I continued until my phone rang. Henry was awake. He needed me.

So I left my needs and secrets and screams in the night. I slipped back into the role of "mom" and went home to care for my son.

I want to go to heaven

My heart stopped when I heard it for the first time. I remember staring at his impatient expression as I struggled to find words. It never got easier. When he said it around family and friends the chatter stopped, the tears welled, and our hearts broke all over again. We never knew exactly what to say when Henry delivered that cold slap of reality.

"I want to go to heaven!"

Time stood still when he said it on Thanksgiving Day. Our extended family had just gathered to pray for the meal. He repeated it later that afternoon to an actor posing as Santa Claus. The jolly old man had been hired to come over and brighten our holidays. But when ol' Saint Nick heard it, he froze like the rest of us. I couldn't bring myself to meet his gaze. I wanted to cry, to apologize, to make it all go away.

I heard him advise Henry softly, "Don't be in a rush." The twinkle in his eye seemed to fade a bit after that. I'm sure he had heard all sorts of Christmas wishes. But nothing in his big red bag could help a terminally ill child exclaiming "I want to go to heaven!"

Ian and I had talked a lot with Henry about heaven. We showed him picture books about heaven. We assured him that he'd be strong enough to run and play again there. We told him that all the houses were sparkly, just as his house was now. We told him that Jesus would take good care of him and that he'd meet all kinds of wonderful people.

I guess, as Henry felt himself deteriorating, the thought of heaven grew more and more inviting. And so we began to hear repeatedly throughout the day, "I want to go to heaven!" Each time I heard it I felt thankful that he didn't seem afraid to die, yet devastated by the reminder that he was *going* to die. I was also worried that he didn't understand something crucial about heaven—he'd be going by himself.

"You know I can't go with you, right?" I once said gently as I ran my thumb across his silky cheek. "You'll have to go first."

Henry thought about this for a minute. Finally he said with importance, "I know who *is* gonna be there." He held up one finger. "God." He held up two fingers. "Gee-jus." Then he paused and scrunched up his little face. "And who's dat other guy?"

"You mean the Holy Spirit?" I asked softly.

"Yeah, dat's it. The Holy Sear-it," he nodded.

When we'd been in the PICU, I'd prayed once that Jesus would visit Henry in his dreams. I think it was in those final weeks that this prayer was answered. I think that's when their special relationship started. That was when Henry began sleeping more and more, consistent with the nature of someone dying from a brain tumor. Bedtime came earlier and naps were more frequent.

During those naps and throughout those final nights, I believe that Jesus sat with Henry, patiently building trust about the impending transition and gently coaxing him ever closer. There were several times that Henry would wake up and demand, "Where's Gee-jus?!" He'd sit up quick and dart his eyes around the room.

"Jesus is right here with us, always," I'd reply. "We just can't see him."

Henry would give the room another once-over before settling back into his pillow. He never seemed satisfied with my answer.

"Baby," I asked once, "were you just *with* Jesus?"

"Yes!" he said.

"Where were you?"

"Wif da stars!" he said. Then he motioned toward the window as his face fell. "But it's daytime outside!"

While he longed to go to heaven and be with Jesus, it seemed as if hesitation set in when his body began to catch up with his wishes. Transitions were never his strong suit, and understandably, the transition from earth to eternity was met with resistance.

Once, in the middle of a deep sleep, he sat up with his eyes still closed. He jutted a finger into the air and began punctuating his words with a jabbing motion. "I. Want. To." he said defiantly. And I had an indescribable sense that I was eavesdropping on a supernatural conversation. But I was only witnessing one side. I couldn't hear the patient, loving tone that addressed Henry. I couldn't hear how inviting the offer had been.

I could only hear his boyish rebuttal as he jabbed a finger forward. "I. Want. Mommy. To. Come. Too."

Escalator of clouds

That night I dreamed about an escalator. For the previous several weeks, department stores had become our Disney World. Escalators were our roller coasters, and Henry loved to ride. He'd hold tight to his grandpa's hand, and they'd ride and ride and ride.

Maybe that's why I dreamed about an escalator. Perhaps my subconscious was trying to mitigate the horror. Perhaps it was trying to ease the impact of wet rattling in my child's lungs. Henry's disease-ravaged brain had issued the death command, and his body was fighting back hard. While destruction was gaining, I was dreaming.

This dream escalator was special. Unlike the ones Henry had ridden in the past, this one was made of clouds. It extended through the sky, past the clouds, and into heaven itself. I dreamed that Henry was slowly ascending, delighted and amazed. He was holding tight to the hand beside him. But on this escalator, there was no sign of Grandpa. Henry was riding with Jesus.

The next morning, Henry awoke and stumbled through the day on legs that refused to quit, even as the shaking intensified. For the next few days he mostly just slept, stumbled around the house, and then slept more. Despite the shaking, he never quit running. He was either running or sleeping until his final day with us.

On that last day, he was done running. That last day, our bed became his paradise . . . but I couldn't let him be. I wasn't ready. He needed a bath. I just . . . he needed a bath. *I* needed him to need a bath.

My dad helped me ease my protesting little boy into the tub. My dad helped me move Henry back to the bed minutes later. My dad was a rock, always strong, always calm. His eyes stayed dry for me, for Henry, for all of us.

He was there when Henry croaked out "I wuv you!" before closing his little eyes, smiling, and offering a weak thumbs-up. Dad was also there when Henry sat bolt upright in his sleep, just minutes later. With those precious eyes still closed, Henry spoke what would be his final words with perfect clarity and strength. He clasped his hands together and said with a delighted smile, "Dat sounds wike fun!"

Henry said that around noon on December 16. And though it was pretty early in the day, Ian and I were already strung out and exhausted. Visitors left. Family retreated to the living room to give us some privacy. Ian and I were alone with our sleeping boy.

There was nothing left for me to do but curl up beside my lavender-scented baby, wrap an arm behind his pillow, and rest my head next to his. I closed my eyes, listened to the roar of his breath, and pictured the cloudy escalator from my dreams.

This time I was standing there beside Jesus and Henry. We were all on the misty ground, holding hands and walking toward that mighty escalator. When we reached the base of it, we paused.

I knew why I was there. I knew what I had to do.

I crouched down and hugged my little man, my baby, my heart. I kissed his forehead and smoothed the hair on his spikey cowlick. Then I stood up again . . . but I couldn't let go of his hand. I turned, weeping, toward Jesus. He took my face in his hands as he smiled warmly and whispered calm assurances. And finally . . . somehow . . . I let go.

I let go and imagined Jesus and Henry stepping upon that giant escalator. I watched as Jesus scooped Henry into his arms and pointed out the wonders of the earth, stars, and universe as they ascended.

I watched as they stepped off and encountered these big, opulent, open gates. Hand in hand, they crossed into the most breathtaking landscape imaginable. There were glassy beaches on their right, billowing meadows to the left, and towering purple mountains ahead . . .

The next thing I remember was the hospice nurse. She was entering our room with a look of alarm. Apparently I'd fallen asleep, and the nurse could tell that time was short.

The next few hours were so surreal. Ian and I could hardly grasp that Henry *was dying*. Our tension shot up. We couldn't catch our breath. We couldn't stop pacing.

"We need to pray," I finally blurted out. So within our desperation, we gripped each other, trembling and crying and begging God for peace and strength.

Afterward Ian said suddenly, "You know, I don't even think Henry's here. I think his spirit left hours ago."

In that instant, we were both flooded with peace. It was like a rush of heavenly air poured through the bedroom window and straight into our souls. We began to relax about caring for Henry's body while it shut down. We had a gentle confidence that our son had been released from his shell. We believed he was already busy crafting, running, and playing with Jesus.

I guess he'd found the strength to make the transition. I like to think it was when my arm was wrapped around him and I was imagining Jesus holding him on a giant escalator made of clouds.

Melting away

Henry's little cousin, "Baby Katato," had squealed wildly the night before. My brother had been lying beside Henry, weeping through praise songs playing on his iPhone and still praying for a miracle, when my sister-in-law walked in. She was holding the baby, who lit up like a thousand Christmas lights and started shouting out happy, gurgling noises. It was as if he alone witnessed the sight of angels surrounding the bed, caring for Henry in his final moments.

If Henry's angels were still present on the evening of December 16, they witnessed much. They saw the huge tears in the eyes of his grandmothers. They noticed those dear women struggle to say good night because they knew it was *goodbye.* They would have seen my dad sit silently beside his little friend, the last to leave our room.

His angels would have seen Ian and me crouching beside the bed as the silence hit. They would have heard the cries to Jesus.

They would have seen Grandpa rise when I entered the living room with the words "He passed."

They would have seen the medical transport guys in our room, the younger one crying softly, the elder one agreeing to forgo the stretcher and body bag.

They would have seen Grandpa and Henry enter the yard of our sparkling gingerbread house one final time. Grandpa was carrying Henry like a baby, leaning forward to shield his buddy's still-warm face from the cold December drizzle.

They would have watched him lay his grandson on the stretcher. He took the sheet that was supposed to cover Henry's body and face and instead pulled it up to his chest. He tucked it around him gently, as if his little friend were simply asleep.

They would have seen that when Grandpa turned back toward the house, he paused for a moment. The festive, colorful ground lights had shorted out. In the misty darkness, only the white lights on the roof remained, casting bright, glowing streaks toward the heavens. It was as if they were presenting themselves as a flag at half-staff, showing reverence for his precious grandson.

Back inside, Henry's family fanned out to find their beds. But his angels would have seen Grandpa still standing at the window, watching as the ambulance drove into the darkness. He was hit by a pang of guilt, remembering the times he'd left Henry waving in that very spot.

Those angels alone would have seen Grandpa's face crumple and the tears begin to pour. He was realizing that the best part of heaven is that there'd be no more waving at windows.

There would be no more goodbyes.

Part III

Triumph by Testimony

NINE

When Worldviews Collide

I'm so thankful I had a new understanding of God before Henry's diagnosis. I'm so thankful that when Henry died, I could fall into God's loving arms without reservation. As I shared in part 1 of this book, I haven't always based my picture of God on the love of Calvary. I haven't always trusted his heart.

I used to believe that everything that happens, even little children dying, occurs in accordance with God's perfect plan. And I was not alone in this. This blueprint worldview has been predominant in Christian history since the fifth-century teachings of Saint Augustine. Today this worldview dominates Christian media, as well as many pulpits.

Had it not been for my new understanding of God, I would have brought my devastated "Why?!" questions to pastors, authors, and even songwriters who believe the world unfolds according to

God's mysterious master plan. I would have combed through their resources, seeking insight to my heart's cry: Why did God allow such hideous suffering to come to Henry? Why didn't God answer our prayers for healing? Why is my baby dead?

The answers would have been crushing.

This chapter explores a sampling of the harmful explanations that Christian culture offers the brokenhearted. It applies them to Henry's fatal tumor and contrasts them with the love of Christ. Let's examine these explanations together.

Henry's fatal tumor was a blessing in disguise

Some Christian leaders would readily explain that Henry's horrific pain and young death were not evil but good. That his death wasn't a tragedy but a gift. That his pain didn't contradict God's will, but his every shriek was perfectly aligned with God's desires.

For instance, John Piper, one of the most influential evangelical leaders in the United States, had words waiting. Those that stung the fiercest were offered in response to a podcast listener. This listener seemed understandably disturbed by some violent biblical accounts of God and asked, "Why was it right for God to slaughter women and children in the Old Testament? How can that ever be right?"

Piper responded:

> It's right for God to slaughter women and children anytime he pleases. God gives life and he takes life. Everybody who dies, dies because God wills that they die. God is taking life every day. He will take fifty thousand lives today. Life is in God's hand. God decides when your last heartbeat will be, and whether it ends through cancer or a bullet wound. God governs. So God is God! He rules and governs everything. And everything he does is just and right and good. God owes us nothing.[1]

According to these words, God slaughtered Henry with an aggressive, malignant tumor because it pleased him. These words also mean that watching my son writhe and die and turn gray in my bed was "just and right and good."

Really?

My radio had words waiting too. Over and over I heard the song "Blessings" on my Christian station. It was number one on the Billboard Christian Songs chart in 2011, and winner of the 2012 Grammy Award for Best Contemporary Christian Music Song. "Blessings" tackles the issue of unanswered prayer by recounting the things we pray for, such as healing, prosperity, and relief from suffering. While this song acknowledges that our prayers are heard, it explains that God loves us "way too much to give us lesser things."[2]

Our family prayed for Henry's healing. We prayed God would ease his suffering. But Henry suffered and Henry died. According to this song, God heard our prayers but he loved us "way too much" to intervene.

God loved us *too much* to alleviate Henry's pain or save his life? The screams of our cancer-ridden child demonstrated God's love better than a healing intervention would have?

Really?

The song continues with a series of questions, contemplating whether the hardships in life are really just God's "mercies in disguise." What if it takes "a thousand sleepless nights," the singer wonders, to know that God is near?

Our family had many sleepless nights that preceded Henry's death. Anxious, pain-filled, exhausting nights. Nights when I couldn't tell whether the pain was coming from the tumor growing in Henry's brain or the trapped fluid building inside his skull. Nights when I scrambled through piles of medications, trying to find that perfect combination that would ease his torment but not stop his heart.

Was that God doing what it takes so that I'd know he's near? Am I really to believe those sleepless nights were God's "mercies in disguise"?

If we hold the blueprint worldview, then we must accept that this is true in every nightmare that anyone has ever experienced. Consider a young couple whose toddler has been kidnapped. Each night they lie awake with questions. They toss and turn in their living nightmare, wondering whether their baby is being raped or mutilated at this very moment. Should they consider their sleepless nights to be God's "mercies in disguise"?

Disguised as what? Evil? Perhaps some would assure me that Henry's death and children being kidnapped aren't blessings in themselves but that each is a necessary component of a blessing God has planned. The real blessing follows the required trauma. After all, rainbows only come after the storms. Rain is required for blessings to bloom, right?

To this I must ask: How many blessings quantify a life? Which ones justify a fatal tumor or a kidnapped toddler? If thousands of lives are somehow bettered, if millions of people find Jesus because of one tortured child, *will that child's torment be worth it*? Will it make the notion that God refused to intervene somehow loving? Praiseworthy?

Am I truly to believe that God is so limited in creativity and resources that he *had* to slay my four-year-old to bring about good? Which blessing exceeds touching my baby's satin face? Smelling his freshly washed hair? Feeling his small hand slip into mine? Must God destroy one of his precious miracles to bring about another?

Why does the blueprint worldview lead us to find ways to mitigate the ugliness of evil? Perhaps it's because the belief that God always gets his way merges good and evil into one. After all, if an all-good God allowed it, then it must somehow be his *best* for us, right? This type of thinking has us struggling to find the virtue encased in every horror. In our eagerness to make things right, we brush aside what is *wrong*. We stare into the face of evil and search for a freckle of good to claim that all is well. We scramble, we hedge, and we slap Band-Aids onto gushing wounds.

But why? Why do so many Christians preach Jesus against the backdrop of a God that looks nothing like him? Do we so badly desire a *God of control* that we readily relinquish the Bible's *God of love*?

Henry's fatal tumor was God's discipline

I remember *Joni* as vividly as I remember anything about my adolescence. I repeatedly checked that dog-eared, battered paperback out of my school's library. I used to stare in awe at the paintbrush in her teeth. Such courage. Such perseverance. Such a pretty smile. I was amazed to see that young woman still smiling after her accident. One dive, one hidden sandbar, and one broken neck had turned an athletic seventeen-year-old into a quadriplegic.

Since her accident, Joni Eareckson Tada has become a bestselling author who has written over fifty books. Her autobiography, *Joni*, has sold over five million copies, has been printed in fifty languages, and was made into a feature film. An international advocate for people with disabilities, Tada is also the founder and CEO of the Joni and Friends International Disability Center, which has served thousands of families worldwide. For decades she has hosted a radio program and has been a featured speaker at Christian conferences across the country. To this day, she perseveres in ministry despite the fact that she now endures chronic pain and has battled breast cancer, all in addition to her paralysis. Sadly, she is thoroughly equipped to address the issue of suffering.

After Henry died, one of my blog followers posted a recent talk of Tada's to my website. I hadn't kept up with Tada's ministry after childhood, so I was surprised when I discovered how prominent it had become in the past few decades. My reader said she hoped that Tada's words would be uplifting in my grief, so I listened to the message that afternoon.

I quickly realized that Tada holds a strong form of the blueprint worldview.[3] In this view, God makes certain that everything happens in alignment with his specific, divine blueprint. He doesn't just passively allow evil; God *guides* evil.[4] He controls the world in painstaking detail as he works out his "mysterious and wonderfully strange plan."[5]

As I explored Tada's teachings further, I also found a recurring theme: suffering is God's discipline. She writes, "I'm convinced that much of the suffering we go through is God's way of disciplining us."[6] She explains that while Jesus saved us from our sin on the cross, "he's got a long way to go with us, and the Father is heaven-bent on conforming us . . . to the image of Jesus Christ."[7]

Just how are we conformed to Christ's image? Tada believes it's through our suffering. She provides an illustration that begins with a stone quarry near her childhood farm in Maryland. It was a busy, noisy quarry, filled with workers mining flagstone for a housing development. Tada compares God to "one of those skilled hammer men" and likens her soul to "a good chunk of rock straight out of the quarry." She insists that God knows her soul is "not as delicate as I would like to think" and confides, "this week . . . when pain was blindsiding me, it was obvious to me that God thinks my soul can still take a good scouring."

Tada tells her audience, "God wields suffering to break apart your rocks of resistance" and that "suffering is his chisel . . . that chips away my pride and your stiff-necked, stubborn rebellion." While that sounds harsh, what follows is even more unsettling. Tada explains that "the hurting and the hammering is not going to end until we become completely like Jesus," and she then admits, "there is no chance of that happening on this side of eternity, so I think we just better get used to it."

She then testifies to how her own agony has helped her to become more spiritually mature because it unveils the sin in her life. She says, "When I am hurting, I am then able to see sin for the poison that it is, because when God takes his sovereign hand and squeezes my lemon hard, out flows . . . a steady stream of frustration."

She believes this is how God uses evil to conquer evil: "My wise and sovereign God takes one form of evil—that is suffering—and he turns it on its head to defeat another form of evil, and that's my sin, my self-centeredness. . . . God's an expert at doing this."

Later in her talk, she transitions from the hammer-man analogy to that of a jewelry maker. After Tada accidently crushed a treasured gold earring, her jeweler gladly pounded the remaining good earring until it matched its broken counterpart. She likens this to a believer's refinement by explaining, "God is the Master

Jeweler. He rules. He orders. He commands. He knows exactly how to handle that hammer, and he is happy to do good toward you." But she warns, "Just remember that his idea of good is to make you more like Jesus, and if our Savior learned obedience through the things he suffered, should the Master expect less from you and me?"

As Tada closes her talk, she offers hope—hope that one day, God's pounding will cease. She assures, "God is using your inflictions to shape you so that you might perfectly fit heaven's landscape where there will be no more hammer, no more chisel . . . only serenity."[8]

Merriam-Webster defines *torture* as "the act of causing severe physical pain as a form of punishment or as a way to force someone to do or say something."[9] If God has chosen paralysis, chronic pain, and cancer to make his daughter conform to his image, then I'd offer that he is a Cosmic Torturer beyond compare. This torture is supposedly aimed at making Tada "completely like Jesus," although that has "no chance of happening on this side of eternity." This means there's no attainable goal in this scenario and that the torture won't stop until she dies.

In my opinion, this is an absolutely heartbreaking interpretation of God's role in Tada's suffering—though I'll quickly admit that this view is *hers to choose*. Tada has suffered greatly, sought answers with sincerity, and developed a resolution about God's role in her pain. Out of reverence, I would not challenge her beliefs if they were held silently in her heart. But they are not. With authority and conviction, Tada teaches this view of God to millions. For this reason, as a member of her worldwide audience, I am compelled to ask some questions.

How does this explanation of suffering apply to Henry's fatal tumor? I often flash back to the weeks before his death, to the nights when shrill screams pierced the darkness of our bedroom. Was Henry's searing pain caused by God's hammer? Was his intense suffering meant to chisel away his stiff-necked, stubborn rebellion? Was it designed to give his soul a good scouring so that he might perfectly fit heaven's landscape?

Or was Henry's fatal tumor not about Henry at all? Was it for me? Was it God's way of ratcheting up my spiritual maturity? Was the Master Jeweler, who knows exactly how to handle that hammer, simply aiming to refine me? Was God using devastation and grief to reveal some underlying sin that needed repentance? If so, God apparently cares more about my spiritual growth than Henry's very life. Am I to be this egocentric? And is God so twisted a teacher that he educates parents by torturing their kids?

Undoubtedly, the New Testament references certain, specific instances of suffering that happened as a result of early Christians spreading the gospel in a superhostile environment. Those believers, in those instances, were told to consider their suffering as God's loving discipline—a refinement of the faith they were already willing to die for.[10]

Should we then conclude that *all* suffering is God's discipline? Should we assume that his discipline takes the form of child molestation, domestic abuse, or debilitating mental illness? What about nations of people starving? Or millions dying in the Holocaust? Or precious young women breaking their necks?

What about when little boys die from big tumors, in their parents' beds? Should we call this God's discipline? Could this ever, ever be called love?

Henry's fatal tumor was part of God's plan to glorify himself

"Already There" is a song featured on the Top Christian Album of 2012 and is performed by the Grammy– and Dove Award–winning band Casting Crowns. For Christians who are in the midst of hard times, this popular song reassures them that God is already on the other side of their struggles. And from God's perspective, all the pieces of our lives fit together according to a "grand design" he has for each of us. "Already There" insists that God brings all of life's chaos together, "like a masterpiece of [his] picture-perfect plan."[111]

I'll never forget Henry's wild eyes, springing awake from heavy sedation. It was torture to watch him cycle through consciousness after the brain surgery that nearly killed him. He'd try to scream and thrash, but a breathing device filled his throat and he was pinned to the bed with wires and tubes. My four-year-old struggled through that terror hour after hour, so bloated, so bewildered, so helpless.

Was this part of the "grand design" that God imagined for Henry? Was my baby's brain cancer just part of the chaos that comprises God's masterpiece? His "picture-perfect plan"? If Henry had lived past age four, would this have sullied perfection? If he'd thrived and grown into a productive and loving adult, would this have been second-rate?

Why would God devise such a plan?

Pastor Rick Warren offers an answer in *The Purpose Driven Life*. This wildly popular blueprint book has sold over thirty million copies and has much to say about God's "master plan." It offers that God's blueprint, which includes even the "death of loved ones," was designed for a purpose.[12]

What purpose? God's glory. Warren explains that showcasing the glory of God is the "ultimate goal of the universe" and asserts that "without God's glory, there would be nothing."[133]

While Christians can agree that everything God *makes* is for his glory, Warren believes this includes a detailed, divine blueprint for every person. He asserts: "There is a Grand Designer behind everything. Your life is not a result of random chance, fate, or luck. There is a master plan. History is *His story*. God is pulling the strings."[144]

Warren also writes: "Regardless of the cause, none of your problems could happen without God's permission. Everything that happens to a child of God is *Father-filtered*." And he goes on to say, "Because God is sovereignly in control, accidents are just incidents in God's good plan for you."[155]

So would this mean that God planned all of our suffering and tragedy? Warren affirms: "God's plan for your life involves *all* that happens to you—including your mistakes, your sins, and your hurts. It includes illness, debt, disasters, divorce, and death of loved ones."[166]

But how does our suffering showcase the glory of God? How did tears falling from Henry's bright blue eyes bring God glory? How did my pleading sobs, seeking a miracle that never arrived, bring God glory?

In agreement with Tada, Warren teaches that suffering builds Christlike character. He writes: "We are like jewels, shaped with the hammer and chisel of adversity. If a jeweler's hammer isn't strong enough to chip off our rough edge, God will use a sledgehammer. If we're really stubborn, he uses a jackhammer. He will use whatever it takes."[177] The greater the hammering we endure, the more Christlike character we can develop.[188] And as Warren explains, "The more you develop Christlike character, the more you will bring glory to God."[199]

I agree that it *is* beautiful when Christians grow and become more like Christ. It *is* beautiful when we partner with God to transform pain into growth. Yet . . . Warren teaches that God is pulling the strings. He believes our lives are unfolding according God's master plan. This plan involves our mistakes, sins, debts, and divorces. In other words, the rough edges of our character were designed by the *same* God who uses sledgehammers, jackhammers, or "whatever it takes" to remove them.

This strikes me as utterly sadistic. Why would God design our rough edges only to pound them away through suffering? What could be the purpose? Apparently . . . glory.

In this view, each life is like a recipe designed to satisfy God's hunger for glory. Warren explains: "The events in your life work *together* in God's plan. They are not isolated acts, but interdependent parts of the process to make you like Christ. To bake a cake you must use flour, salt, raw eggs, sugar, and oil. Eaten individually, each is pretty distasteful or even bitter. But bake them together and they become delicious."[20]

Here I am left to wonder: In the "delicious" cake of my God-glorifying character development, which ingredient was *my son*? And where was Henry's cake?

Warren also explains that God only promises *his children* that he'll work everything together for good. On the other hand, "All things work together *for bad* for those living in opposition to God who insist on having their own way."[211]

So did God work everything together for Henry's good? His life ended with a painful brain tumor and childhood death. That seems like Henry's life worked together for bad. Was he not a child of God?

Some blueprint subscribers would clarify that Henry was, in fact, a child of God, and that his early death was just God's way of calling him home. After the bloody massacre at Sandy Hook Elementary School that claimed twenty-six lives in 2012, President Obama delivered a touching speech to the community of Newtown, Connecticut. Near the speech's close he quoted Jesus, saying: "Let the little children come to me . . . and do not hinder them, for to such belongs the kingdom of heaven." He then read the names of the ruthlessly slaughtered students and concluded, "God has called them all home."[222]

I wonder if the surviving loved ones left that day with questions about God's goodness. God calls children home by having them gunned down? Odds are that some of those survivors turned to popular Christian books for guidance. Unfortunately, in *The Purpose Driven Life*, they would have learned that it all happened for one purpose. God's glory.

And though the survivors would undoubtedly be baffled that God glorifies himself through a seemingly random act of pointless violence, Warren assures, "You know you are maturing when you begin to see the hand of God in the random, baffling, and seemingly pointless circumstances of life." They'd then be slapped with a cheery "Don't give up—grow up!"[23]

But is *this* what God's quest for glory really looks like? Is God driven by a self-seeking fame of sorts? Does he meticulously control the universe just to show everyone who's in charge? What if the notion that God devised a "master plan" to glorify himself through our trauma-induced refinement actually *conflicts* with how God revealed himself in Scripture? What if God's glory is his love?

Scripture states that God *is* love (1 John 4:8, 16), and that love was defined by the cross (1 John 3:16). It also says that the cross is the "wisdom of God" and the "power of God" for those who follow Jesus (1 Cor 1:23-24). Doesn't this mean that the all-wise God was *most glorified* when he died the shameful death of a God-forsaken criminal? That the all-powerful God was *best glorified* in his weakness, displaying a love that triumphs through sacrifice? Yes, Jesus himself affirms this when speaking of his impending death on Calvary (John 12:23-33).

When we look to the cross, we see that God's "glory" isn't harmful. And it's not self-absorbed. It's other-oriented. It's something that Jesus freely gives away. We see this in Jesus' prayer for his disciples. Just before he was arrested, Jesus prayed to the Father, "I have given them the glory that you gave me, that they may be one as we are one—I in them and you in me—so that they may be brought to complete unity" (John 17:22-23). God's "glory" is the freely shared, enemy-loving, self-sacrificing, victorious love displayed on the cross![24]

With Warren, I affirm that God's purpose in creation was to increase his glory. But I'd offer that this doesn't occur by designing the "rough edges" of our lives and then using the "jackhammer" of traumas to remove them. God increases his glory by *expanding his love*!

I must accept that Henry's fatal tumor was part of God's blueprint or reject the gospel

I don't know the couple who sent us *Choosing to See: A Journey of Struggle and Hope*. Somehow they'd heard about our loss. They reached out because they also stagger under the crush of child death. Their son was nearly four when he drowned. Those parents know the full weight of empty arms. And now those arms pack boxes. They send Christian books to bereaved parents. They reach *from* grief *toward* grief, beautifully finding a measure of comfort by offering comfort to others.

Choosing to See by Mary Beth Chapman was in this box of comfort. Chapman is an author, speaker, adoption advocate, and the wife of Christian music legend Steven Curtis Chapman. This memoir seemed to call out to me because it highlights the story of her little girl's tragic death. Maria Chapman was just five years old when her big brother accidentally hit and killed her with his truck in the family's driveway.

As I read the memoir, I was completely undone by Chapman's unmasked humanity. She had me rooting for her success in the book's early chapters, deeply grieving the loss of her daughter toward the middle, and inspired by her charitable outreach toward the book's close. I found myself longing to embrace her, thank her for her courage and vulnerability, and whisper together about our shared hope—that we will one day hold our children again.

Yet though we share a sacred ache, I am compelled to dialogue with Chapman's central message. This is because *Choosing to See* spans beyond a memoir and contains strong teaching elements. Some very pointed statements, combined with Chapman's status as a renowned Christian leader, have created a book that instructs multitudes of grieving people about how to interpret God's role in tragedies.

According to Chapman, tragedies like the one her family experienced are all part of God's perfect plan. She writes:

> I can only imagine the discussions that [Mary] and Joseph would have when [young Jesus] wasn't listening, how they probably

begged God to let the cup pass from them, but in the end yielding up the prayer we all hesitate to pray when it comes to our children . . . Your will be done. UGGHH!!!! I don't want to. I didn't want to [on the day Maria died], and I still don't want to now. Yet somehow we did, and somehow we will continue to.[255]

Chapman also mentions a walk on the beach after Maria's passing. As she wandered, she cried out to God, "Why? What now? How? What?" She follows with an account of God's responses. Some of those responses are truly beautiful, but others look very little like the love of Calvary. Chapman shares that God responded: "Why? Because I am God and I know all and am in control and know what is best. Even though it looks like a mess . . . it is My mess"; "I allow what I allow for reasons you can't even comprehend"; "I put this bright sun and this cloudless morning in place and will bring the storms in as well. I do not need to speak, for I already have and you have not only heard Me, you have seen Me and My power at work. If I control all of this, then I was here [the day Maria died]. It hurts, but I am all you need."[266]

She writes later about her sadness, anger, and confusion that God's plan "had to involve Maria's big brother, who absolutely adored her." She asks, "God, where are you and why in the world would you choose us to walk this out . . . it isn't fair!" But she then reminds herself (and her readers): "I know God loves me and my family. I know God is sovereign and He knows what is best for us. I know He has our days numbered and makes *no* mistakes."[277]

She also shares these heartbreaking reflections from a year after Maria's death: "The pain is still there . . . most of the time as sharp as ever. . . . God allowing the chisel and hammer to do His beautiful work in and amongst our friends and family." She adds later:

"Could it be that this little girl was simply given to us for a short time so that she would ask Jesus into her heart, and then as simple as that was, leave just two months later to go be with Him? Hard to fathom, but completely something only God could orchestrate!"[288]

She signs off one section with a chilling quotation from missionary James Hudson Taylor: "May this be your experience; may you feel that the Hand which inflicts the wound supplies the balm, and that He who has emptied your heart has filled the void with Himself."[299]

As much as it saddened me to see a grieving mother process her loss through the blueprint worldview, I closed that book with an even larger concern. This prominent Christian leader equates the blueprint worldview with *the gospel itself*. She writes about the impromptu speech she gave shortly after Maria's death: "It's all true! It's all true! The gospel is true. If we believe anything about our faith, we have to believe that we know where Maria is right now and that God didn't make a mistake. He didn't turn His head, He was in complete control."[30]

Along with the multitudes of other grieving parents who have received this memoir as a gift, I apply these words to my own loss. This message suggests that I *have* to believe that when Henry died, God was in complete control. I *have* to believe that God didn't make a mistake as he killed (or specifically allowed the death of) my son. Chapman is clear that if I believe *anything about the gospel*, I must believe this.

I have to ask: *Really?*

Even if this belief stands in stark contrast to the love displayed on Calvary? Even when I consider the ministry of Jesus, spent wholly with hurting and afflicted people? Not once did he suggest that God had given them their afflictions. Rather, he and the gospel authors attributed them to Satan or to demons (Mark 9:25; Luke 11:14; 13:11-16; Acts 10:38).

Do I have to believe that God was meticulously controlling the moments when Henry screamed? When he nearly bled out on a surgeon's table? When his roaring breaths went silent? To believe otherwise is to reject the gospel?

Bestselling author Ann Voskamp agrees with this blueprint position . . . and she goes a step farther. According to the line of thinking that Voskamp espouses, I must *thank God for Henry's fatal tumor.*

In *One Thousand Gifts*, a Christian memoir that spent sixty weeks on the *New York Times* bestseller list, Voskamp poetically articulates her blueprint perspective. As I read her faith journey, I was inspired by her authentic desire to practice the presence of God through a detailed gratitude journal. Yet I was frankly sickened by her take on God's role in radical suffering.

Voskamp asserts that the "crux of the gospel" is the acceptance that everything is God's grace. She stresses the "hard discipline" of receiving even "ugly" things (such as cancer) as God's "grace and gift" in order to receive the "*fullest* salvation." She asserts that to do otherwise is to be a "blasphemer," and insists that "anything less than gratitude and trust is practical atheism."[311]

In this view, evil doesn't actually exist. Voskamp writes, "That which seems evil only seems so because of *perspective*, the way the eyes see the shadows. Above the clouds, light never stops shining."[322]

Voskamp recalls the morning when she concluded that the "crux of Christianity" is "to remember and give thanks, *eucharisteo*."[333]

Almost immediately, she began to consider the objections of those who have profoundly suffered.

These imagined people ask her:

When your memories have an old man groping for your crotch, hot, foul breath on your face, and your skin crawls? Give thanks?

And an ultrasound screen stretches still and you're sent home to wait for the uterine muscles to contract out the dead dreams?

Or the woman you lay down with, shared the naked and un-ashamed, she beds another man, hands you back the wedding albums, and says she never knew love for you, what then?

Remember and give thanks? For what? What if the remembering doesn't kindle gratitude?[344]

Voskamp counters these protests by explaining that God earned our trust when he gave us Christ, and says that "we can give thanks in everything because there's a good God leading, working all things into good." She assures us, "Every moment, every event, every happening. It's all in Christ and in Christ we are always safe."

But the voices with whom she is pretend-dialoguing continue to object, so she hushes, "Trauma's storm can mask the Christ and feelings can lie." She then tells the pretend-molested child, the pretend-grieving mother, and the pretend-jilted husband that their traumas were, in actuality, good things. They just need some perspective.

Voskamp writes: "I draw all the hurting voices close and I touch their scars with a whisper: sometimes we don't fully see that in Christ, because of Christ, through Christ, He does give us all things good—until we have the perspective of years. In time, years, dust settles. In memory, ages, God emerges."[355] She later reiterates, "God reveals Himself in rearview mirrors."[366]

I'm sorry, but *what*? A child being molested is *good*; the victim just needs the "perspective of years"? A dead baby in the womb is clearly *God revealed* as the "dust settles"? A shattered marriage was given by God as part of "all things good"?

In Voskamp's blueprint perspective, "Trauma's storm can mask the Christ and feelings can lie." Are these lying feelings the wholly understandable feelings of anger, sadness, and shame that victims of trauma face? Does the "crux of the gospel" dismiss these authentic feelings as lies? Does it insist that victims mutter *thanks* to a god who supposedly doled out their inflictions?

I submit that this is a gross misrepresentation of Scripture's *good news*—and one that revictimizes the wounded among us.

Voskamp assures her readers that "sometimes we don't fully see that in Christ, because of Christ, through Christ, He does give us all things good." Yet I'd offer that the repeated use of the word *Christ* does not make this evil concept a godly concept. We cannot claim "Christ" while divorcing God from any sense of right and wrong.

Jesus Christ was the exact representation of God (Heb 1:3), and God *is* love (1 John 4:8, 16). Love does not molest children and demand thanks. Love does not kill babies and demand thanks. Love does not shatter marriages and demand thanks.

The notion that we must develop a peaceful resignation to all our experiences and the belief that all things happen for a greater good are concepts compatible with ancient stoicism, but they stand in direct contrast to the ministry of Jesus. God-in-flesh *rebuked evil*; he didn't give thanks for it. He healed the broken; he didn't break the healthy (and then require their gratitude!).

To all of these leaders and writers and to every other precious soul, I'd like to pose this exciting, hope-filled question: What if the love of Jesus directly mirrored the one who sent him?

What if God's essence is a love we can recognize?

What if God doesn't orchestrate child molestation, fatal accidents, adultery, and empty wombs beneath broken hearts? What if God in Spirit holds the same standards of morality as his flesh-and-bones representation?

What if the New Testament *rightly* points us to a God who is as gentle as the father is to the prodigal son? As caring as a lovestruck groom to his unfaithful bride? As compassionate as Jesus, the powerful, humble servant who came to bring life to the fullest?

What if God's love is something we can readily recognize, receive, and reflect? Now that would be good news!

Worth believing

I recently read that "no theology is worth believing that cannot be preached standing in front of the gates of Auschwitz."[377] I would add: or proclaimed at the funeral of a four-year-old.

I'm so thankful that when Henry died, my theology—my picture of God—was worth believing. In fact, this picture of God remained staggeringly beautiful in the midst of our anguish and was boldly proclaimed at Henry's funeral.

As I faced one of my worst nightmares, I understood that God was perfectly revealed in the love of the cross and that Henry's fatal tumor was not part of a mysterious, divine blueprint. By this point, four words had been etched into my soul: *love, risk, rejection,* and *war.*

I knew the God of love created from love to expand his love. He took a hope-filled risk by creating this world and free agents. But because of a rejection of God's love, we live on the front lines of a cosmic war. It's a war that God will ultimately win.

The resurrection demonstrates that God's love cannot be conquered by brute force. We can be confident that the enemy-loving, self-sacrificing God of Calvary will one day restore his creation. Until then, we have the assurance that his character is good and his heart is filled with a love we can recognize. This made *all* the difference as I walked the painful path to Henry's death.

Instead of thinking that God slaughtered Henry with a malignant brain tumor because it pleased him, I knew that God was working creatively to bring the most good possible out of this evil, within the boundaries of his beloved, free creation.

Instead of thinking that God simply remained silent while Henry cried out because somehow it brought God the most "glory," I knew Jesus' ministry of healing truly represented God's heart toward disease.

Instead of believing that God specifically allowed Henry's death to "discipline" or refine me, I was assured of his Calvary-like love for me.

Instead of assuming that God wanted me to choke out a "thanks" for sending Henry's fatal tumor while scattering his ashes, I knew that God shared my feelings of injustice and my deep, groaning ache. Grief is right in a world gone wrong.

Because I understood God's loving character, I could declare, "This is from God!" when we witnessed miracles like those precious windows into Henry's transition from my arms to the Father's arms. I could also say with confidence, "This is *not* from

God," when crippling pain, disease, and death came to my son. I understood that God's heart was broken and that he battled against the disease that ravaged Henry Joseph Kelley, the remarkable child that God himself had breathed into life.

While I don't question the hearts of those who propagate the blueprint worldview, I seriously question the worldview being propagated. This view says that God's plan was to crush Henry to mysteriously glorify himself. This view would have crushed my passion for God! Had I held this view when my son died, my broken heart would have turned away from the One who broke himself for me.

Most importantly, this blueprint worldview doesn't look like Jesus. A god who plans our agony in detail to glorify himself doesn't look like Jesus, the one who healed the sick and raised the dead! The one who healed the ear of his arresting officer before he prayed for his assailants' forgiveness with his final breaths! It doesn't look like Jesus!

So when it comes to our worldview, and to our picture of God, let's start with the cross. Let's take our cue from Paul and claim to know nothing "except Jesus Christ and him crucified" (1 Cor 2:2). Let's remember that Jesus was the "radiance of God's glory and the exact representation of his being" (Heb 1:3). Jesus himself said, "Anyone who has seen me has seen the Father" (John 14:9)!

The blueprint worldview brings comfort to some. I understand that. But the warfare worldview offers all the assurances that the blueprint view offers. The only thing a Christian loses with the warfare worldview is a polluted picture of God. We have to admit that if we follow blueprint thinking to its logical conclusion, it's possible that the same plan that called for the Holocaust could also call for devastating calamity in our own lives. To hold the notion that the universe unfolds according to God's blueprint *and* that this blueprint will never call for one's own personal tragedy is to embrace delusion. Such a worldview offers no real protection.

I've shared some of the painful things I faced while holding the blueprint worldview. While there were times it offered comfort, it also caused me to question God's goodness and to doubt his love. By the time I faced the most excruciating pain of my life, I'd rejected the blueprint worldview. I lost Henry while holding a renewed picture of a Jesus-looking God and the warfare worldview. I can say this without hesitation: *there is no comparison!*

While I was losing Henry, my soul was anchored in a God whose heart I could trust. I could place my confidence in God's ability and desire to bring life to the fullest, no matter what an enemy had done. I could rest assured that the God of infinite intelligence is never unprepared and wisely meets all tragedies with a plan to bring good out of evil. He accomplishes his purposes not by using brute force to control all events but by relying on his superior wisdom.

Not only did this knowledge ease my ache; it also unleashed a wellspring of passion that even death can't damper! I understood that God's purpose in creation, his *pursuit of love*, pushes past death and soars into eternity. This provides the greatest consolation I have ever known.

While my earthly adventure with Henry has come to an end, that's not this story's end. I believe this story ends in an eternity with Henry and with my breathtaking Savior: a God who is unfailingly good and who demonstrates unfailing love.

·· TEN ··

Passionless Hope

Three months after Henry died, we decided to sell the house. I just couldn't walk past the empty bedroom anymore. The bed was always made. The floor was always picked up. It was just as I'd always wanted . . . but not like this.

Now I *ached* for messy floors and disheveled sheets. Now the room's cleanliness was a testament to his unrelenting absence. It was an orderly shrine to the chaos of grief. I knew we had to leave.

So we staged our home beautifully and priced it aggressively, and after two weeks on the market, we had a contract. With almost rude abruptness, the time had come to say goodbye.

I had gotten what I asked for. We would be free from the tomb of Henry's quiet bedroom. We would be free from the constant triggers of painful memories. Free from the sudden flashes of our giggling boy: running barefoot through our backyard, streaking his sticky hands across the fridge, spilling glitter on the kitchen floors. I had gotten what I asked for . . . and suddenly I needed to be alone.

Ian agreed to take Miriam to our new apartment as I cleaned and emptied our home of its final possessions. And as I scrubbed and polished and delayed the inevitable, I listened to a sermon.

The pastor in my earbuds talked about prophetic speech. He read from Ezekiel 37, where a prophet follows the Spirit of God through a valley that's filled with dry bones.

"Can these bones live?" God asks Ezekiel.

Ezekiel looks over the stacks of brittle remains, stripped of all flesh, breath, and potential. "Sovereign Lord, you alone know," he replies.

God tells him to prophesy breath, tendons, flesh, and skin over the bones. So in obedience, Ezekiel begins to speak life into the lifeless, hope into the hopeless. And the bones begin to rattle. They join together before his eyes. Tendons and flesh appear and skin covers them. Soon whole bodies are lying motionless at Ezekiel's feet.

Then God says, "Prophesy to the breath."

Once more Ezekiel uses his voice in obedience, and the bodies fill with breath. Resurrected souls rise to their feet, and God proclaims them to be the people of Israel.

It was such a gripping and bizarre story. But the pastor explained how it applies to the life of every Christ-follower. He said that we, just like Ezekiel, are called to prophetically *speak hope*. We must gaze upon those situations in life that seem hopeless and proclaim the hope of the Lord. He likened it to Martin Luther King Jr. sharing aloud his dream of racial reconciliation.

I got completely lost in the sermon, and before I knew it, everything was spotless. I had wiped the small marker-stained fingerprints off the outlets. I had buffed scuff marks from riding toys off the floorboards. I had rinsed colorful chalk smears off the outside columns. I had swept the back porch of the spilled-over sand from the kids' sand table and discretely scattered it across the yard.

And, somehow, I had to say goodbye. Another goodbye. But unlike the goodbye I'd said to Henry months earlier, I knew I'd feel this one fully, deeply, and without the anesthetic of shock.

So I wandered through one empty room after another, bombarded with rich memories and bankrupt dreams. This was the house where my babbling toddler had grown into a chattering little boy. It was where we'd created crayon masterpieces and squished play dough and built block towers and conquered potty training. It was where he'd proudly helped me stir soups and wash dishes and water plants. It was where he'd met Miriam. It was where we'd celebrated birthdays and holidays with family and friends. It was where we'd laughed hard and cried loud.

It was where Henry passed from this life into eternal life.

As flashes of our life lapped over me, I experienced the full force of crippling loss. I sank to the floor in our master bedroom, where I bawled and moaned and rocked rhythmically with the waves of desperation. The pain was so thick and consuming that I struggled for air and truly wondered if I could rise from the floor.

I remember crying out toward the ceiling, "*How?* How can I do this?!" My body was crumpled in a heap on that beige carpet . . . until I remembered. I remembered the sermon of hope that had helped me scrub our home into someone else's house. I remembered Ezekiel. And I began to speak the hope of the Lord into the most hopeless moment of my life.

"I have hope," I whispered with the next gasp of air.

My sobs settled.

I lay motionless.

Those little words had helped pull me together, but I didn't have the strength to rise.

"I have hope," I repeated a little louder. Then I sat up and filled my lungs with a powerful breath.

"I have hope!" I declared, finally finding the strength to stand.

I repeated the process in every other room. Each time I was flattened by a fresh downpour of memories, and I spoke of hope over and over until I gained the strength to rise. I honestly don't know how I would have left that house without speaking aloud *hope*.

Hope is where I needed to start. I needed to remember my hope for Christ's return and my hope of a reunion with Henry. I needed to hear anew Scripture's promise that one day I'll join Christ, the "firstborn" of the new creation, as a beloved sister. And in the meantime I could trust that Jesus is preparing a place in the Father's house. I needed to keep in mind that one day the bride of Christ will be made radiant and will participate eternally in the wedding supper of the Lamb. Yes, I needed to hear about Christian hope.

Yet today, as I write and reflect on what fuels me through this pain, I've realized that while hope picks me up off the floor, *passion* is what compels my fingers to write. Hope is sufficient for me to press forward, but *passion* compels me to reach out to you.

And it weighs heavily on my heart that Christians usually discuss hope against the backdrop of the blueprint. They speak of hope while holding the unspoken notion that God causes or specifically allows radical suffering and evil for mysterious higher purposes.

While I could find the *hope to survive* within this blueprint framework, my faith would be stripped of the *passion to thrive*. How could I passionately proclaim God's unfailing love if I believed his detailed, divine plan called for Henry's intense pain and young death? I couldn't.

The good news is that Christians needn't resign themselves to a hope-filled, passionless faith. We can have both. We are called to both. And the Scripture-based, Calvary-centered warfare worldview offers both. Regardless of the traumas we may endure, this understanding of God's ways equips us with hope for the future *and* with passion for God today.

Unfortunately, as we discussed in the last chapter, the majority of Christians consider evil and radical suffering to be part of God's "perfect plan." Many believe God causes or specifically allows things like sexual abuse, the Holocaust, and fatal brain tumors for an unknown "greater good." They proclaim, "His ways are higher than our ways!" and "All things work together for good!" Is this what the Bible teaches? Let's take a closer look at these claims in the sections that follow. Then we'll examine how these pat answers, and the blueprint worldview they stem from, offer victims a passionless hope.

His ways are higher than our ways

The phrase "His ways are higher than our ways" is adapted from Isaiah 55:8-9. The entire passage reads: " 'For my thoughts are not your thoughts, neither are your ways my ways,' declares the Lord. 'As the heavens are higher than the earth, so are my ways higher than your ways and my thoughts than your thoughts.' "

Do these verses support the notion that everything that happens, including radical suffering, is simply a part of God's mysterious and perfect plan? Is evil somehow good in God's mind because his thoughts are "higher" than ours are?

Let's examine the passage in context. In the beginning of the chapter, we find God inviting *all* people who are thirsty, even those without money, to have fine food and drink (vv. 1-2). He speaks of how other nations will be drawn to Israel because the Israelites are so richly blessed by God (vv. 4-5). And he shares his willingness to mercifully pardon all who will repent from their wicked ways (v. 7).

God is expressing his desire to use Israel as a means of fulfilling his dream—a dream of drawing all nations together under his loving lordship. While many of the ancient Israelites prided themselves on having unique status with God on the basis of their nationality, God was reminding them that his ways were different from, higher than, their own. He was expressing his desire to reach the *whole world* through the chosen nation of Israel.

This must have been difficult to comprehend. As humans, we often struggle to forgive those who are unfaithful to us. But here God shares his desire to shower mercy upon all who turn away from their unfaithfulness to him. It's his great forgiveness and heart for the entire world that is *higher* than our own thoughts and ways.

So when God said through the prophet Isaiah, "My ways are higher than your ways," he was *not* instructing people to piously resign themselves to a divine blueprint. God was not saying that he has a mysterious, "loving" plan that calls for every disease, instance of suffering, and evil act. Rather, God was explaining that his ways are higher because he loves the whole world more than the Israelites could imagine!

Unfortunately, this passage is frequently misused in an attempt to disregard hard questions about God or to justify jumbled beliefs. But by examining it in context, we can see that these verses do *not* imply that horrific evil is actually "loving" because it's included in some divine, cosmic blueprint. Love cannot sometimes be evil. Love cannot sometimes be *not love*.

The idea that evil is actually loving when it's planned by God makes love something mysterious—something we can't recognize. But love is something we must recognize, because Scripture commands us to be imitators of God and love as he does (Eph 5:1-2).

We can only follow commands that we understand. We can only *show* love if we *know* love. And we do. God's love was defined by the cross. It's a love that ascribes worth to another, sometimes at great cost to oneself.

Isaiah 55:8-9 does not ask us to believe that God abides by a different standard of right and wrong. It doesn't assert that God's love is sometimes the opposite of what we think love means. It's referring to the fact that God is *more* forgiving and *more* merciful than we realize.[1]

All things work together for good

Pain needs purpose. Joni Eareckson Tada wisely asks, "Who can live without purpose?"[2] I'd add: Who can live in pain without purpose? Profound pain needs profound purpose.

Yet I reject that Henry's death was planned by God. I don't believe that his fatal tumor was part of a mysterious cosmic blueprint designed to bring God glory.

So does my pain lack purpose? Is this tragedy meaningless collateral damage in a war that wages throughout this vastly complex universe?

No.

Is my grief pointless?

Not for a second.

Thankfully, I don't need to believe that God planned my pain for it to have meaning. That's because pain can *acquire* tremendous purpose during and after it transpires. And because God is infinitely intelligent and never unprepared, it follows that he had an eternal plan to bring purpose *to* my pain in case it transpired.

All I need to do is partner with his efforts.

To many, this may sound radical. Some of you may be wondering, does Scripture support this? Doesn't the Bible say that all things work together for good? Wouldn't that mean that there is a God-given purpose behind all things? Painful or not, they're all part of the master plan, right?

Romans 8:28 is the key text for this discussion. It's one of the most popular verses in the Bible and is often cited in support of the idea that every specific pain happens for a mysterious higher purpose. For instance, in *The Purpose Driven Life*, Rick Warren quotes the New Living Translation: "God causes everything to work together for the good of those who love God and are called according to his purpose for them." As I mentioned in chapter 9, from this Warren concludes: "The events in your life work *together* in God's plan. They are not isolated acts, but interdependent parts of the process to make you like Christ. To bake a cake you must use flour, salt, raw eggs, sugar, and oil. Eaten individually, each is pretty distasteful or even bitter. But bake them together and they become delicious."[3]

Warren's conclusion is that God is the Master Baker and our life circumstances are God's ingredients. And this makes sense *if* Romans 8:28 is applied using a translation like the one above and is examined apart from the rest of the New Testament. Thankfully, this is not the only option. Other Bible translations don't imply that God is the cause of every pain and tragedy in our lives. The Revised Standard Version, for example, reads: "in everything God works for good *with those* who love him, who are called according to his purpose."[4]

Whoa! That's a major difference!

The first translation portrays a God who single-handedly determines everything that happens and always gets his way. If he desires to cook up something (or some*one*) for his "glory," he simply tosses together a cup of good grades with a tablespoon of financial stability. Then, to balance the recipe's sweetness, he adds a pinch of fatal brain tumor and a splash of marital strain. In this view, what seems bitter or arbitrary to us ends up being delicious to God.

The second translation, however, does not imply that God is all-controlling. Rather, it emphasizes that God is always ready to partner with those who love him (regardless of who or what caused their circumstances) to bring about good.

Both translations are linguistically possible in the original Greek. So which one is right? The answer to this question is critical, because it profoundly influences our picture of God and guides our reaction to painful situations.

According to New Testament scholar Timothy Geddert, the confusion lies around the Greek verb for "work together." He explains that this verb is *not* used to describe one person "working various ingredients together"; rather, "it is about *more than one party* 'working together' on a common project." This is consistent with how the verb is translated when it appears all other times in the New Testament. And when the noun associated with that verb is used in the New Testament, it is always used to depict two or more parties working together. Geddert concludes, "Romans 8:28 is not about God fitting all things together into a pattern for our benefit. It is about God and those who love God working as partners, 'working together' to bring about good in all situations."[5]

The first interpretation can breed complacency toward evil or offer the misplaced assurance that all bad things are mysteriously working toward our earthly good. It can even compound victims' crises with a crisis of faith as they struggle to accept that it was their heavenly Father who brought about their nightmare.

By contrast, this second rendering of Romans 8:28 can be seen as a challenge issued to Christians. It spurs God's people to action—to finding ways to join in God's good work. When we encounter people who feel separated from God's love, we're to consider ourselves "co-workers" with God, sent to assure them, as Geddert suggests, in "concrete and tangible ways that God still loves them."[6]

I've found this interpretation of Romans 8:28 to be compelling and convincing. And unlike the Master Baker interpretation, it's consistent with God's self-revelation in Jesus! He's a God whose essence *is* the self-sacrificial love of Calvary. He doesn't plan evil for a mysterious higher good but instead collaborates with his children to bless the victims of this war-torn creation.

We can remain confident that no matter what happens, God has a plan to bring good from it. He's infinitely intelligent. So no matter how unexpected a tragedy seems to us, we can trust that God has been preparing a plan to bring good out of it, in case it happened, from the foundation of the world. He is never unprepared, and the purpose he can bring to an evil event is just as good *as if* the event had happened *for that very purpose*.

What beautiful hope! We can partner with God to bring purpose to our pain! We can be coworkers with God, comforting every traumatized soul, not allowing one tear to be wasted, and compassionately meeting each pain with hope and healing.

Pain needs purpose. Profound pain needs profound purpose. As Christians, we must not sit back stoically when tragedy strikes, believing we are witnessing the unfolding of God's divine blueprint. Rather, we must understand that Romans 8:28 commissions us to spring into action as the hands and feet of Christ.

Our job is to partner with God's efforts in moments of crisis, acting as his ambassadors to bring about good. In other words, we are called by the God of profound love to partner with him in profound pain, and to endow it with profound purpose.

A sea of unanswered questions

"Did you watch it?" I asked Ian one afternoon. It was about four months after Henry's death. Earlier that day someone had sent us a video profiling several Christian parents who had also lost children.

"Not yet. Let's watch it together," Ian said as he joined me at the computer. After a few quick clicks we found ourselves glued to the screen, hungry and hesitant. We were searching for clues, wondering how our lives would play out. These parents had walked our painful path for years, some for decades.

We leaned in, listening past sorrowful piano notes and churchy sound bites, straining for answers. Would our pain fade? Would it always be so intense? Could we ever feel happy again?

As we scrutinized the parents' tones and studied their faces, we found flashes of familiar anger. We recognized streaks of pain, coated in quiet sadness. We noted an earnest desire to honor God.

We saw hope for restoration in eternity. But despite everything that we identified with, something seemed . . . off.

Something was lacking as the parents robotically resumed their old hobbies of gardening, golfing, and taking nature walks. Something was scary about the dullness of their expressions, their mouths turned downward, and the way they seemed to be idly passing the time. Something was painfully absent in their eyes when they spoke of God.

But what? I thought about it for days. There had been so much I recognized from my own grief—the pain, hope, anger, faith, and sadness. But what was missing from their stories that seemed to punctuate my life and permeate my loss?

Finally, it hit me. *Passion.* In their eyes and smiles and body language I'd seen hope but no passion. And when it came to God's role in their loss, defeat seemed to coat their cookie-cutter answers. I remember one father weakly offered something like "God taught me that he was all I needed."

These testimonies were meant to encourage us. They were success stories of parents who had faced the worst and hadn't abandoned their faith. Unfortunately, their understanding of God's role in their tragedy seemed to be robbing them of their passion for God.

They all embraced the common notion that God had specifically allowed their suffering for a mysterious higher purpose. After all, an all-powerful God has the ability to unilaterally step in and prevent tragedy, right? So if God didn't intervene to save their children, it must mean that it was all part of his plan. And with an assumption like this, those parents' lack of passion is completely understandable. How could they be passionate about a God who stamped "approved" on their worst nightmare? I couldn't.

The idea that a good God specifically allows horrors like brain cancer, deadly tornados, and school massacres must be reexamined. I believe this notion acts as a quiet undertow, tugging the passion of broken Christians into a sea of unanswered questions. It shakes our trust in God's character and causes us to doubt his love. It also paints a picture of God that doesn't look like Jesus. But Jesus was the exact representation of God's essence (Heb 1:3). So whenever we examine God's role in suffering, we must start with a picture of God that looks like Jesus.

Let's do that with a real-world example. Let's imagine that Jesus was physically present at Sandy Hook Elementary School on the morning of December 14, 2012. Let's pretend he knew the shootings were planned and he possessed the power to stop them. But he didn't. Instead, let's say he did in *bodily* form what many claim that God does in *spirit* form. Picture Jesus nodding in approval (saddened or not) as a deranged gunman took twenty-six lives. Perhaps he whispered to the shooter after twenty-five slayings, "I'll allow one more," because twenty-six victims was somehow the specific number that would bring him the most glory. Does this sound like Jesus?

Of course not!

Yet this is how we portray God when tragedy hits and we stoically profess "This is all part of God's plan" and "God is in control." It seems to me that within this understanding, the best that Christ-following, traumatized persons can aspire to is stoic resignation. And they are left with a stark realization regarding God's character: it's mysterious.

If God is good, why didn't he intervene when that psychopathic man was loading his automatic rifle? It's mysterious. If God is loving, why didn't he find a way to warn the victims beforehand? It's mysterious. Why did God protect some children and not others? It's mysterious.

When it comes to God's character, *mystery* leaves battered hearts primed for passionless hope.

Mystery allows room for hope that suffering will one day cease. But it fails to embolden victims to passionately embrace and proclaim the love of God—the same God who specifically allowed every second of their devastation. The kind of "love" that steps aside while evil transpires would evoke rage, dismay, and confusion if we saw it exhibited by humans. These feelings are no less vivid when the one who's supposedly complicit is God.

This is why we cannot gloss over our understanding of God's role in evil and radical suffering. In fact, I've found that the more convinced I am that God is opposed to evil, the more compelled I am to share his love.

I believe this is what distinguishes my grief experience from the grief I saw in the video. Within my grief, there's a belief—a belief that creates a spark. It's an ember that glows red-hot when I speak of God's role in Henry's death. God didn't plan this. God didn't do this. God didn't want this. God wasn't passive in Henry's death, and he wasn't trying to teach me something by watching my son die. God loves us! He loves us with a love we can recognize.

Henry wasn't healed on earth, but not because a divine blueprint called for his death. I believe God did everything possible to maximize good and minimize evil as a vicious disease thwarted his loving will.

Why do I believe this? Because God *is* Calvary-like love. He always has been. He always will be. *God looks like Jesus*, laying down his life, even for those who hate him. And the love of God wins in the end. The resurrection demonstrates that this powerful, transformative love cannot be conquered by brute force.

We can rejoice in the hope that God will eventually bring an end to suffering. But until that day, we can also passionately embody God's love by becoming the hands and feet of Christ, bringing comfort, aid, and a beautiful understanding of God to all who are wounded.

God's love is pure. His character is trustworthy. He battles to bring good out of every evil and calls us to join him.

This is my hope *and* this is my passion.

Passionate hope

The blueprint worldview teaches that God is love . . . *and* that he planned all the evil. It says that God is beautiful . . . *and* that he controls all the ugly. It calls God a loving father . . . one who specifically allows every school massacre, kidnapping, and painful death. As a person who has experienced devastating loss, I could conceivably find hope within a blueprint framework. I could hold hope in eternity. Hope that my suffering will end one day. But I could not find passion.

I could find joy. There's still joy in serving others. Yet while I could serve them, I wouldn't be able to passionately and authentically proclaim God's beautiful character to them.

I could find purpose. From the depths of my grief I could find purpose in sharing my hope with others. I could offer comfort, and listen with empathetic ears. I could testify about the good that has come from my immense suffering. But I could not passionately, gleefully, and truthfully proclaim the awesome love of God

. . . the God who supposedly planned Henry's intense pain and young death.

I could not accept that the God of the blueprint is a God of love.

If you are still holding tightly to the blueprint worldview, let me again invite you to wrestle. Why? Because there's a war happening all around us. Good and evil are clashing at every turn, and God is inviting us to be his coworkers. He's inviting us to wrestle with our questions, doubts, reservations, and fears so we can move past a soiled image of God and discover the passion that overflows when our minds and hearts are in agreement. This passion shakes us, wakes us, and compels us to get busy being the very hands and feet of Christ.

Hope is important. Speaking hope is vital. I've learned this first-hand. And in the spirit of speaking hope, I'd like to share my hope that each of you will wrestle with your understanding of God's role in suffering. My prayer is that you won't quit until you land solidly upon a picture of God that looks like the crucified Christ.

ELEVEN

The Lord Gives . . . and Takes?

*T**he ultrasound tech* looked devastated. "I'm so sorry," she whispered to the happy couple. "There's no heartbeat."
It was agonizing to watch. I was curled up on the couch in front of my favorite reality TV show. It featured a large Christian family that I, along with millions of other viewers, had grown to love over the years. I'd cheered for each new life they'd brought into the world. And to now witness their loss was nothing short of gut-wrenching.

I held my breath as the couple's expressions morphed from joy to bewilderment and finally broke into pain. As she lay flat on the ultrasound table, the mother wiped her tears and whispered, "The Lord giveth, and the Lord taketh away, blessed be the name of the Lord."

The couple joined hands and took their pain to God. They thanked him for the short time they'd been given with their developing baby. The father said, "I pray we'll handle this the right way, and be able to encourage the children to handle this the right way." The mother repeated with greater resolution, "The Lord giveth, and the Lord taketh away; blessed be the name of the Lord."

Despite my tears, I stayed glued to the screen. I followed them out of the doctor's office and into their living room. Over an intercom, they summoned their large brood together. The youngest kids were bouncing around while waiting for the announcement. The room was filled with excited cries of "Is it a boy or a girl?" and "Is it twins?"

When everyone was gathered and silent, the mother explained, "The baby died." Again, I witnessed joyful faces fade to shock and then break into pain. After a brief conversation, the father concluded solemnly, "The Lord giveth, and the Lord taketh away; blessed be the name of the Lord."

The Lord gives, and the Lord takes away; blessed be the name of the Lord. I heard those words first as a young child, nestled between my parents at church. I was trying to make sense of what was happening. I think they were too. It soon became clear that the couple at the microphone had tragically miscarried.

The Lord gives, and the Lord takes away; blessed be the name of the Lord. I've read those words several times on social media. Friends have posted them, sometimes weeks after we've rejoiced over their pregnancies. Those words signaled that it was time to join them in their mourning.

The Lord gives, and the Lord takes away; blessed be the name of the Lord. Is accepting this sentiment what it means to handle grief "the right way"? Are we supposed to offer stoic resignation, even praise, toward a God who orchestrates the death of babies? Is this what the Bible requires? Is this what God desires?

Where did this phrase come from? Why is it held up as the pinnacle of Christian grieving?

For answers, we need to turn briefly to the book of Job. Here we find the Bible's superhero of suffering: a prosperous, righteous man who lost nearly everything in one horrible day. How does Job respond? His earliest response includes the phrase "The Lord gave, and the Lord has taken away; blessed be the name of the Lord" (Job 1:21 ESV).

Many Christians believe Job's initial response models how believers must react when tragedy strikes. And this is compelling when we examine the verse that follows: "In all this Job did not sin or charge God with wrong" (1:22 ESV). In fact, the point seems further confirmed when God speaks to Job at the book's close. There God chastises Job's friends for *not* speaking rightly of him, "as my servant Job has" (42:7 ESV).

So ... seems pretty clear, right? Job encountered tragedy. Then he praised God for sending it. In doing this, he never sinned. And God later confirms that *Job spoke rightly.*

Therefore, with regard to Henry's death, I should echo Job's words and thus accept Job's picture of God. That's how I can avoid sin and grieve rightly. Right?

But what if the author of the book of Job wrote, "The Lord gave, and the Lord has taken away; blessed be the name of the Lord," not to advocate this reaction but to *refute* it? What if this masterfully written work was penned to push back on this common response? What if the book of Job is meant to teach us about a very different view of God's role in suffering?

These are the questions we'll examine in the sections that follow.

How to approach the book of Job

There are different types of literature that compose the Bible. Categories for biblical books include law, history, poetry, and several others. In order to best honor, understand, and apply Scripture to our lives, we must examine each book in a manner that suits its category.

The book of Job is classified as wisdom literature, like Proverbs and Ecclesiastes. This is important to note, mostly because of what the book is *not* intended to be: historical literature. Job's character could have been based on an actual person who suffered greatly, but most scholars agree that this book, "while probably reflecting deep experiences of suffering, is not a biographical or historical account." They have called the book of Job " 'once upon a time' literature," "a 'what if?' book, a 'let's suppose for the sake of argument' book," and even a "thought experiment."[1] Unlike the person of Jesus, whose historical integrity is central to our entire faith, the point of Job's tale does not depend on its historical accuracy.[2] And in fact, if we treat this *wisdom* book as a *history* book, we just may miss its point.

It seems clear that the author of Job was concerned with God's relationship to evil and suffering.[3] So it follows that we can view his literary work as an invitation to wrestle with this issue. Like Jesus' parables (for example, the prodigal son), this story exists to impart a lesson.[4]

For some, examining the book of Job from this perspective may be new or uncomfortable. I understand. For most of my life, I simply assumed that the book of Job was a journalistic report of historical events, written to instruct Christians how to grieve. Yet because this book's inspired purpose is not to recount history, we needn't believe that all the events described actually transpired.

For the remainder of this chapter, let's try something different. As we examine this book, I encourage you to step *out* of Job's shoes and *into* the theater. Let's behold this incredible tale together and ask ourselves what the author is trying to communicate. Let's analyze this book in a way that suits its literary style and poetically instructive purpose. I believe this book reveals something profound about God but that we must be aware of its distinct presentation to catch the overarching lesson.

The book of Job is structured in a unique way. The prologue (introduction) and the epilogue (ending) are written in common language. These narrative pieces compose the story's framework. The middle of the book is written in a poetic style. It consists of lyrical speeches from Job, his friends, and God. These speeches provide a playground for our mind's wanderings about God's role in suffering.

In the next few sections we'll explore the book's narrative framework before turning our attention to the poetic speeches of God.

A divine wager

The prologue (Job 1–2) begins with a description of its main character, Job. He's a righteous and super-wealthy guy. Job has seven sons, three daughters, lots of servants, tons of animals, and a heart totally devoted to God.

One day Job is blissfully living the good life when, unbeknownst to him, a council assembles in the heavenly realms. But as the angels are gathering, an uninvited guest arrives: Satan.[5]

God asks Satan where he's come from. Here I can just imagine Satan putting his feet up on a crystal conference table as he says, "Oh, you know, here and there, just roaming around on earth and whatever."

At this point we can almost hear the angels growing quiet. They begin to fixate on the exchange between God and Satan. None of *them* would speak to God with such irreverence.

"Have you considered my servant Job?" God asks Satan. Then God begins to brag on Job's righteousness and obedience, no doubt before a nodding crowd.

"Job only obeys you because you protect and bless him," Satan snorts (and the angels gasp!). We can even picture Satan pausing for effect before he sneers, "If you quit coddling Job, he'd curse you to your face."

Can you hear the ripples of "Ooooooooo" and the whispers of "Oh, it's *on!*" reverberating among the heavenly hosts? And within this profound work of "dramatic fiction," God has no choice but to lift his protection from Job.[6]

After all, if God just ignored Satan or cast him aside, a sliver of doubt would be left in the minds of the heavenly hosts (and therefore the reading audience). They'd wonder: What if Satan has a point? Do people just obey God because of what's in it for them? Does God simply control humans, blessing them when they please him, cursing them when they don't? Maybe God rules with fear instead of love.

So in the blink of an eye, Job's bread and butter become burnt toast. He loses his herds and flocks to fire. He loses his servants to desert savages. He even loses his children in a building collapse. Eventually he loses his health too.

But before we get further into the tale, let's ask ourselves: Does the prologue to the book of Job provide any clues about how to grieve "the right way"?

Many Christians would say yes. They believe the prologue supports the profession that the Lord gives, and the Lord takes away.

Why? Because in this poetic tale, the main character's affliction was "Father-filtered." Satan inflicted Job, but God specifically allowed it. Should we then assume the same is true for every trauma in our lives?

I'd offer that this option could only be considered *if* we regard the prologue as a historical, cosmic event. But if we decide to regard the prologue as history, we run into some major problems.

Namely, we can't just take *one* piece of the prologue and apply it to our understanding of how God operates. If it's describing an actual event, we should consistently apply *all* the details provided to how the universe is run. But this leaves us with at least three questions:

- Did God really not know where Satan was before he arrived at the council meeting? Does God therefore not know what Satan is up to on earth?

- Does Satan have the cunning to sucker God into wagers that result in murder and destruction? Is Satan therefore smarter than God?

- Does Satan have to get God's permission every time he acts to inflict suffering on earth? This seems odd, as we know that humans are free to sin without obtaining permission from God. If Satan cannot at least do the same, how could he be the "highest ruling official" of the earth, as Jesus claimed?

On the other hand, if we approach the prologue as most scholars do, we face none of those questions. And in the same way, we don't treat God's specific permission of Job's tragedies as an example of how God actually operates. Instead, we understand that this gripping introduction is meant to set the stage for Job's encounter with radical suffering.[7]

We can appreciate this text's inspired meaning without treating it like a heavenly court reporter's transcript. Just as we would misunderstand Jesus' parables by pressing them for literal details, so it is with the book of Job. The central point is where we need to lock in our attention. God's wisdom and justice are on trial, and the question is whether God will be vindicated.

I believe that symbolism here is key. Job and his friends have no knowledge of the divine wager, and this arguably represents the notion that significant actions transpire outside of human awareness. Unfortunately, those actions sometimes result in extreme human suffering. And due to this brilliant literary setup, Job and his friends, as well as the book's reading audience, are primed to wrestle with God's role in pain.[8]

Job spoke rightly

In the shock of sudden loss, Job professes, "The Lord gave, and the Lord has taken away; blessed be the name of the Lord." And at the book's close, God proclaims that *Job spoke rightly*. Many Christians hold that these verses provide proof that God desires this type of response when tragedy strikes.

Yet, if we consider the entire book of Job, this proof leaves us with at least three concerns. The first is that although Job speaks humbly at the book's opening, the shock of loss soon wears off. And while Job never wavers in his belief that God is all-controlling, he does waver in his devout submission to God. Soon into the poetic section of the book, venomous accusations start flying from Job's lips.

Why then did God affirm that *Job spoke rightly?*

Was Job *right* when he called God ruthless? Someone who slaps him around? Someone determined to kill him (30:20-23)?

Was Job *right* to claim that God stalks him like a lion (10:16)? Attacks him violently (16:14)? Angrily tears him apart (16:9)?

Was Job *right* to call God his enemy (6:4-7; 13:24; 16:7-14; 19:6-20)? Someone who is senselessly terrorizing him (9:17-18, 34; 13:21)? Persecuting him (30:21)? Out to destroy him (10:8)?

Was Job *right* to assert that God is unjust and mocks the pain of the innocent (9:22-24)? Ignores the prayers of the wounded (24:12)? That he's a destroyer of hope (14:19)?

Job spoke rightly?

Finally, after all of these accusations, God arrives on the scene. And what does he do? Does he affirm Job's early respectful tone and rebuke his later outrageous charges? No. After delivering his own poetic speech, God simply declares that *Job spoke rightly.*

So when we consider God's blanket approval of Job's *right* speaking, we have to challenge the assumption that God seeks pious praise in the wake of trauma. Job was just as skilled at hurling nasty charges against God!

The second problem we find is that Job's friends share his picture of a micro-controlling God. But God doesn't praise them. In fact, God rebukes Job's friends for *not* speaking rightly. So whatever this verse means with regard to speaking rightly, it cannot be in professing the image of an all-controlling God.

Third, we should note that at the end of the story, our hero repents. Job says to God, "I spoke of things I did not understand, things too wonderful for me to know" (42:3). He concludes, "I despise myself and repent in dust and ashes" (42:6). If Job's character was intended to be our model for Christian grieving, it seems odd that the author would have him repent in the end.

At this point, I believe we've established that Job's famous phrase—"The Lord gave, and the Lord has taken away; blessed be the name of the Lord"—does not necessarily express accurate theology. But this leaves us wondering, how could Job be both *right* and *incorrect*? What did God mean when he said that *Job spoke rightly*?

The answer: Job gave it to him straight. He was honest with God, even when it wasn't pretty. Amid other charges, Job accused God of being fickle and terrorizing. Yet amazingly, Job's harsh allegations weren't the issue with God. They had naturally flowed from Job's *faulty* picture of God.

Job had started with the assumption that God single-handedly determined everything that came to pass. In that day, the prominent wisdom was that those who prospered were receiving reward for their righteousness. On the other hand, those who suffered were viewed as getting punished for their wickedness.[9] But Job knew that he was righteous and was being afflicted without cause, so he railed against God's "justice."

Because God understood Job's flawed assumptions, he knew Job's accusations were not only logical but, more importantly, honest.[10] He therefore praised his servant for *speaking rightly*. And when Job responds, we find him repenting from his misguided presumptions, not from the candidness of his rants.[11]

The book of Job demonstrates that God calls us to be honest, not stoic. We are called to openly air our feelings toward God and wrestle with him when necessary. The author of Job understood this, as did the author of Genesis. There we find Jacob wrestling with God all night long on the riverbank. King David understood this as well. He held nothing back in his laments in the book of Psalms.

The God of the Bible *is* relational love. He seeks intimacy, and sometimes in this war-torn world, intimacy can only occur in the painful wake of honest railing. To *speak rightly* is to speak our heart's truth to God even when our thoughts about him are misguided.

God restored Job

As the drama of the book of Job concludes, we're told our hero has a happily-ever-after ending. Job's friends and siblings comfort him with lavish gifts. Job gains more herds than ever before. He's blessed with ten more children (and his new daughters are described as the fairest in all the land). We're told that the Lord restored Job's fortunes and gave him twice as much as he had before (42:10).

Does this story's epilogue support the phrase "The Lord gives, and the Lord takes away; blessed be the name of the Lord"?

Some say yes.

They point to God's overall justice. They say that although God specifically allowed Job's radical suffering, God later restored him. In fact, some might insist that Job was better off. Surely he was more mature, plus his possessions were greater and his daughters were prettier. So God gives and he takes away... but he's not *unreasonable*. In the end, God restored Job.

God... restored... Job.

Let's let that sink in.

God restored Job.

His thousands of dead animals... *restored*?

His slaughtered servants... *restored*?

His fatally crushed children... *restored*?

All the grief, anguish, and trauma . . . *restored*?

Really?

To say the least, if we accepted that the epilogue accurately represents the way God operates, we run into a major problem. That is, we'd have to embrace a terrifying picture of a God with a horribly skewed sense of right and wrong. We'd have to believe that God deals coldly with his creation, exchanging human souls in equal numbers to redeem losses (and endowing female attractiveness as icing on the apology cake).

As a survivor of child loss, it is clear to me that Job's loss was not restored. Replacing one loved one with another does not restore loss. Arithmetic does not apply to human lives!

For me, one hundred new sons couldn't replace Henry. And I'm certain that any parent who has lost a child and then goes on to have another baby will insist that their new addition does *not* replace their deceased child. A new child can bring joy and perhaps ease a family's pain, but one life cannot erase and replace another.

We must acknowledge that the epilogue presents a picture of God who is utterly unaware or unconcerned with the nature of humanity's pain. And *this* stands in direct opposition to God's self-revelation in Jesus.

On the other hand, if we accept that the fairy-tale ending of this inspired story doesn't reflect history any more than the prologue does, then we do not run into these problems.[12] We might conclude it's simply the author's overly tidy ending to his "let's suppose for the sake of argument" book. Or we might see these lavish blessings as a public vindication of Job.[13]

Regardless of whether the epilogue contains symbolic elements, we can be confident that, just like the prologue, we find no reason to apply its details literally. And we certainly can't point to Job's "restoration" as evidence that God demands praise while smiting his servants.

But what's the alternative? What does God desire? What *is* the point of the book of Job?

The point of the book of Job

We turn now to consider God's two poetic monologues (38:1–40:2; 40:6–41:34). In the process we will make a beautiful discovery. Previously, we examined God's declaration that *Job spoke rightly*. This approval even included Job's near-blasphemous accusations, because they were logical and honest. God knew that they stemmed from his faulty theology. But as we behold the whirlwind that encompasses God's presence, we find that God loved Job *too much* to leave his faithful servant with those fundamental misconceptions.

It's crucial that we weigh God's consecutive speeches against everything else presented in the book. Why? Because many believe that they present the author's point of view. They contain the book's intended lesson.[14]

Scholars have asserted that each part of the book of Job presents a different picture of God for the audience to evaluate.[15] This makes sense if we step back and consider the pieces separately. For instance, the prologue and the epilogue show God politely contending with sinister cosmic forces (Satan) and being willing to specifically allow death and destruction to win bets, though he'll sometimes "restore" an innocent victim caught in the cross fire. In Job's speeches, we find a God who acts single-handedly, often in cruel and arbitrary ways. And with Job's friends, we find a God who is justly (not arbitrarily) micro-controlling humanity through divine reward and punishment. In their eyes, it's impossible for a righteous person to suffer, so the victim is always to blame.

As we, the audience, progress through the story, we find our-selves considering each character's carefully articulated position. And finally, in this section, God steps up to the microphone to speak for himself. So as God speaks, let's strain to hear the author's voice. Let's listen for the point of the book. Many believe the lesson is woven into the whirlwind.

In poetic fashion, God radically enlightens Job with two key revelations. The first is that creation is not simple—it's complex! Job and his friends had an easy explanation for everything that hap-pened, including suffering: it came single-handedly from God. But God refutes this simplistic belief by pointing to the vast complexity of creation.

He highlights Job's (and the audience's) ignorance by asking de-tailed questions about creation, such as whether Job has seen God's warehouses of hail and snow (38:22). He asks Job if he knows when mountain goats give birth (39:1) or how long a doe gestates (39:2). In posing questions such as these, God is eloquently illustrating, in terms that Job could understand, that the universe is so complicated and multifaceted that the *why* behind anything that happens goes beyond our full comprehension. There are no simple explanations.

Today we can naturally conclude that everything we face is en-tangled with the effects of sin, the consequences of humanity's free choices, and nature's free processes (processes that often operate in opposition to God's ideal).

Now, to some readers, this concept may feel overwhelming at first. I understand. And so does God. I believe this is why God tells

Job to *brace himself* before he opens Job's eyes to this understanding (38:3). Perhaps it's because trading simple answers for the awareness of creation's complexity (and acknowledging a huge amount of human ignorance) can feel frightening at first. Yet I submit that the reward is discovering a God whose character is not randomly cruel nor manipulative.

This leads to the second revelation in God's speeches. Job learns that God is not acting single-handedly in the universe but *is involved in cosmic conflict* against a powerful adversary.

The idea that God is involved in cosmic conflict exists throughout the book of Job.[16] It starts in the prologue with an *uninvited* heavenly agent *unexpectedly* approaching God and wagering an *unplanned* bet. While we can't search the prologue for literal historical details, we can acknowledge the symbolic reference to things happening outside of human awareness that result in radical suffering (suffering that is *outside* the ideal will of God).[17]

Although the name Satan is only used in the prologue, some argue that his is not a minor character in this drama. He doesn't just appear in the prologue and then disappear altogether.[18] Rather, he is present throughout the book in the mention of cosmic mythological creatures such as Behemoth and Leviathan.[19] For the author's ancient Near Eastern audience, these creatures would have been well-known representations of chaos and death. The great Behemoth has been linked to Mot, the god of death, and Leviathan to a "guise of Satan."[20]

In God's speeches, these creatures are vividly described as immensely powerful and extremely daunting. As one scholar notes, they are so fierce that even God has to handle them with "kid gloves."[21] In fact, God is seen as praiseworthy precisely because he is the only one who is able to battle them. In contrast to Job's accusation that God is a tyrant, God shows himself as the victor![22]

He's a God who fully understands the complexity of the universe and the forces of evil that threaten creation. He's a God who is battling evil and is equipped to restore all things under his loving lordship.

In the New Testament, we find God delivering the deathblow to his enemies through the work of Calvary (Col 2:13-15). In the end, we'll see that victory fully realized. But for now, Christians can triumphantly echo Job's closing declaration that "no purpose of [God's] can be thwarted" (42:2).[23]

We can be confident that despite the aggression of fierce enemies, God won't allow his plan to create and sustain the world, for the purpose of expanding his love, to be destroyed.

Bless the name of the Lord

The Lord gives, and the Lord takes away; blessed be the name of the Lord. That was Job's view. At first he said it piously. Then he shouted it bitterly. Yet even as his composure crumbled, our hero's heart kept repeating: *The Lord gives, and the Lord takes away.*

Why did the author give Job this persistent message? I hope this chapter has demonstrated that it was *presented* to be *refuted*.[24] In the whirlwind, Job receives a distinct alternative to his faulty picture of God. God is not micro-controlling. He's not sending calamities; instead, he is battling evil. And when we compare these revelations to God's full revelation in Jesus Christ, we find that the pictures align.

On the other hand, when Christians embrace and proclaim Job's faulty picture of God, I submit that we point to a God who looks very little like Jesus. Jesus didn't orchestrate disease or death.

He treated the sick and afflicted as casualties of war. He used his power to heal, encourage, and triumph over death through the power of love.

So what should we say? How should we react when loss and pain and trauma come?

I'd offer that we are welcome to praise our loving Father who *gives* good gifts (James 1:17). But we can also honestly, even angrily, cry out when nature or people *take* something precious. And we can *bless the name of the Lord* by serving each other in humility, seeking ways to receive and reflect the perfect love of God.

TWELVE

A Beautiful Answer

I remember being surrounded by people and yet completely alone. It was the day we unloaded the wheelchair instead of the stroller and the feeding machine instead of a baby carrier. It was the day we brought Henry home from the hospital, just as we'd done years earlier. The first time we brought him home was to begin his life. This time we'd brought him home to die.

Amid that painful homecoming celebration, loneliness set in. Smack in the middle of well-wishers, family members, and medical professionals, I felt consumed by a stark isolation. My husband felt it too, and we often silently held hands across the chasm.

Those days were intensely private, completely public, and there was no time to process. So when a hospice chaplain kindly offered to visit, I jumped to accommodate with sky-high expectations.

I yearned to be reminded of God's heart, his perfect goodness. I needed to hear someone insist that God deeply values all living creatures and would never wish this on our son. I craved a fresh source of strength and passion, a presence to testify to God's fierce love for us.

But that isn't what happened.

Instead, this chaplain simply sat with us. He asked us how we were doing and listened well. He shed tears. He was sympathetic. He was empathetic.

And when he left, I remained untouched, weary, and alone.

When sitting is not enough

The chaplain didn't do anything wrong. In fact, he did well the job he was trained to do. It's also the approach that many Christians take when approaching devastated people. They simply sit in quiet solidarity with a person in pain. After all, telling a grief-stricken person that their trauma is part of God's perfect plan would be, at best, extremely insensitive. If this is the only option, then silence becomes the better approach.

There was a time when I would have embraced silence as the *only* suitable approach. In my secular counselor training, I mastered reflective techniques in which I rephrased people's laments, refrained from offering answers, and simply listened as they wrestled with hard questions. I knew how to be completely present. I could enter fully, reverently, into pain.

These skills are foundational and necessary. And there are times that simply offering oneself as a sounding board is best. When a comforter doesn't know what to say, silence can be best. When a comforter doesn't know what a victim believes about God, silence can be best.

Rick Warren affirmed the role of silence a couple of days after a deadly tornado swept through Moore, Oklahoma. He tweeted, "In deep pain, people don't need logic, advice, encouragement, or even Scripture. They just need you to show up and shut up."[1]

His advice was retweeted more than three thousand times in just a few days, showing that many recognize the wisdom here. I agree that to "show up and shut up" can be the best immediate course of action, particularly with regard to sudden, unexpected tragedy. Sometimes we *speak* best about God's love through silent tears, hearty hugs, helping hands, and donated dollars.

But it's important to remember that in time, the dust will settle. In time, the shock will dissipate. And the pain-filled questions will arise. They always arise. When that time comes, are we prepared to offer more than silence?

Are we able to help those who crave more than company in their pain, fear, and desperation? Those who yearn for someone to go beyond holding their hand and sharing their tears? Can Christ-followers be a better a source of strength and passion in those moments? Can we coherently testify to God's fierce love for us?

I believe we can. But we must realize that the process of becoming a better comforter begins *before* tragedy hits. It begins the moment we reject the blueprint and start to search for better explanations of God's role in suffering.

Too comfortable with the questions

But what is the answer? Where is God in the midst of our pain? If God is love, why is there so much hate? If God is strong, why doesn't he protect the weak?

In other words, when the problem of evil collides with real life, what do we say? How can we help?

Circulating in some Christian circles is a quotation that attempts to address these questions by *not* answering them. The quote originates from a famous poet, Rainer Maria Rilke, who once advised a young man:

> Be patient toward all that is unresolved in your heart and . . . try to love *the questions themselves* like locked rooms, like books written in a foreign tongue. Do not now strive to uncover answers: they cannot be given you because you have not been able to live them. And what matters is to live everything. *Live* the questions for now. Perhaps then you will gradually, without noticing it, live your way into the answer, one distant day in the future.[2]

I've read this quotation in faith memoirs and heard it proclaimed from pulpits. It shows up in articles and blog posts, and its essence is tweeted between young Christians in faith crises. The advice has become "Live the questions!"; "Press into the questions!"; and "Lean into mystery!"

Many who embrace this advice are reacting to the strong form of the blueprint worldview. They are rejecting the notion that God plans and ensures specific evil acts. They believe God is love and therefore doesn't cause evil. But they also hold that our loving God could stop evil, but for some reason . . . he doesn't. And therein lies the mystery.

They find themselves sincerely stuck. And so there's an allure to the idea that we can simply "live the questions." But I submit that this poetic resolution disguises a very real decision to *quit wrestling* with reasonable objections.

This perspective dresses up the choice to avoid seeking answers as somehow mystical, spiritually mature, or even exceptionally pious. Yet if a good God always gets his way, and evil is transpiring all around us, I don't see how any amount of living with that incoherence will lead to answers on "some distant day."

I believe these sincere Christ-followers are stopping short of discovering a passion-evoking, coherent answer to the problem of evil. And this also renders a deep disservice to their traumatized brothers and sisters.

After all, what if the questions become "How could a good God allow my brilliant, beautiful four-year-old to be ravaged by brain cancer?" or "Why didn't God intervene before the gunman shot my kindergartener during circle time?" or "Why didn't God stop that massive tornado from killing my family, destroying my home, and obliterating my neighborhood?"

In these cases, could we encourage others, as Rilke advises, to "love the questions themselves"? If the questions become this vivid, and this gut-wrenchingly personal, can we really expect victims to simply "live the questions" because perhaps they will gradually live their way "into the answer one distant day"? Rilke expresses a beautiful sentiment, but I submit that in regard to shattered lives and teetering faith, it's utterly insufficient.

To develop meaningful faith, we must indeed enter into a place of questioning. Honest, courageous questions can shelter us from the harsh rains of bad teaching or keep us from growing overconfident in our own convictions. The problem arises when we make a home within our shack of ambiguity. When we resolve to do nothing more than to "live the questions," what can we give? When devastated people are wrestling with God's role in their pain, what can we offer?

Sure, we can guide them away from the notion that God orchestrated their pain. But then what? If we have avoided finding answers to these questions, then we have nothing to offer the broken hearts around us except silence.

In contrast to the silence that accompanies the shock of sudden trauma, this ongoing silence is not reverent. It is not helpful. It's a silence that comes from our contentment with "locked rooms" and "books written in a foreign tongue."

It's a chosen silence, not a necessary silence. And when we take a hard look at the world's heinous suffering and consider those who abandon their faith when the questions are not answered, it becomes clear that it's time to abandon silence.

It's time to make some noise.

The most important question in the world

In contrast to the poetic advice of twenty-seven-year-old Rainer Maria Rilke, bestselling author and noted agnostic Bart Ehrman engages "the questions" and seeks answers. In fact, he asserts that the problem of evil is humanity's "most important question." He writes:

> If there is an all-powerful and loving God in this world, why is there so much excruciating pain and unspeakable suffering? The problem of suffering has haunted me for a very long time. It was what made me begin to think about religion when I was young, and it was what led me to question my faith when I was older. Ultimately, it was the reason I lost my faith.[3]

Rather than attempting to "love the questions themselves like locked rooms, like books written in a foreign tongue," Ehrman bravely attempted to pick the locks and translate the books. He brazenly examined evil in detail, scoured the Bible for an adequate explanation, and ultimately rejected the Christian faith over this "most important question."

That's a startling story. And it could certainly strike fear in the hearts of Christ-followers who hold deep questions. What if our faith can't handle the answers?

Could it be fear that's propelling this movement of silence? Is fear luring folks into contentment with mystery concerning God's role in suffering? If so, we know that God didn't give us this spirit of fear (2 Tim 1:7). So at least for the sake of those hurting around us, let's jump headfirst into the "most important question" one final time.

Appealing to the suffering God

Some Christians reject this challenge, however, and take a different approach. They explain God's role in radical pain and suffering by . . . changing the subject. Rather than offering a direct answer, they instead point to the suffering that God experienced on Calvary. They remind broken people that God didn't give himself a pass when it comes to human suffering. They point to the cross and recount the suffering of Jesus (sometimes in gory detail).

I completely embrace the importance of Calvary. The fact that God left his heavenly throne and humbly became a human who was beaten, hammered to wood, and died an agonizing death means my Creator chose to *know* suffering. The knowledge that God has not exempted himself from pain is an integral part of my faith. After all, what kind of comfort could an emotionless, indifferent, or aloof God offer?

Yet awareness of God's suffering doesn't directly ease my pain, just as hearing about other parents who have lost children does not ease my pain. I do feel a sense of solidarity with bereaved parents, and solidarity can ease the isolation of grief, but learning about their pain brings no comfort. So also the knowledge of God's suffering brings no comfort. It can only offer a sense of solidarity.

Victims are often pointed to this solidarity with God. We are encouraged to avoid seeking answers and instead seek God's presence. And yet, as a victim of trauma, I cannot safely enter into God's presence until I establish that God is not the one causing or specifically allowing my pain. I cannot enter into solidarity with a Divine Abuser.

Consider this analogy. Suppose a girl named Emma is being horribly abused by her father. Suppose Emma's mother could stop the abuse, but she remains complicit for reasons that she regards to be a higher good, such as family unity or financial security for all involved.

Now suppose Emma approaches her school counselor, Mr. Smith, and confides her pain. Mr. Smith compassionately tells her that there are no good explanations for why her father causes her suffering, or why her mother specifically allows it. But he assures Emma that her parents love her very much. He also encourages her to spend more time with them, soaking in their presence. When Emma expresses her hesitation, Mr. Smith tells her a secret he's learned about her parents. He's sure it will justify their harmful actions and make everything right: Emma's father and mother were also once terribly abused.

Does this knowledge ease or erase the pain of Emma's abuse?

No.

Does it mean her parents are trustworthy and safe?

Absolutely not.

When Emma is abused at home in the future, should she try to enter into solidarity with her parents because they've also suffered abuse?

To ask that of a victim is grotesque.

Emma's knowledge of her parents' abuse offers *perspective* toward their dysfunctional behavior, but it fails to justify their abusive actions or harmful character.

The point is that when it comes to the problem of evil, appealing to a suffering God alone does not satisfy. It can't answer the cries of the wounded, those asking whether God is their cosmic abuser, or whether he simply fails to intervene.

Isn't this why we wrestle with God's role in suffering? We want to know whether God's heart is trustworthy, whether his arms are safe. What answers does the blueprint worldview provide?

When mystery fails

The strong form of the blueprint worldview asserts that God is loving and all-powerful. In this view, God's power is used to meticulously control everything. Nothing happens outside of God's will. He planned all things, even grotesque evil and radical suffering, to glorify himself. This means he's like Emma's father in our imagined scenario—the ultimate source of the abuse.

It also means that God's actions can only be considered loving and just by changing the definition of these terms to incorporate everything God (supposedly) does, even if it goes against everything we understand about love, including the Bible's definition of love. Since these strange versions of love and justice go beyond our ability to comprehend them, this view must appeal to mystery.

Would this appeal to mystery satisfy Emma? Would it provide her comfort? Would she seek a closer relationship with her dad if assured that the horrific abuse he planned and orchestrated daily was simply a mysterious manifestation of his love?

I hope not. That's so disturbing.

Let's turn to the weak form of the blueprint worldview. This view asserts God is loving and all-powerful. In this view, the evil that transpires is not what God desires, yet he chooses *not* to intervene for mysterious higher purposes.

In this view, God could be compared to Emma's mother—someone who doesn't *want* Emma to be abused, yet fails to stop or prevent it. Here God is the mother who perpetually does nothing even as her own child screams, cries, and begs for help. In this view, God is the mother who watches intently as Emma's horrific suffering unfolds, deciding that allowing Emma's terror ensures a greater good that her child can't yet comprehend.

Would *this* answer satisfy Emma? Would she acknowledge her mother's loving goodness even though her mother failed to intervene in her relentless abuse? Would Emma suddenly find her mother safe?

I don't see how. How could she view her mother as trustworthy? As someone who seeks her daughter's overall flourishing? Isn't this what love does? Instead, her mother repeatedly demonstrated that she is untrustworthy. She cannot be trusted to protect the innocent. Is the same true of God?

It seems impossible to reconcile God's complicity in radical suffering and God's self-revelation in Jesus, who spent his ministry healing the sick, feeding the hungry, and raising the dead. This isn't a God who passively endures evil; this is a God who goes to the greatest lengths possible to defeat it!

We must also ask ourselves: What higher good is God supposedly ensuring when children are tortured, kidnapped, or starved? And this begs the follow-up questions: Would less suffering be less effective? Is each specific tragedy, in its exact depth of pain, necessary for God to establish his purposes? If so, why? If not, why not ease the torment of so many?

By attempting to explain how a loving God has specifically allowed every horror throughout history, this view must also appeal to mystery.

While both the strong and the weak forms of the blueprint worldview affirm that God is all-powerful, they must rely on mystery to explain how he is loving. But how can we trust someone whose character is mysterious? How can we love someone whose "loving" actions often seem evil?

Again, isn't this the reason we ask the "most important question" in the first place? We want to know if we can trust God's heart. We want to know if his arms are safe. Can *any* Christian worldview explain God's role in suffering without ultimately rendering his character mysterious?

A beautiful answer: The warfare worldview

Can any answer satisfy? It's true that no answer can erase the pain of loss or remove the sting of trauma. But I have found one explanation that has enabled me to face my worst nightmare and emerge with an even stronger sense of God's pure love and a fiercer conviction to share it with a broken world.

I found this in the warfare worldview. This view addresses "the most important question" in a way that resonates deeply with the mind and heart. It's highly consistent with Scripture and firmly rooted in the love of Calvary.

It's a view that doesn't press into mystery; it presses into *Jesus*! And if you can't imagine Jesus nodding yes to a deadly tornado, or a child's malicious tumor, or a deranged gunman taking aim at kindergarteners, then we shouldn't imagine God doing so either. In this view, when it comes to God's character, there is no mystery!

Rather than believing that nightmares transpire as part of a blueprint, this view acknowledges that evil comes from wills other than God's. Instead of asserting that God sometimes simply watches while his creation suffers, this view understands that God is battling, always battling, to bring good out of evil.

The warfare worldview explains how the world is filled with evil and radical suffering while God is both all-loving and all-powerful. As we discussed in chapter 3, it does this with four words: love, risk, rejection, and war.

The God of love created from love in order to expand his love. He took a hope-filled risk by creating this world and free agents. Due to the rejection of God's love, we live on the front lines of a cosmic war. It's a war that God will ultimately win. The decisive blow was delivered on the cross. Yet, until the final coming of the kingdom of God, we still struggle with forces of evil.

I asked in the beginning of this book whether God lacked the *power* or the *desire* to spare Henry. By now I hope it's clear that I don't believe terminal brain cancer was God's desire for Henry. I don't believe my son's death transpired according to God's specific plan for Henry's life. Instead, I believe God did everything possible to heal my son, to relieve his pain, to save his life. That's what any loving parent would have done. I believe God battled, and I believe God lost. For whatever reason, in that particular instance, he could not heal my little boy. If he could have, but would not, then he failed to exhibit perfect love.

It may sound shocking or off-putting to assert that God *can't* do something. But consider this: if God *could* prevent a rape, stop a bullet, or heal a malignant tumor, but *won't*, he's failing to demonstrate love (at least a love that humanity can comprehend). And if we know anything about God, it's that he *is* love. It's his very nature. Everything he does (or doesn't do) perfectly reflects his love. For God *not to love* is for God not to be, well, God.

I don't believe this understanding contradicts the fact that God is all-powerful, however. In this view, God is all-powerful in the sense that he is the *source* from whom all power originates. He alone created from nothing. The all-powerful God *chose* to create a world in which his ideal will can be thwarted.

Why? For the purpose of expanding his love! And Scripture assures us that this powerful love wins in the end. For now, God uses his infinite intellect to wisely war against evil. He's always looking for creative ways to partner with us in bringing about good (Rom 8:28). After all, Jesus was always willing to compassionately heal those afflicted by disease, and we know that Jesus embodied the heart of the Father (Heb 1:3).

Just as Jesus *could not* perform miracles sometimes (Mark 6:4-6), or had to attempt healings more than once (Mark 8:22-25), so too God's heart of restoration is often *not* victorious due to an unfathomably complex cosmos and countless variables lying outside our awareness.[4]

So when it comes to Emma in our scenario, God is neither her father nor mother. He was present with her during every second of her horror, but he wasn't orchestrating or enabling Emma's abuse. Neither option is loving. Instead, God was continuously doing in spirit form what he once did in bodily form: battling evil. He was doing everything possible to maximize good and minimize evil, given the constraints of the world he created. Emma can be assured that her abuse (just like anything that looks less beautiful than the groom dying to save his unfaithful bride) originated in wills other than God's.

Most importantly, we can be confident that one day God will restore everything under his loving lordship. We will be reunited with Christ (Col 3:4) and see God face-to-face (1 John 3:2; Rev 22:4). The "old order" of things will be done. There will be no more crying, death, grief, pain, or curse (Rev 21:4; 22:3).

That will be a day beyond compare. It's the end God had in mind from the beginning. There will at last be no more sorrow and no more tears—just a shared, loving eternity.

Mystery and the warfare worldview

Would this answer satisfy Emma? She still may ask: But why me? Why are some children abused and others cherished? I could ask: Why Henry? Why do some children suffer and die and others thrive? How does the warfare worldview account for specific evils?

In regard to the *why* behind specific evils, the warfare worldview appeals to mystery. Yet unlike the other answers often given, *mystery* is used here in regard to the incredible complexity of the universe. Let's consider again the prologue to the book of Job. Here an *uninvited* heavenly agent *unexpectedly* approaches God and wagers an *unplanned* bet. While we've rejected the notion that this describes a literal, historical event, we can acknowledge the symbolism of events transpiring outside of human awareness that can result in radical suffering. Just as Job was never enlightened to the details surrounding the source of his suffering, so also we will face unique pain without an explanation of the numerous factors responsible for bringing it into existence.

Though the warfare worldview must appeal to mystery to address the "why me" question, the *heart* and *character* of God are never claimed to be mysterious. On the contrary, this view points to the cross for our ultimate revelation of God's essence. It advocates a love that pours itself out unto death, and a power that uses wisdom instead of brute force. While a love like this may sound too good to be true, it's a love that is revealed clearly, offered freely, and never mysterious.

Pick the locks

If our view of God's character and use of power can't hold up to radical suffering, it's worthless. By suffering, I'm not referring to getting a demotion at work or tolerating a gossipy neighbor. I'm talking about kids who starve, children sold into the sex trade, and people who are kidnapped and systematically tortured for years. I'm talking about the suffering that exists when your child screams from the tumor ravaging his brain. I'm talking about the moment you cry out to Jesus while you watch him die.

As Christ-followers, let's prepare for the storms in life. We must be ready to offer more than silence when broken people ask about God's role in suffering. Let's acknowledge the questions, and yet resist making a home among them. Let's boldly pick the "locked doors" of the mind. We have the power to coherently reassure people of God's love!

Ultimately, we can point people to Jesus, who—while perfectly encapsulating God's essence—used wisdom and self-sacrifice to battle the one who comes to "steal, kill, and destroy." Jesus treated the sick and afflicted as casualties of war. He consistently demonstrated compassion and exercised his power to heal. This is the Father's heart toward those experiencing radical suffering.

This is the hope-filling, passion-evoking, uncompromising love of God.

THIRTEEN

If I Could Do It All Over

I could hear faint crying in the distance as I headed to check on my new patient. I was finishing my first shift as a maternity nurse, which was odd, because I'd received no medical training.

It was nearly midnight when I checked the chart in front of room 13. It showed that the new patient had spent the last twelve hours in labor and delivery and had arrived on our unit with a small but healthy baby boy.

After a few soft raps, I pushed open her door and found . . . my younger self. Young Jess was staring back at me from the raised head of a hospital bed. And as the best of dreams go, I acted as though this was expected, and she didn't seem to recognize me.

Her shadowy frame was supporting a newborn. The embrace was lit by a ribbon of stale fluorescent light, spilling from the bathroom to mingle with the radiant glow of tangible love.

New motherhood. It was enough to draw even the most intro-
verted women into conversation.

"Do you have kids?" young Jess asked me.

"Two," I said, sliding into the vinyl rocker beside her. The little
bundle in her arms was learning to nurse with gusto. I'd forgotten
how tiny he was, and how stunningly perfect.

"Henry's my first," she beamed. "We waited eight years to have
him, until I was able to stay home." She stroked the temple of her
lifelong dream. "Now that he's finally here, I never want to say
goodbye . . . not even for a day."

I closed my eyes against a crippling mixture of sorrow and jeal-
ousy. I wanted that time back. Sitting down had been a mistake. I
rose to leave but she stopped me with a question. "Any advice?"

I paused and looked them over. "He's latched on fine. You're doing great."

"No, I meant about being a mom. Anything I should know?"

Oh, there was so, so much . . .

I wanted to advise her to avoid the rat race of perfect parenting,
to not stress so much over Henry's sleep schedule, his picky eating,
or the fact that potty training would seem like a sick joke only suck-
ers embarked upon. He'd get it eventually.

I wanted to tell her not to mistake inexperience for ineptitude,
and to shake it off when the pediatrician points out that she's
turned Henry slightly orange from all her homemade sweet potato
baby food.

I wanted to tell her that when her industrious boy begs for glue,
scissors, glitter, sand, baking soda, food coloring, and lots of tiny
beads to make a special project, *just say yes*. Say no when it's too
overwhelming, but as often as possible, say yes. I wanted to share

that she'd never remember cleaning the messes but that his de-lighted smiles would stay etched on her heart for eternity.

I wanted to tell her that one day, when both kids are screaming and she hasn't showered in forty-eight hours and the whole family is hungry and tired and the house is a disaster, not to misinterpret the stresses of raising young children as her failure as a mother.

I wanted to beg her not to melt down when four-year-old Henry wets the bed, even after he refused to use the potty. She'll strug-gle to forgive herself when she learns that incontinence is a chief symptom of hydrocephalus.

I wanted to tell her that when Henry sometimes screams in the faces of kids who approach him and melts down when she attempts adult conversations, and when she's torn about leaving him for date nights and refuses to spend a night away with her husband because she's afraid of how Henry will do without her, and when it becomes logistically simpler to let calls go to voice mail and to withdraw from most activities, and when her social circle starts shrinking and she finds herself more and more isolated—well, I wanted to tell her that in those moments she's not alone. She's never alone. I wanted to tell her that God is always close and that he's whispering, "Nothing can separate you from my love."

I picked up a stuffed seahorse from her nightstand and pressed its belly. The toy lit up with an amber glow and began to play sooth-ing lullabies. That seahorse would lure Henry to sleep for years, and even accompany him into brain surgery while she and Ian were forced to stay behind. Henry would develop a deep sense of security and comfort from his seahorse, though it offered no real protection.

I realized that I mostly wanted young Jess to wrestle with her picture of God. It would be two years before she learned that God's heart was fully represented in the person of Jesus Christ. Until then, she'd hold the notion that everything occurs in accordance with God's perfect plan, his "meticulous divine blueprint," as though God would orchestrate or nod in approval at what was to come.

Young Jess believed that God controlled everything, and that sometimes brought her comfort. But I wanted to gently suggest that her belief provided no more actual safety than a glowing, musical seahorse. And, in fact, that view had caused her to doubt God's goodness and the purity of his love.

I wanted to tell her that the universe is *not* unfolding precisely as God pleases. It's messy and painful and chaotic, seeped in the spoils of a cosmic war—a war that exploded in the pursuit of love.

I wanted to warn her that this is a gruesome war where fatal accidents happen, hideous crimes are committed, and young children can be stricken with brain tumors while their parents watch them die.

I wanted to warn of the grief and anguish to come, of the moments when a loving eternity would seem an eternity away. And after young Jess shakes her fist at God and shouts, "This better be worth it!" I wanted to assure her that it will be, and that in the meantime God is responding with, "Nothing can separate you from my love."

I wanted to assure her that though she'll be deeply wounded in battle, she'll learn that God works flexibly and astoundingly around every obstacle in her path, and he'll bring tremendous purpose to every pain she will suffer.

And once she understands that God's heart is trustworthy, and that his power is demonstrated through perfect, self-sacrificial love, every other measure of comfort will pale in comparison. This love will fill and surround her as she faces the unimaginable, and it will unleash a wellspring of passion that even death can't destroy.

She'll begin to discover the freedom to peacefully, completely exist within each moment. Even when Henry's earthly life speeds toward an end, she won't need to grasp fearfully at time. Like water, it will slip through her fingers regardless.

Instead, she'll learn to run an open hand through the waters of time, because a loving God has conquered sin, pain, cancer, and death. She will be assured that when one beautiful moment passes, another breathtaking adventure awaits. Each will be flooded with God's love!

So instead of staring down at her shoes and fretting about her earthly path, she'll begin to allow God to lift her head. That's when she'll find infinity spanning wide in every direction. She'll understand that God's purpose in creation, his pursuit of love, pushes past death and soars into eternity, redefining safety and security once and for all.

"It's just . . . I'm so new to this," young Jess interrupted my thoughts. "I want Henry's life to be perfect. I know it's impossible, but I just want to protect him from every pain, and every disappointment, you know?"

She laid baby Henry up on her shoulder and rubbed his back with gentle circles. I gazed at his tiny nose, the faint red birthmark between his eyes, the gentle way his chest rose and fell with each baby breath.

"I know," I said softly. "But the best we can do is to tell our little ones, 'Nothing can separate you from my love.'"

"You're right," she said through a blissful yawn. "Do you mind taking him to the nursery until his next feeding?"

My throat constricted at the chance to hold him. "Of course," I breathed. I burned to feel his skin against mine, to whisper "I love you" to his living body one more time. But as I extended my trembling hands . . . I awoke.

I awoke with the growing familiarity of empty arms and an aching heart. Yet through the hush of softened sobbing, I heard a gentle whisper, a reminder echoing in my heart: *Nothing can separate you from my love.*

Bathed in love

Though this wasn't a literal dream, it's a scenario I've played and replayed in my imagination, trying to determine what I'd tell my younger self if given the opportunity. In the end, I'd ask of my younger self what I'm asking of you: Will you wrestle with your picture of God?

I eventually did. There were months of study, questions, and wrestling with doubts. But when I rose from the mat, I beheld with fresh clarity a picture of God based on the love of Calvary.

Now I can see the Father's eyes filled with adoration. I feel his hands moving softly. Our God is as gentle as I was while bathing my dying son. He's a loving parent who yearns to soak us in his warm presence. He wants us to radiate the scent of his care and affection, as sweet as lavender baby lotion. He aches to raise us from the waters of pain, cradle us in his arms, and gaze upon the manifestation of his eternal dream—*humanity*—created in his image, participating in his love.

He sees our flaws, our wounds, our ten-inch scars and lopsided smiles, but they don't make him turn away. There's nothing we can do to repel his love. His arms are always extended, his lips whispering delight in us, repeating his promise to never leave. He is tenderly attuned to our every breath . . . our every breath.

This is the God we can walk beside, look to, lean into, fall into. This is the God who carries, cleanses, wraps, raises, holds, heals, and loves without fail, without pause, without condition. This is a God who went to the furthest extent possible and faced the greatest evil to rescue us, to restore our covenant.

This is Jesus.

Triumph by testimony

For all of us, pain comes. Loss comes. How can we triumph in this war-torn world? How do we claim the victory when our lives have been devastated? By the grace of God, we turn to the most powerful weapon in our arsenal: our testimony.

Revelation 12:11 speaks about Christ-followers who are victorious over Satan. It says: "They triumphed over him by the blood of the Lamb and by the word of their testimony; they did not love their lives so much as to shrink from death."

This verse came to life for me one recent evening. I was sitting outside, whispering my pain into prayers. At first those prayers seemed to evaporate into the oranges, purples, and deepening blues of the streaky night sky. But I continued anyway. "I just miss Henry so much," I confided. "I want to talk to him *so bad.*"

And within the silence that followed, my spirit felt a gentle whisper: *Do it.*

So I did. I imagined Henry's dimpled smile, his dancing blue eyes, and the cowlick of straw-blonde hair on the crown of his head. He was leaning against a column beside me. He looked happy, calm, and ready to hear his mama talk.

"Hi," I whispered, my tear-soaked face breaking into a smile. "I love you so much! And I miss you so, so much. I want to hold you ... *so badly* ... I want to hug you and squeeze you and give you *ten kisses*! I promise I will again." And then, to my surprise, this tumbled out: "But for now, Mommy has to stay."

And with that simple confession, life and passion swept into my soul. "I have to stay a little longer," I reiterated with fresh clarity and building momentum, "and tell people that God loves them. Some people don't know how *much* God loves them. So I'm going to stay here awhile longer ... and tell them."

And I realized that this is where I find victory. When I share the love of Jesus, defeat dissolves and triumph emerges. When I profess the truth that Henry's death was not sent by God for a mysterious higher purpose, I find passion. I find strength.

When I hear from people all over the world whose lives are being transformed as they reexamine Scripture and realize that the character of God was fully revealed on Calvary, I find momentum. When I pause to contemplate the stunningly beautiful, enemy-loving, self-sacrificing essence of God, I find joy.

So I share Jesus. I share my personal relationship with the Creator of the universe, who walked this earth long enough to demonstrate how we are to love one another, and then gave his life to defeat the powers of darkness.

I share the knowledge that my pain will be met with purpose. I don't believe that Henry's life was savagely taken for a mysterious greater good. But I believe that this pain will be met with purpose as I partner with God to spread the knowledge of his great love.

And this helps me let go of what can't be ... at least for a moment. Though I pick up my old hopes and dreams again and again, in the moments when I release them—when I release Henry into God's care—God meets me there in a powerful way.

Since Henry's death, I've had good days and bad days. Yet regardless of how I feel, I choose to stay, and to tell people that God loves them. I choose to share my heart, even as I continue to wrestle.

As I move forward, I'm still processing, questioning, and learning to admit that I might be wrong. In fact, for the first time in my life I've found the freedom to move beyond a faith centered on certainty. I'm confident that love encircles me as I grow. And as I confront new questions and doubts that arise, I keep rediscovering a passion that remains. Over and over, I land on the undeniably beautiful image of a powerful God who took on humble human form and taught us how to love. And on that cross, when his radical love seemed most foolish, we found that it couldn't be stamped out by brute strength. That other-oriented, transformative love overcomes even death.

That worn wrestling mat holds a place of honor in my soul. It's where the God of love and I continue to throw down in an arena of honesty, grace, patience, and limitless love. That's where my story began, and it's where my story will continue.

The book you hold in your hands sprang from that sacred space. It's my offering, my testimony, my triumph over evil with the love of the cross. I hope it blesses you, challenges you, and compels you to wrestle. I pray it directs you to a God of perfect love.

••••

Common Questions
about the Warfare
Worldview

1. How can you assert that God's primary attribute is love? Isn't God's love simply one attribute among many?

The Bible tells us that God's essence is love (1 John 4:8, 16). This is given as a definitive, unqualified character statement. Love is also the predominant theme of the Bible. God created out of love, with the desire to extend the love of the trinity to humanity (John 17:20-26). Because of his great *love*, God brought the Israelites out of slavery and made them into a nation (Deut 7:8; Hos 11:1; Isa 63:9) and called them to bless the whole world (Gen 12:2-3; Gal 3:8-9). God sent Jesus because he so *loved* the world (John 3:16) and didn't want anyone to perish (John 3:16; 2 Pet 3:9; 1 Tim 2:4;

Ezek 18:23). When Jesus laid down his life, he demonstrated his love (Rom 5:8). And God offers those who accept his love an eternity of existing in this love (Rev 21:3-4; 22:3-5)!

Our amazing God is abounding in love (Ps 103:8) and loves us with an everlasting love (Isa 54:8; Jer 31:3). He is reluctant to get angry (Exod 34:6; Ps 103:8) and eager to show mercy. When he does get angry, his anger is temporary, but his love is permanent (Ps 30:5; Isa 54:8). So while God may exhibit other attributes, such as "justice" or "wrath," they must all be seen as expressions *of* his love rather than as existing *alongside* his love.

Peter Kreeft expresses it well when he writes:

> Love is God's essence. Nowhere else does Scripture express God's essence in this way. Scripture says God is just and merciful, but it does not say that God is justice itself or mercy itself. It does say that God *is* Love, not just a lov*er*. Love is God's very essence. Everything else is a manifestation of this essence to us, a relationship between this essence and us. This is the absolute; everything else is relative to it.[1]

God's very nature and character is love. It is his foundational attribute. And his "love" is not some mysterious label we must slap on everything that God supposedly does. Rather, it's a love we can recognize! This love is defined by the cross (1 John 3:16). It's an other-oriented love that does not insist on its own way (1 Cor 13:5). It cannot be forced. Neither can it be changed.

We can choose to accept or reject God's love, but we cannot turn it off. God loves us the way the sun shines and the rain falls: indiscriminately (Matt 5:43-45; Luke 6:35-36). His love isn't dependent on anything we do. By definition, God's agape love is motivated by the giver rather than the one who receives it.

God loves because he *is* love. He is the father in the parable of the prodigal son—always waiting with open arms and an open heart for us to return to his love.

2. Isn't God all-powerful? How can the will of an all-powerful God ever be thwarted? Aren't you denying God's sovereignty?

Scripture states that God does what he pleases (Isa 46:10; Ps 115:3; 135:6; Job 23:13; Dan 4:35). He "works out everything in conformity with the purpose of his will" (Eph 1:11). Job famously declared to the Lord, "No purpose of yours can be thwarted" (Job 42:2), and King Nebuchadnezzar said of God, "No one can hold back his hand or say to him: 'What have you done?' " (Dan 4:35).

What does this mean? Does God meticulously control everything? Is he the author of sin and evil?

No, this can't be the case, because as we discussed in chapter 3, God *is* love (1 John 4:8, 16). He is light, and "in him there is no darkness at all" (1 John 1:5). He cannot be tempted by evil and doesn't tempt anyone (James 1:13). He is not a God of confusion but of peace (1 Cor 14:33) who "does not willingly bring affliction or grief to anyone" (Lam 3:33). With him, evil may not dwell (Psalm 5:4). His eyes "are too pure to look on evil" (Hab 1:13). He is righteous in all his ways and kind in all his works (Ps 145:17). So God *can't* be the author of sin and evil.

And in seeming contrast to the verses that assert God's will cannot be thwarted, the Bible also speaks often about how God's will *is* thwarted and that it grieves him. For instance, we see God's dismay when the Israelites did not return his love (Matt 23:37-39; Rom 10:21). They repeatedly hardened their hearts against God

(Heb 3:8, 15; 4:7), and this rebellion grieved his Holy Spirit (Isa 63:10). So also the Pharisees and experts in the law "rejected God's purpose for themselves" when they weren't baptized by John (Luke 7:30). Before Stephen was stoned to death, he declared that the priests of the Sanhedrin were just like their ancestors—always *resisting* the Holy Spirit (Acts 7:51). And when Paul advised the church in Ephesus regarding Christian living, he urged believers not to "grieve the Holy Spirit" (Eph 4:30).

In addition, Jesus instructed his disciples to pray that God's will be done on earth as it is in heaven (Matt 6:10), which assumes that it is currently not! And just as sometimes Jesus could *not* perform miracles (Mark 6:4-6), or had to attempt healings more than once (Mark 8:22-25), so too Scripture portrays that God's loving will is often not victorious due to opposing forces outside of our awareness (Dan 10).

Finally, Scripture explicitly states that God doesn't want anyone to perish but desires all to be saved (2 Pet 3:9; 1 Tim 2:4; Ezek 18:23), but we know that some do perish. That's because, by the very nature of God's own design, his loving will is sometimes thwarted by the free choices of free agents.[2]

How can we reconcile these two seemingly opposed streams of Scripture? How can we affirm that God "does what he pleases" while honoring the texts that demonstrate that God's will is sometimes thwarted?

I believe the answer lies in God's overarching purposes for creation. It seems God desired the one thing that cannot be gained with all the brute force in the universe: love. I established through Scripture (in chapter 3) that the God of *love* created out of *love* for the purpose of expanding his *love*. Scripture tells us that love does not insist on its own way (1 Cor 13:5). God cannot force anyone to love him. Love must be chosen. Therefore, the creation of free agents, who can thwart God's will to some degree, was necessary for love.

I believe we can affirm the verses that proclaim our all-powerful God is able to do whatever he pleases. Yet these passages *don't* assert that it pleases God to control everything. It seems that it pleased God to create free agents. And God's choice to limit his power was intrinsic to that creation process. It was an organic, necessary part of endowing true freedom. God chose to *limit himself* by creating free agents who, inherent to their very nature, have the capacity to thwart the loving will of God.[3]

Theologian and author John Sanders explains this well:

> If God wants a world in which the possibility exists that God may not get everything he wants, then in an ultimate sense this divine will is not thwarted. It is important to note that if in some cases God does not get what he wants, it is ultimately because of the decision God made to create the sort of world in which God does not get everything he wants.[4]

In other words, God willed the *possibility*, but not the *actuality*, of his will being thwarted. Yet when we speak about an all-powerful God, it may feel strange to assert that he can be limited by anything.

Perhaps it helps to consider this analogy. Imagine you win a full scholarship to the university of your dreams. The conditions of your scholarship state that you are free to pursue any degree you wish. You eagerly move onto campus to pursue your lifelong goal of becoming a veterinarian. But when you try to enroll in classes, you discover that scholarship recipients are blocked from all courses outside of the engineering department. Frustrated, you contact the scholarship committee only to be told repeatedly, "You are free to pursue any degree offered, as long as it's engineering." Were the conditions of your scholarship accurate and honest when they stated that you were free to choose any major? If you ultimately decided to pursue engineering, could you say that it was because you freely chose to do so?

Just as a scholarship committee cannot force recipients to "freely choose" engineering, God cannot force created beings to "freely choose" love. Endowing freedom to agents organically limits God to a certain degree.[5] One could say that God is limited by the freedom of his created agents just as he is limited by the inability to make hot snow, still wind, bright darkness, or round triangles. Those are intrinsic impossibilities, things that by definition *can't* exist. And as C. S. Lewis said about these sorts of impossibilities, "nonsense remains nonsense even when we talk it about God."[6]

Instead of viewing this as something that weakens or lessens God, scholars such as Lewis proclaim that God's creation of agents who can reject him is a "miracle" and "the most astonishing and unimaginable of all the feats" that we attribute to him.[7] It seems God's power is not manifested in being crushingly irresistible but in endowing his beloved with the freedom to resist him.

So although many Christians equate God's sovereignty with meticulous control, we can see how this definition of sovereignty does not allow for the possibility of love. When we consider the term *sovereignty*, we can consider the mightiest kings in history, sovereign over their kingdoms. They didn't have meticulous control of every detail that transpired. Meticulous control is not necessary for effective leadership. Meticulous control does not require wisdom or creativity, only power.

It seems the most biblically accurate view of God's sovereignty, his ruling authority, is in understanding that God's power is manifested through creative, wise, Calvary-like love. Paul tells us that the cross is the "wisdom" and "power" of God to those of us who are being saved. When God puts on display his infinite wisdom and omnipotent power, it looks like God getting himself crucified at the hands of enemies, out of love for enemies. This is the *exact opposite* of the kind of controlling power the world—and, unfortunately, much of the church—has always assigned to God/gods.

To the world, the cross is foolishness (1 Cor 1:18-25). That's because the world respects brute force—a "might makes right" mentality. But the cross was all about wisdom, creativity, and other-oriented love.

In God's wisdom, he created free agents. This allowed for the possibility that his loving will might sometimes be thwarted. Nevertheless, because God is infinitely intelligent and can perfectly anticipate all possibilities, he always has a creative, perfect, eternally prepared plan to bring good out of evil. And by taking the risk of creating free agents, God is assured of ultimately achieving his highest purpose in creation: he will share eternity with those who have freely chosen his love!

So while some start with an assumption that God meticulously controls everything and are then left to wonder, "How does a sovereign God love?" I believe theologians Jerry Walls and Joseph Dongell have it right when they ask, "Given the full revelation of God in Scripture . . . how would a God of perfect love express his sovereignty?"[8]

3. *What about the man born blind in John 9? Didn't Jesus affirm that God caused the man's blindness?*

In the ninth chapter of John's gospel, we read that Jesus and his disciples encounter a man who had been blind from birth. In verse 2 the disciples ask, "Rabbi, who sinned, this man or his parents, that he was born blind?" Verses 3-4 follow with, " 'Neither this man nor his parents sinned,' said Jesus, 'but this happened so that the works of God might be displayed in him. As long as it is day, we must do the works of him who sent me. Night is coming, when no one can work.' "

This famous passage seems to indicate that God planned the man's blindness in order that God might glorify himself later through a miraculous healing. Some say this supports the notion that all things are part of a divine master plan, and then conclude that God is mysteriously behind good *and* evil.

We can see this assumption in John Calvin's assessment of this gospel account. He believed that both God's "divine severity" and his mercy were highlighted here. When the man was blind, he was apparently an example of the former, used to teach others to become humble and "learn to fear" God. Alternatively, with his healing, God's goodness and mercy were put on display. Calvin believed this is how God "glorifies his name" in the "theater of the world." And he was convinced that we have no right to argue with God, "whether he appears as merciful or severe."[9]

In Calvin's assessment, God struck an unborn baby with blindness. A child spent his life in darkness because he was God's instrument of severe glory. A man's adulthood of disability and begging was God's tailor-made backdrop for a glory-increasing miracle.

Despite the fact that this makes God a moral monster, this disturbing interpretation leaves us with at least two concerns.

First, how can we reconcile this with God's self-revelation in Jesus? We find throughout the Gospels that Jesus revealed God's character by categorically *coming against* disease, oppression, and death with healing, freedom, and life. Jesus consistently rebuked diseases as coming from Satan and/or demons (Mark 9:25; Luke 11:14; 13:11-16; Acts 10:38), and Matthew 9:35 tells us that "Jesus went through all the towns and villages . . . healing every disease and sickness." Jesus never harmed anyone. In fact, Peter summarized Jesus' ministry to Cornelius by saying that Jesus "went around doing good and healing all who were under the power of the devil, because God was with him" (Acts 10:38). According to Peter, to be afflicted is to be "under the power of the devil," not the power of God. God's power is displayed when one is set free from the devil's power by being healed. If Jesus perfectly revealed God's essence to us (Heb 1:3), how do we align this revelation with a God who blinds babies to glorify himself?

Second, to accept that God caused the blindness that Jesus healed is to pit Jesus against the Father. And this contradicts Jesus' teaching in Matthew 12:24-28. There Jesus tells the Pharisees that he could not drive out demons with Satan's power because every "city or household divided against itself will not stand." If we grant that the man was blind by God's decree, and then healed by God-in-flesh, we must ask: Is God divided against himself? If so, Jesus is standing in opposition to his own teaching!

Nevertheless, the text seems to indicate that God was behind the man's blindness. So what are we to believe? Is this the smoking gun for those who believe that everything unfolds according to God's master plan? Did Jesus himself affirm the blueprint worldview?

Thankfully, many scholars don't believe this passage insinuates that God blinded this man from birth in order to glorify himself later with a miraculous healing. Let's take a closer look to gain some more insight. You may be surprised to find some important parallels to the infamous book of Job.

When the disciples ask "Who sinned?" they are revealing their understanding of how God operates. Like Job and his friends, the disciples' question presupposes that God unilaterally acts upon the world, meticulously punishing sin and rewarding righteousness. They want to know if the man born blind was paying for his own sins or for the sins of his parents.

In the New International Version, the response reads: " 'Neither this man nor his parents sinned,' said Jesus, 'but *this happened so that* the works of God might be displayed in him' " (emphasis added). There are a couple of points to note here. First, the words "this happened" do not appear in the original Greek, but were supplied by translators. Second, the phrase "so that" reflects the fact that translators are interpreting the original Greek word *hina* to be purposive. They then use that word to link the *purpose* of the man's blindness to the works of God displayed in him.

Yet scholars hotly debate how John 9:3 should be interpreted. Many argue that the best rendering of this verse does *not* imply that God is the author of this man's blindness. They believe that translations such as the NIV invite tremendous confusion with Jesus' answer and offer a bizarre explanation for God's role in suffering.[10] So how do they interpret this verse? They do so in different ways.

Gary Burge, author of the NIV Application Commentary on John, appeals to punctuation placement. It should be noted that the original Greek text did not have punctuation. It was simply an unbroken string of letters. This means that translators had to decide where to insert periods, commas, and so on. There were also no chapter and verse divisions. Verse numbers weren't even added to the New Testament until the sixteenth century. And as we'll see, those decisions about punctuation and verse division can have monumental consequences.

Burge advocates an interpretation that places a period after the first part of Jesus' response. This would apply the purposive clause "so that the work of God . . ." not to the man's blindness (v. 3), but to *Jesus' purpose for doing God's work* (v. 4). This version reads: " 'Neither this man nor his parents sinned,' said Jesus. 'But so that the work of God might be displayed in his life, we must do the work of him who sent me while it is still day.' " In other words, "God had not made the man blind in order to show his glory; rather, God has sent Jesus to do works of healing in order to show his glory."[11]

Other scholars and theologians go a different route in absolving this text of a blueprint reading. They assert that in this case *hina* is not meant to be purposive, but imperative (issuing a command). This means that "so that" is replaced with "but let." After the disciples ask if it was the man or his parents who sinned, Nigel Turner believes the text should read: " 'Neither,' Jesus had replied, 'but let the works of God be made manifest in him.' " Turner notes how this "releases the text from the fatalism which had obsessed it, and dissolves the picture . . . [of] a man destined from birth to suffer for the sole purpose of glorifying God when he was healed."[12]

In both approaches, we find Jesus shutting down the disciples' line of questioning altogether, just as God dismissed Job's faulty theology when he spoke out of the whirlwind. Jesus dismisses the disciples' false assumptions and refocuses their attention to God's light shining into the man's darkness.[13] He reframes the matter at hand and demonstrates that, regardless of the cause, the man's blindness was about to become a vehicle of revelation.[14]

While most modern English translations of John 9:3 may draw one toward the notion that God is mysteriously behind good *and* evil, the above interpretations align with the remaining gospel accounts of an incarnate God who is categorically opposed to afflictions like blindness. Indeed, Jesus was sent to "destroy the devil's work" (1 John 3:8). He is the light of the world (John 8:12), doing God's work in the daylight of his presence (John 9:4-5) while perfectly embodying the God of light, in whom there is no darkness (1 John 1:5).

4. Isn't God all-knowing? If so, how could he change his mind or take a risk? Wouldn't that mean he doesn't know the future?

I fully affirm that God is all-knowing and has infinite intelligence and complete knowledge of everything that exists. Scripture is clear that God knows all things (1 John 3:20). Many Christians understand this to mean that God created a world in which everything in the future has been eternally settled. While God certainly could have created this type of world if he had chosen to do so, there are compelling reasons to believe that he did not. Other Christians hold that God chose to create a world in which the future consists partly of possibilities, all of which are perfectly known by God. Therefore, the notion that God changes his mind or takes risks pertains only to the nature of the future God chose to create, not the scope of God's knowledge.

The major point of contention between these two views is whether the future choices of free agents are "things" to be known.

Some assert (and I'm inclined to agree) that these choices exist as *possibilities* rather than as *settled realities* and are perfectly known by God as such. People sometimes assume that God has to know the future in absolute, settled detail in order to promise that he can bring good out of our suffering and be victorious in the end. But this assumption inadvertently underestimates God's intelligence. Because God has infinite intelligence, he can anticipate each and every one of the future's innumerable possibilities as if each and every one were the *only* possibility—or in other words, as if each and every one were a settled fact. So whatever comes to pass, God has an eternally prepared plan to respond to it, just as he would if he knew it as an eternally settled fact.

A helpful analogy might be two undefeated chess masters, Jill and Kate, who are scheduled to compete in an upcoming championship match. An investigation into Jill's winning streak reveals that she has only played against computer opponents. Before each game, Jill either programmed the computer's moves or somehow obtained a printout of the moves the computer would make. Because she always knew exactly what would transpire before she began, Jill was always completely prepared and consistently victorious.

A similar probe into Kate's past victories reveals that she has always played against live opponents. Unlike Jill, Kate doesn't rely upon her ability to program or foreknow her opponent's moves. Instead, Kate's incredible success springs from her profound ability to anticipate all possible moves her opponents *might* make. Because Kate has a plan in place to meet any potential move, she is always completely prepared and consistently victorious. She has even been known to successfully predict the number of moves it will take to defeat her opponent.

As you consider the impending showdown, which player would you put money on to win? Who seems to possess superior wisdom, creativity, and skill? Which one seems more praiseworthy?

Hopefully, this example has helped to illustrate how the choice to design a partially open future puts no limits on God. In fact, it actually renders his wisdom more praiseworthy! God doesn't need to restrict himself to *one* finite blueprint to ensure victory. For a God of infinite intelligence, constructing a trillion trillion plans is no more mentally taxing than creating just one. And given the fact that only one of those trillion trillion possible futures becomes an actuality, one could say that in this view, God *over-knows* the future.

Why would God design things this way? To allow for the possibility of love. And by allowing his created agents the freedom to choose or reject love, God hasn't limited his intelligence but rather has demonstrated its vastness!

While this may resonate philosophically, what does the Bible say? Does it address the nature of the future? Yes, and in fact we find two scriptural motifs concerning this subject: one of future determinism (the future is settled), and one of future openness (the future consists of possibilities).

The first motif shows that God can predetermine and foreknow whatever he wants and that there are many things about the future which are already settled. However, the second motif establishes that the future is not *exhaustively* settled. There are aspects of the future that are left to be decided, namely the choices of free agents. This means that the future is composed partly of settled realities and partly of possibilities. In other words, the future is settled to the degree that God wants it settled, and open to the degree that God has chosen to leave it open.

Since this approach may be new to readers who have always held that the future is exhaustively settled, let's examine a small sampling of the scriptural support for a partially open future.

To begin, there are several instances in which God expresses genuine regret in relation to how things turned out, sometimes even in regard to his own prior decisions (Gen 6:5-6; 1 Sam 15:11, 35). We also see instances of God conveying frustration when his people resist him (Exod 4:10-15; Ezek 22:30-31), as well as surprise or disappointment at how certain situations unfolded (Isa 5:1-7; Jer 3:6-7, 19-20). These emotions are experienced when circumstances turn out *differently* than one expected, not when everything goes according to plan. So this begs the question: If God exhaustively foreknew (or predetermined) every response of each person or people group, how could God ever truthfully express feelings of regret, frustration, disappointment, or surprise?

Another aspect of this openness theme is that God is frequently portrayed as testing his people to determine whether they will remain faithful (Gen 22:1-12; Exod 16:4; Deut 8:2; 13:1-3; Judg 2:20–3:4; 2 Chron 32:31). But if God perfectly foreknows, as an eternally settled fact, every response people will have, why would he test them? A common answer is that the testing wasn't for *God's* benefit, but rather its purpose was for *his people* to learn something about themselves. Yet these verses say nothing of the sort. The text is explicit that the testing happened so that *God* could know their hearts.

We also find that God sometimes asks non-rhetorical questions about the future (Num 14:11; Hos 8:5). He speaks, and even thinks, in terms of what *might* or *might not* happen (Exod 3:18–4:9; 13:17; Jer 26:2-6; 38:17-18, 20-23; Ezek 12:1-3). This is strange if we hold that every detail of the future is eternally settled. If that were the case, shouldn't we expect God to speak only in terms of what *will* or *will not* happen?

Perhaps most notable are the numerous times God *changes his mind* due to prayer or in response to dynamic circumstances (Exod 32:14; 33:1-14; Num 14:12-20; Deut 9:13-29; 1 Sam 2:27-36; 2 Kings 20:1-7; 1 Chron 21:15; Jer 26:19; Amos 7:1-6; Jon 3:2-10). Other times God says that he will alter his plans if circumstances change (Jer 18:7-11; 26:2-3; Ezek 33:13-15). In fact, Bible authors understandably portray this willingness to change as an attribute of God's greatness (Joel 2:13-14; Jon 4:2). Isn't the notion that God changes his mind incompatible with the belief that all events are eternally settled in God's mind?

While some Christians assert that the passages mentioned above are merely figurative, they must go beyond a plain reading of the text to do so. This approach is understandable if we have sufficient reason to think a passage can't mean what it seems to mean, such as verses that depict God as having eyes or arms. Since God is spirit and doesn't literally have eyes or arms, this type of language is used, poetically or metaphorically, to tell us something about God, such as his awareness or protection. But if a passage describes God changing his mind or experiencing disappointment, what are we to learn about God other than the fact that he changes his mind and experiences disappointment? The only thing that forces people to think the passages above are figurative is that their plain meaning conflicts with a preconceived notion of what God is like.

On the other hand, Christians who accept the literal meaning of the texts above must conclude that the future is partially open. And if we concede that the future is partly composed of possibilities, then the assertion that God takes risks or changes his mind is consistent with the fact that God knows all things.

We can say that God knows the future in the sense that he knows future certainties as certainties and future possibilities as possibilities. And, most importantly, we can rest in the knowledge that our infinitely intelligent God is thoroughly prepared to meet any evil with good and to eventually bring all things under his loving lordship, no matter what (perfectly foreseen as possible) obstacles arise.[15]

5. How do you respond to verses such as Psalm 139:16, which seem to clearly state that God knows and plans our lives in advance?

Psalm 139:16 in the NIV reads: "Your eyes saw my unformed body; all the days ordained for me were written in your book before one of them came to be." This popular verse is often cited in support of the blueprint worldview, and at first glance, it seems pretty compelling. It seems to provide explicit biblical proof that at least the length of our lives are determined by God before a single moment transpires. Do we have any reason to doubt this conclusion? I believe we do.

First, we should note that this verse is located in the book of Psalms and thus belongs to the poetry genre of Scripture. This is not a quotation from Jesus as he taught his disciples. It's not an excerpt from one of Paul's letters to the church about practical matters. Rather, these are the creative words of love-filled poetry. This alone should give us pause in regarding them as explicit, literal support for doctrinal statements or metaphysical realities.

Nevertheless, I believe it's important to study these lyrical writings and seek to understand the author's heart. And as we do, let's take care to examine them in context.

When we start at the beginning of Psalm 139, we find that David (credited as the psalmist) first describes how God's presence is always surrounding him. God's hands guide him and hold him. God is intimately involved in every aspect of his life. In verse 13, David begins to describe the intimate setting of his formation, the presence of God even in the womb. He praises God for his magnificent handiwork. David knows he is "fearfully and wonderfully made" (v. 14). He marvels about how his frame was not hidden from God when he was "made in the secret place" and "woven together in the depths of the earth" (v. 15). Verse 16 begins with David professing that God's "eyes saw my unformed body." Then, in the context of this intimate illustration of a Creator's love, we come upon the phrase in question.

At this point, it would be consistent for David to continue referencing his physicality, praising his Creator for knowing each part of David's developing fetal form, even before it came into being. But the original Hebrew is ambiguous here. The text does not supply the subject matter that was recorded in God's book, so this is left open to the judgment of translators. Some translations, such as the NIV, portray the subject as being David's *days*. Other translations, such as the NEB, KJV, and NJPS, make the psalmist's *body parts*, not his days, the subject of what is recorded. For instance, the NJPS reads: "Your eyes saw my unformed limbs; they were all recorded in Your book; in due time they were formed, to the very last one of them." This poetic rendering conjures images of a master sculptor who beholds a block of clay and imaginatively *sees* the form to be created, even before skilled fingers make their first impressions.

Making David's body parts the subject matter of what was written in God's book fits perfectly with the flow of this poem. By contrast, there is nothing in this poem that would lead us to expect David to suddenly make a pragmatic statement about how God determined how long he was going to live. Yet this is what the translation of verse 16 in the NIV and other versions of the Bible require us to believe. While the grammar allows for either, I believe translations that continue the focus on the formation of David's body are more consistent with the passage's context.

Even if one remains convinced that Psalm 139:16 is referencing David's "days," verse 16 *still* does not provide support for the blueprint worldview. It's important to note that for ancient Hebrews to say God "ordained," "planned," or wrote something "in his book" did not mean this thing was unalterably settled. For example, as I discussed in question 4, we find a number of occasions when God announced a plan and then changed his mind. Similarly, we find some passages of Scripture suggesting that God can change what is written in his book (Exod 32:33; Rev 3:5). And, most relevant to our understanding of Psalm 139:16, we find a number of verses that demonstrate that the number of our days is *not* set in stone. For instance, we find God pronouncing that Hezekiah was going to die, and then deciding to extend his life for an additional fifteen years (Isa 38:1-5). We also read that a person's "strength" plays a role in determining one's lifespan (Ps 90:10). In Proverbs, we read that a fear of the Lord "adds length to life," but the life of the wicked will be "cut short" (Prov 10:27). We're warned to avoid wickedness so that we don't "die before our time" (Eccles 7:17) and told that the bloodthirsty and deceitful "will not live out half their days" (Ps 55:23). In keeping with the scriptural trend regarding the variability of our life span, we can be confident that whatever God ordained for David spoke only of his hopeful plan, rather than of an unalterable number of days.[16]

Ultimately, I don't believe this disputed line of biblical poetry provides sufficient evidence that God preordains everything that comes to pass. In fact, arriving at this conclusion presents a significant problem: namely, we'd be forced to reject the plain reading of the numerous biblical texts that support the notion that our lives are not fixed but can be altered by various circumstances.

As I've researched verses like this that on the surface seem to support a blueprint worldview, I've concluded that there are always other—and arguably better—interpretations to consider.[17]

....

Reflection Questions

This six-week discussion guide is designed to help initiate group discussion or individual reflection for those wishing to go deeper with the topics presented in this book.

Week 1

Reading: Introduction and Chapter 1

1. How would you describe your understanding of God's role in suffering?

2. Several common sayings about God's role in suffering are mentioned in this section such as: "Everything happens for a reason," and "God won't give you more than you can handle." When have you heard these or similar expressions? How were they helpful or harmful?

3. The author describes several experiences that helped shape her picture of God. Can you think of a moment in your life that strongly affected your picture of God?

4. The author highlights an emotional debate with her high school Bible teacher. At the end of their conversation, she accepted the teacher's position and buried her objections. When have you heard spiritual teaching you didn't agree with? How did you respond?

Week 2

Reading: Chapters 2–3

1. When you hear the word *God*, what image comes to mind? What words would you use to describe God? What about when you hear the word *Jesus*? What image comes to mind? What words would you use to describe him?

2. Read Hebrews 1:1-3. How does viewing Jesus as an exact representation of God's essence compare to your picture of God?

3. Reflect upon instances of evil or radical suffering that you or someone you know attributed to God's perfect plan. Consider what it would look like to see that suffering as coming from wills other than God's. Where can you say, "An enemy has done this"?

4. How have you viewed Calvary in the past, and how did that view influence your impression of God's character? What are your thoughts about God as a lovestruck groom?

Week 3

Reading: Chapters 4–8

1. The author talks about withdrawing from church because her views of God differed greatly from those around her. Have you ever felt as if your questions or doubts about God set you apart from other Christians? If so, how did you handle it?

2. The author describes an experience she had while using imaginative prayer beside Henry's hospital bed. What are your thoughts about engaging your imagination in prayer? If you already practice this habit, how have you found it helpful?

3. Read Romans 8:1-2. If you struggle with shame or condemnation, what would it look like to fully, repeatedly, apply this verse to those areas of your life?

4. The author mentions practicing the presence of God as the neuro-oncologist gives her grim news about Henry's prognosis and treatment options. She imagines God's hand taking the form of the couch cradling her. Other times she associates sunlight streaming through the window or the breath of the people around her as reminders of God's life, goodness, and love. How do you—or how can you begin to—associate everyday objects and encounters with reminders of God's presence and unfailing love?

Week 4

Reading: Chapter 9

1. Believers are called to be unified, and yet they often disagree. What does it mean to be unified? Can Christians practice unity in the midst of disagreement?

2. When disagreement surfaces, how can we take care to honor *messengers* while challenging *messages*? How can we best facilitate meaningful conversations with productive outcomes?

3. Several prominent Christian leaders are discussed in this chapter. What Christian leaders have been most influential in your life? What messages have been a blessing, or have caused pain, in your life?

4. As you consider the blueprint and warfare worldviews through the lens of loss, what stands out the most? What questions are you wrestling with in this moment?

Week 5

Reading: Chapters 10–11

1. Read Isaiah 55.

   a. When have you heard the phrase "God's ways are higher than our ways"? How did that experience (or experiences) affect your picture of God?

   b. When you interpret Isaiah 55:8-9 in the context of God's desire to spread his love, how is your picture of God changed?

2. Read Romans 8:28.

   a. How have you interpreted this verse in the past, and what impact did that have on your picture of God?

   b. Compare the "Master Baker" understanding of Romans 8:28 to the interpretation that urges us to be God's coworkers by meeting pain (regardless of who or what caused it) to bring about good. How does each version compare to the character of God revealed in Jesus?

3. Read Job 1:20-21.

   a. When have you heard the phrase "The Lord gives and takes away"? How did it influence your picture of God?

   b. When you consider that Job's famous words were *presented* to be *refuted*, what impact does that have on your impression of God and his role in suffering?

   c. How does each approach line up with the character of God revealed in Jesus?

Week 6

Reading: Chapters 12–13

1. It can be difficult to know how to comfort someone in crisis. In the aftermath of a tragedy, when do you feel it is best to be silent? When is it best to speak? When have you needed comfort? If others have offered their silent presence during your time of need, how did their silence help or fall short?

2. In the blueprint worldview, *mystery* is often used to account for why God causes or specifically allows each instance of horrific

suffering (rendering God's character mysterious). In the warfare worldview, mystery is used to account for why one individual is affected instead of another (rendering God's character always good while acknowledging that the cosmos is incredibly complex).

a. Where have you encountered mystery as an explanation for suffering?

b. Where do you embrace mystery?

c. Are there any questions you've avoided due to fear that the answers wouldn't satisfy?

3. Consider the analogy of Emma and her parents.

a. In the past, how has your picture of God compared to Emma's father or mother?

b. What thoughts or feelings have you experienced when you've been encouraged to trust God in the midst of suffering?

4. In week 2 of this study you were asked: When you hear the word *God*, what image comes to mind? Over the past several weeks, how has that image changed? How does your current picture of God compare to the love of Jesus?

5. Who in your life can support you as you question? Who can wrestle alongside you? How can you support each other as you question and wrestle?

....

Acknowledgments

There are many who invested time into reading early drafts of this book and offering constructive feedback, including Matt Anderson, Shelley Boyd, Terri Churchill, Lisa Como, Paul and Laura Davidson, Paul Eddy, Cindy Gustaphson, Marina Hannus, Josias Hansen, Joe and Liana Hilgenkamp, Jamie Horn, Barbara Schendel-Kent, Daniel Kent, T. C. Moore, David and Erica Morrow, Natalie Williams, and Micah Witham. Thank you all for your willingness to engage with me. Because of you, this book is a far better product.

Special thanks to Paul and Laura Davidson, Betty Davidson, and Amy Kingery, whose memories helped compose and confirm my retelling of Henry's story. Thanks also to Joe and Michelle Davidson for your steadfast prayers and support. And to my husband, Ian—your love, patience, and encouragement carried me through this process. I appreciate you more than words can express.

My exceptional agent, Greg Daniel, deserves a huge thanks for taking a chance on this new author. I'm also beyond grateful for the invaluable insights of my editor, Valerie Weaver-Zercher, for the hospitality shown by Amy Gingerich, and for the entire Herald Press team, who made this publishing venture a joy to embark upon.

A special note of appreciation goes to Greg Boyd. Through his books and podcast sermons, Greg challenged my old assumptions about God and introduced me to a beautiful, renewed picture of God based on the person of Jesus Christ. Greg, your ministry has transformed my understanding of God's character, and this knowledge was a beacon of hope and peace in my darkest days. Thank you for your inspiring leadership, for believing in this project, and for pouring your time and energy into offering feedback.

Finally, to every person who followed Henry's story, who walked with us, encouraged us, and prayed for us, I am in your debt. With all my heart, I thank you.

····

Notes

Introduction

1. See Gregory Boyd, *Is God to Blame? Moving Beyond Pat Answers to the Problem of Suffering* (Downers Grove, IL: InterVarsity Press, 2003), 41–49; and Gregory Boyd, *Satan and the Problem of Evil: Constructing a Trinitarian Warfare Theodicy* (Downers Grove, IL: InterVarsity Press, 2001), 11–13.

Chapter 2: Wrestling with the Jesus-Looking God

1. In researching the biblical passages that seem to depict God acting violently toward Jesus, I've come to realize that there are always nonviolent, and arguably better, interpretations for them. For an analysis of the verse in question, Isaiah 53:10, that doesn't result in the portrayal of God crushing his Son, see E. Robert Eckblad, "God Is Not to Blame: The Servant's Atoning Suffering according to the LXX of Isaiah 53," in Brad Jersak and Michael Hardin, *Stricken by God? Nonviolent Identification and the Victory of Christ* (Grand Rapids, MI: Eerdmans, 2007), 180–204.

Chapter 3: An Enemy Has Done This

1. Old Testament scholar Terence Fretheim provides a thorough analysis of the biblical theme of God changing his mind in "The Repentance of God: A Key to Evaluating Old Testament God Talk," *Horizons in Biblical Theology* 10 (1988): 47–70. For further discussion of the topic in this book, see "Common Questions about the Warfare Worldview," question 4.

2. What follows is a presentation of the warfare worldview that stems from the trinitarian warfare theodicy articulated by Gregory Boyd. It is intentionally written to be accessible to general audiences. For more detailed information, see Gregory Boyd, *Is God to Blame? Moving Beyond Pat Answers to the Problem of Suffering* (Downers Grove, IL: InterVarsity Press, 2003). On an academic level, see Gregory Boyd, *God at War: The Bible and Spiritual Conflict* (Downers Grove, IL: InterVarsity Press, 1997); and Gregory Boyd, *Satan and the Problem of Evil: Constructing a Trinitarian Warfare Theodicy* (Downers Grove, IL: InterVarsity Press, 2001).

3. For further information, see "Common Questions about the Warfare Worldview," question 1.

4. For more on how God's desire to expand his love required the possibility that his will may sometimes be thwarted, see "Common Questions about the Warfare Worldview," question 2.

5. See Terence Fretheim, *Creation Untamed: The Bible, God, and Natural Disasters* (Grand Rapids, MI: Baker Academic, 2010), 1–8.

6. For further information about the warfare theme that runs throughout the Bible, see Boyd, *God at War*.

7. This is not to say that God *never* specifically allows suffering. Scripture outlines some instances in which God allows suffering, such as the torturing and crucifixion of Jesus, the thorn in Paul's side (2 Cor 12:7-10), and the hardship of the Hebrew Christians (Heb 12). In these specific instances, reasons are provided as to why the suffering occurred. They are not attributed to a mysterious, divine plan. We face problems if we assign God's specific permission to *all* suffering—most notably, this view contradicts the ministry of Jesus.

8. See Gregory Boyd, "Covenantal Love," sermon, Woodland Hills Church, April 25, 2010, http://whchurch.org/sermons-media/sermon/covenantal-love.

9. Imaginative prayer is a powerful tool for spiritual development and rejuvenation. For a more extensive review of this topic, see Gregory Boyd, *Seeing Is Believing: Experience Jesus through Imaginative Prayer* (Grand Rapids, MI: Baker Books, 2004). In this book, Boyd encourages Christ-followers to rest along their path of spiritual growth. He explains that rather than relying solely on their actions to become closer to God, they must utilize their God-given imagination. Boyd outlines how believers may engage their imagination through prayer to experience a richer, more vibrant, and intimate relationship with Jesus.

Chapter 6: Henry's Tiger

1. Cultivating a moment-by-moment awareness of God's presence can transform the life of a Christ-follower. For more on this topic, see Brother Lawrence

and Frank Laubach, *Practicing His Presence*, Library of Christian Classics, vol. 1 (Jacksonville, FL: SeedSowers, 1973); and Jean-Pierre de Caussade, *The Sacrament of the Present Moment*, trans. Kitty Muggeridge (New York: HarperCollins, 2009). For an easy-to-read, modern take on practicing the presence of God, see Gregory Boyd, *Present Perfect: Finding God in the Now* (Grand Rapids, MI: Zondervan, 2010). In this book, Boyd reflects on the history of this practice, shares key Scriptures that instruct believers to adopt this moment-by-moment awareness, and provides practical advice about how to make this monumentally important goal an ongoing reality.

Chapter 7: Henry the Snowman

1. To view this Emmy Award–winning story, see Jaye Watson, "Henry's Last Holidays," video, 3:31, from a broadcast by 11Alive on October 31, 2012, http://www.11alive.com/video/1938229804001/0/Henrys-last-holidays.

Chapter 9: When Worldviews Collide

1. John Piper, "What Made It Okay for God to Kill Women and Children in the Old Testament?" transcript and podcast video, 5:36, Desiring God, February 27, 2010, http://www.desiringgod.org/interviews/what-made-it-ok-for-god-to-kill-women-and-children-in-the-old-testament. For an alternate (and recommended) interpretation of the violent depictions of God in the Bible, see Gregory Boyd, *Crucifixion of the Warrior God: A Cruciform Reinterpretation of the Divine Violence in the Old Testament* (Downers Grove, IL: InterVarsity Press, forthcoming).

2. Laura Story, "Blessings" (Brentwood, TN: INO Records, 2011).

3. While some Christians believe that God *specifically allows* evil because he will use it for a mysterious greater good (the weak form of the blueprint worldview), Calvinists such as Tada believe that God *foreordains* and guides evil to ensure his purposes are met. She credits noted Calvinist Loraine Boettner with helping her develop an understanding of God's role in her diving accident. Tada says that while reading Boettner's *The Reformed Doctrine of Predestination*, she realized that her suffering "was the key to unlocking the hieroglyphics of God's foreordained will." Joni Eareckson Tada, "Understanding God's Sovereignty" in *Indelible Ink*, ed. S. Larsen (Colorado Springs: WaterBrook Press, 2003), 8.

4. See Tada, "Understanding God's Sovereignty," 8–11; and Joni Eareckson Tada, "Turning Evil on Its Head," Ligonier Ministries, June 1, 2006, http://www.ligonier.org/learn/articles/turning-evil-its-head/.

Those who have read/heard Tada's teachings may note that she sometimes uses language suggesting that God *allows* or *permits* suffering. Yet it is important to note that she interchangeably uses terms describing God as one who "allows" and "permits" suffering with someone who "designs" and "ordains" our pain. See Joni Eareckson Tada, "A Deeper Healing" (speech, Strange Fire Conference, Sun

Valley, CA, October 2013); and Joni Eareckson Tada, "A Deeper Healing" (keynote speech, National Religious Broadcasters Convention, Nashville, TN, March 2013).

One should be aware that in a Calvinistic framework, terms such as *permit* and *allow* in relationship to God's control take on a distinct and obscure meaning. Since Calvinists hold that everything has been predetermined by God, "God's permission, then, is simply his choice to allow things to unfold as he has already determined they will." J. Walls and J. Dongell, *Why I Am Not a Calvinist* (Downers Grove, IL: InterVarsity Press, 2004), 125–34. See also Roger E. Olson, "Yes to God's Sovereignty; No to Divine Determinism," chap. 4 in *Against Calvinism* (Grand Rapids, MI: Zondervan, 2011).

5.   Tada, "Understanding God's Sovereignty," 11.

6.   Joni Eareckson Tada, *A Place of Healing: Wrestling with the Mysteries of Suffering, Pain, and God's Sovereignty* (Colorado Springs: David C. Cook, 2010), 118.

7.   This quotation and all following quotations in this section are from Joni Eareckson Tada, "God's Jewels" speech, True Woman Conference, October 2008, transcript and audio, 33:44, https://www.reviveourhearts.com/events/true-woman-08/gods-jewels/.

8.   Among other analogies, Tada compares our suffering to "divine sandblasting" needed to clean the "layers of dirty film over our souls" (*A Place of Healing*, 86–88). She likens God to a painter who will "bruise" and "batter" his early sketches to achieve his desired results (ibid., 118–19), and to a master sculptor who uses "suffering," "illness," and "disability" as his tools to shape us into the image of Christ (ibid., 67). She also praises the notion that God specifically designs trials to destroy our character flaws just as chemo is specifically designed to kill cancer cells; see Tada, "A Deeper Healing" (keynote speech, National Religious Broadcasters Convention, March 2013). Perhaps most concerning is her public declaration that her diving accident and resulting paralysis are God's discipline for her teenage antics, such as making beer runs with friends; see Joni Eareckson Tada, "Sin and Suffering," Joni and Friends, podcast audio and transcript, 3:59, June 10, 2011, http://www.joniandfriends.org/radio/5-minute/sin-and-suffering.

Across the numerous books, articles, essays, talks, and blog posts authored by Joni that I have read and heard, I found only one line in one book that says that "not all suffering is God's discipline," but this is never nuanced and no alternative explanation is provided. In fact, in the remainder of that section, Tada encourages Christians to appreciate and persevere through their suffering and says that "if the pain and discomfort of your difficult circumstances persist . . . God's up to something pretty special in your life!" (*A Place of Healing*, 118–19).

9.   *Merriam-Webster Online* s.v. "Torture," accessed September 23, 2015, http://www.merriam-webster.com/dictionary/torture.

10. Tada points to Hebrews 12:7-9 while explaining that much of the suffering we endure is God's discipline. Yet while Christians commonly lump all suffering together, I'd offer that there are (at least) two distinct types of suffering that a Christ-follower may experience: (1) suffering related to persecution for one's faith and (2) suffering related to sources like abuse, disease, and natural disasters.

While there may occasionally be some overlap between the two, it's important to note that suffering for one's faith involves *choice*. It results when people "take up their cross" and follow Jesus regardless of threats to their personal safety. It is the organic consequence of following Christ in a war-torn world. Suffering due to abuse, disease, or natural disaster *does not involve choice*, however, and it affects believers and nonbelievers alike. There is no evidence that Christians have higher or lower rates of illness, disease, or devastation related to natural disasters.

It should also be noted that suffering by persecution for one's faith is *consistent* with the ministry and message of Jesus. In contrast, assuming that suffering related to abuse, disease, or natural disasters was designed by God *contradicts* the ministry and message of Jesus. He never suggested suffering comes from God. To the contrary, he uniformly healed the sick and rebuked many ailments as coming from Satan and/or demons.

Hebrews 12 concludes that section by explaining that God's discipline "is for our good, in order that we may share in his holiness" and that it "produces a harvest of righteousness and peace for those who have been trained by it." As we consider tragedies like the death of children, we see how different such trauma is from what this passage describes. For starters, the death of children will not "work together for their good," because death strips them of an opportunity to participate in the refinement process. To assert that their deaths refine their parents is to suggest that God cares more about parents' growth than bringing the child "life to the full," or even life at all! Second, in many cases, immense grief and radical suffering leave behind a lasting wake of devastation rather than a "harvest of righteousness and peace." While healing and comfort can follow for the brokenhearted, and while purpose can be brought to the pain, this is vastly different from suggesting that God sows evil and death to reap a harvest of righteousness.

For more on this issue, see also Gregory Boyd, *Is God to Blame? Moving Beyond Pat Answers to the Problem of Suffering* (Downers Grove, IL: InterVarsity Press, 2003), 80–83.

11. Mark Hall, Matthew West, and Bernie Herms, "Already There," performed by Casting Crowns (Nashville: Beach Street/Reunion Records, 2011).

12. Rick Warren, *The Purpose Driven Life: What on Earth Am I Here For?* expanded ed. (Grand Rapids, MI: Zondervan, 2002), 194–95.

13. Ibid., 56.

14. Ibid., 194. Emphasis in the original.

15. Ibid., 193. It's also important to note that Warren, like Tada and other Calvinists, seems to hold a distinct and obscure definition for terms like *permission* in regard to God's role in our suffering (see chap. 9, n. 4). Warren self-identifies as a "Monergist" instead of a "Calvinist." In an extended interview on the doctrines behind *The Purpose Driven Life* with noted Calvinist John Piper, Warren agreed with Piper on nearly every doctrinal issue raised, from unconditional election to a micro-controlling view of God's sovereignty. He noted in the interview that he only avoids the Calvinist label because of the negative connotations that it carries; see John Piper, "John Piper Interviews Rick Warren on Doctrine," Desiring God, video, 1:38:42, May 27, 2011, http://www.desiringgod.org/blog/posts/john-piper-interviews-rick-warren-on-doctrine.

16. Warren, *The Purpose Driven Life*, 194.

17. Ibid., 195.

18. Ibid., 195–96.

19. Ibid., 59.

20. Ibid., 195.

21. Ibid.

22. Barack Obama, "Remarks by the President at Sandy Hook Interfaith Prayer Vigil," December 16, 2012, transcript, Office of the Press Secretary, The White House, http://www.whitehouse.gov/the-press-office/2012/12/16/remarks-president-sandy-hook-interfaith-prayer-vigil.

23. Warren, *The Purpose Driven Life*, 198.

24. For more information on how the crucifixion reveals God's attributes, see Boyd, *Is God to Blame?* 38–39.

25. Mary Beth Chapman and Ellen Vaughn, *Choosing to See: A Journey of Struggle and Hope* (Grand Rapids, MI: Revell, 2010), 212–13.

26. Ibid., 221–22.

27. Ibid., 235, emphasis in original.

28. Ibid., 238–39.

29. Ibid., 251.

30. Ibid., 153.

31. Ann Voskamp, *One Thousand Gifts: A Dare to Live Fully Right Where You Are* (Grand Rapids, MI: Zondervan, 2010). Emphasis in the original. Quotations from pp. 100, 125, 40, 125–26, 40, and 148, respectively.

32. Ibid., 88.

33. Ibid., 153.

34. Ibid., 153–54.

35. Ibid., 155–56.

36. Ibid., 157.

37. Author unknown, quoted in Olson, *Against Calvinism*, 25.

Chapter 10: Passionless Hope

1. See Gregory Boyd, *The Myth of a Christian Religion: Losing Your Religion for the Beauty of a Revolution* (Grand Rapids, MI: Zondervan, 2009), 78–80. For more information about how Isaiah 55:8-9 does *not* describe a love that humans cannot recognize but rather attests to a love that is *greater* (i.e., more merciful and forgiving) than the Israelites' expectations, see John Sanders, *The God Who Risks: A Theology of Divine Providence* (Downers Grove, IL: InterVarsity Press, 2007), 27–28; and Richard Rice, "Biblical Support for a New Perspective," in Clark Pinnock et al., *The Openness of God: A Biblical Challenge to the Traditional Understanding of God* (Downers Grove, IL: InterVarsity Press, 1994), 42–43. John Goldingay notes that this passage is similar to Psalm 103:11, in which God's great love and forgiveness is being compared to the height of the heavens. He acknowledges that although it may seem unbelievable, Yhwh's plans and ways "are spectacularly centred on a compassion that issues in pardon." *The Message of Isaiah 40–55: A Literary-Theological Commentary* (New York: T and T Clark, 2005), 553–54.

2. Joni Eareckson Tada, *A Place of Healing: Wrestling with the Mysteries of Suffering, Pain, and God's Sovereignty* (Colorado Springs: David C. Cook, 2010), 34.

3. Rick Warren, *The Purpose Driven Life: What on Earth Am I Here For?* expanded ed. (Grand Rapids, MI: Zondervan, 2002), 195.

4. Emphasis mine. Other translations that depict this divine-human co-operation include the NEB, GNB, REB, NIV margin, NJB, and Goodspeed. Roger Forster and Paul Marston support this rendering of Romans 8:28 and say it is a "call to action" for Christians "to work with God to bring good into the world." *God's Strategy in Human History*, vol.1, *God's Path to Victory*, 3rd ed. (London: PUSH Publishing, 2013), 27. Robert Jewett writes, "Paul's wording implies divine and human co-responsibility in the face of adversity." *Romans: A Commentary, Hermeneia—A Critical and Historical Commentary on the Bible* (Minneapolis, MN: Fortress, 2007), 527. John A. T. Robinson adds, "the idea of God cooperating with us is thoroughly Pauline, as is our description as 'co-operators with God' (1 Cor 3:9)." *Wrestling with Romans* (Philadelphia: Westminster, 1979), 105. Dale Moody asserts that the synergistic emphasis of the NEB is "just right" when it says God "co-operates for good with those who love God." *The Word of Truth: A Summary of Christian Doctrine Based on Biblical Revelation* (Grand Rapids, MI:

Eerdmans, 1981), 314, 342. It should also be noted that the NIV's translation, "in all things God works for the good of those who love him," does not imply causation. It simply states that whatever happens (good or bad), God is working for good.

5. Timothy Geddert, *Double Take: New Meanings from Old Stories* (Hillsboro, KS: Kindred Productions, 2007), 173–78. Emphasis in the original. Geddert explains that in Romans 8:28 the Greek verb for "work together" is *sunergei*. He points out that, in the New Testament, *sunergei* is always used in regard to two or more parties "working together" (Mark 16:20; 1 Cor 16:16; 2 Cor 6:1; James 2:22). Geddert also notes that the noun associated with this verb, "*sunergos* i.e. co-worker, helper, fellow worker," is used in this same manner every time—to portray "two or more parties that are working along with each other." (*Double Take*, 176; Geddert cites Rom 16:3, 9, 21; 1 Cor 3:9; 2 Cor 1:24; 8:23; Phil 2:25; 4:3; Col 4:11; 1 Thess 3:2; Philem 24; and 2 John 8). See also Forster and Marston, *God's Strategy*, 25–27.

6. Geddert, *Double Take*, 177.

Chapter 11: The Lord Gives . . . and Takes?

1. All the quotations in this paragraph except the final one come from Terence Fretheim, *Creation Untamed: The Bible, God, and Natural Disasters* (Grand Rapids, MI: Baker Academic, 2010), 68. John H. Walton offers the phrase "thought experiment" in *Job*, The NIV Application Commentary (Grand Rapids, MI: Zondervan, 2012), 26.

2. See Walton, *Job*, 24–27.

3. Tryggve Mettinger, "The God of Job: Avenger, Tyrant, or Victor?" in *The Voice from the Whirlwind: Interpreting the Book of Job*, ed. Leo G. Perdue and W. Clark Gilpin (Nashville, TN: Abingdon, 1992), 39.

4. Terence Fretheim, *God and World in the Old Testament: A Relational Theology of Creation* (Nashville, TN: Abingdon, 2005), 221.

5. Rather than the NIV's translation "angels," most interpretations refer to these celestial beings as "sons of God"; see Walton, *Job*, 63–64.

6. For more on the prologue of the book of Job being a work of "dramatic fiction," see Fretheim, *Creation Untamed*, 68. Concerning the need for God to accept the challenge presented by Satan, Gregory Boyd writes, "in the context of this narrative this assault can be refuted only by being put to a test." *Is God to Blame? Moving Beyond Pat Answers to the Problem of Suffering* (Downers Grove, IL: InterVarsity Press, 2003), 86.

7. Walton asserts that we cannot consider the opening scene in heaven to be "a source of information about God's activities and nature" (*Job*, 26). Robert Fyall

notes that it would be "illegitimate" for us to glean from the prologue's wager that God is a "cosmic dramatist interested only in a suspenseful story and so indifferent to the lives even of his servants that he plays with them to win a bet." *Now My Eyes Have Seen You: Images of Creation and Evil in the Book of Job*, New Studies in Biblical Theology 12 (Downers Grove, IL: InterVarsity Press, 2002), 35.

8. See Boyd, *Is God to Blame?* 85–87.

9. For more on how the ancient Israelites believed the retribution principle was the "main determining factor for God's activity" and tended to allow its converse corollary to "formulate their theodicy," see Walton, *Job*, 44–48.

10. Walton asserts that God's declaration that "Job spoke rightly" meant that Job's words were "sensible, logical, or able to be confirmed or verified" given his picture of God, and that Job's words were "understandable but not correct" (ibid., 173–74, 433–34). Fretheim offers that God's praise was for Job's courageous, honest "lamenting" rather than an endorsement of Job's theological position (*God and World*, 221–23, 246, 360, n. 158). C. L. Seow demonstrates that God's praise affirms the lament tradition, which involves speaking *to* God (as Job did) rather than *about* God (as Job's friends did) by affirming even these extreme laments that "border on blasphemy." *Job 1–21: Interpretation and Commentary* (Grand Rapids, MI: Eerdmans, 2013), 87–92. And Boyd affirms that Job's words were considered by God to be "straightforward" or "honest," unlike the self-serving words of Job's friends; see Gregory Boyd, *Benefit of the Doubt: Breaking the Idol of Certainty* (Grand Rapids, MI: Baker Books, 2013), 87–88.

11. Fyall asserts that Job's repentance, after he encounters God in the whirlwind, was based on his "ignorance and presumptuousness" (*Now My Eyes Have Seen You*, 53). It is Job's acknowledgement that "his idea of God had been limited," and it's a response consistent with one who receives "an awesome revelation" (ibid., 178). Fretheim offers that Job's confessions in the prologue (1:21; 2:10) probably reflect "conventional piety" and that in 42:5 we find Job standing "in judgment over his prior piety, declaring it hearsay" (*God and World*, 225). See also J. C. L. Gibson, "On Evil in the Book of Job," in *Ascribe to the Lord: Biblical and Other Studies in Memory of Peter C. Craigie*, ed. L. Eslinger and G. Taylor, JSOT Supp. 67 (Sheffield, U.K.: Sheffield Academic, 1988), 414.

12. Fretheim, *God and World*, 231.

13. Fyall, *Now My Eyes Have Seen You*, 103.

14. Fretheim, *God and World*, 223; Fyall, *Now My Eyes Have Seen You*, 18; Mettinger, "The God of Job," 48; Walton, *Job*, 410. While these commentators agree that the author's perspective is found in the God speeches, they do not necessarily agree on what that perspective is.

15. Fretheim notes that the "evaluation of the perspectives of others" is a "key thread" in this book and that "readers of Job are . . . invited to engage in a hermeneutics of evaluation" in their interpretation (*God and World*, 222).

16. Fyall asserts that "the battle with evil is a major motif in the book as a whole" (*Now My Eyes Have Seen You*, 20). He links Satan to the "abundant references to spiritual powers" throughout the book (ibid., 37), namely in the mention of ancient Near Eastern deities such as "Leviathan (3:8); Yam and Tannin (7:12); Sea (9:8 and 38:8-11); Rahab (9:13 and 26:12); the gliding serpent (26:13)" (ibid., 168). See also Mettinger, "The God of Job," 39–49; and Gibson, "On Evil in the Book of Job," 399–419.

17. Fyall describes the heavenly court as "the realization that there are powers in the universe other than God and that they exercise great influence on the course of events" and notes that it is "not only the narrative device for setting the plot in motion but the controlling reality behind the whole book" (*Now My Eyes Have Seen You*, 34, 37).

18. Ibid., 20.

19. Some scholars assert that Behemoth and Leviathan are simply depictions of natural animals (i.e., hippo, crocodile). Fyall offers that these creatures, "while containing elements drawn from physical characteristics and habits of animals," should arguably be regarded as "embodiments of the powers of death and evil" (ibid., 128–29). In chapters 6–8 of *Now My Eyes Have Seen You*, Fyall makes an extended case for how Behemoth and Leviathan are references to mythological creatures that ancient Near Eastern audiences would have recognized as sources of rebellious cosmic powers. He notes that "the Hebrews had a profound knowledge of the mythological language of their day and they used it in a powerful and creative way to express their new revelation of a transcendent deity, his power as Creator, his providence and his battle with evil at both a cosmic and an earthly level" (ibid., 137). See also Mettinger, "The God of Job," 39–49; and Gibson, "On Evil in the Book of Job," 399–419.

20. Fyall, *Now My Eyes Have Seen You*, 18, 141, 157.

21. Gibson, "On Evil in the Book of Job," 417.

22. Mettinger, "The God of Job," 39–49.

23. For more on this verse, see "Common Questions about the Warfare Worldview," question 2.

24. See Fretheim, *God and World*, 224–26. For more on how the retribution principle was presented in the book of Job in order to be overturned, see Gibson, "On Evil in the Book of Job," 412. For further study about how the retribution principle works well as a theology (offering a picture of God's nature) but fails to render a complete theodicy (explanation of God's role in evil), see Walton, *Job*, 39–48.

Walton notes that the "role of the book of Job is to perform the radical surgery that separates theology from theodicy" (ibid., 41). Gregory Boyd offers that Job 1:21, as well as the book as a whole, was written to expose the inadequacies of the belief that God unilaterally controls both good and evil, as well as the resulting implication that God's character is arbitrarily cruel and mysterious; see Boyd, *Satan and the Problem of Evil, Constructing a Trinitarian Warfare Theodicy* (Downers Grove, IL: InterVarsity Press, 2001), 403–6.

Chapter 12: A Beautiful Answer

1. Rick Warren, Twitter post, May 22, 2013, 2:07 a.m., http://twitter.com/RickWarren.

2. Rainer Rilke, *Letters to a Young Poet* (New York: Penguin Group, 2011), 18.

3. Bart D. Ehrman, *God's Problem: How the Bible Fails to Answer Our Most Important Question—Why We Suffer* (New York: HarperCollins, 2008), title, 1.

4. For more on how the loving will of an all-powerful God could be thwarted, see "Common Questions about the Warfare Worldview," question 2.

Common Questions about the Warfare Worldview

1. Peter Kreeft, *The God Who Loves You* (original edition *Knowing the Truth of God's Love*, Ann Arbor, MI: Servant Books, 1988; reprint San Francisco: Ignatius Press, 2004), 95. In relation to God's wrath, Kreeft also writes, "It is real, but it is not part of God Himself. God is not half love and half wrath, or 99 percent love and 1 percent wrath. God *is* love. Wrath is how His love appears to us when we sin or rebel or run away from Him. The very light that is meant to help us appears to us as our enemy when we seek the darkness" (ibid., 128). For more information about God's love being his essence/foundational attribute, see Richard Rice, "Biblical Support For a New Perspective," in Clark Pinnock et al., *The Openness of God: A Biblical Challenge to the Traditional Understanding of God* (Downers Grove, IL: InterVarsity Press, 1994), 18–22; and John Sanders, *The God Who Risks: A Theology of Divine Providence* (Downers Grove, IL: InterVarsity Press, 2007), 177–82.

2. For more on scriptural support for God's will being thwarted and a discussion of key passages that supposedly support the blueprint worldview, see Gregory Boyd, *Is God to Blame? Moving Beyond Pat Answers to the Problem of Suffering* (Downers Grove, IL: InterVarsity Press, 2003), chap. 9; and Gregory Boyd, *Satan and the Problem of Evil: Constructing a Trinitarian Warfare Theodicy* (Downers Grove, IL: InterVarsity Press, 2001), 93, 394–416.

3. Boyd, *Is God to Blame?*, 178.

4. Sanders, *The God Who Risks*, 243.

5. For more on freedom being, by its very definition, irrevocable, see Boyd, *Is God to Blame?* 115–21; and Boyd, *Satan and the Problem of Evil*, 178–86.

6. C. S. Lewis, *The Problem of Pain* (New York: Harper Collins, 1940), 18.

7. Ibid., 129–30.

8. J. Walls and J. Dongell, *Why I Am Not a Calvinist* (Downers Grove, IL: InterVarsity Press, 2004), 219.

9. John Calvin, *The Gospel according to St. John*, trans. T. H. L. Parker, 2 vols. (Grand Rapids, MI: Eerdmans, 1959), 1:239.

10. Gary M. Burge asserts that most English translations of John 9:3, including the NIV, "invite gross confusion with Jesus' answer." *John*, The NIV Application Commentary (Grand Rapids, MI: Zondervan, 2000), 272. John C. Poirier notes that traditional translations imply a bizarre theodicy in " 'Day and Night' and the Punctuation of John 9:3," *New Testament Studies* 42 (1996), 288–94.

11. Burge, *John*, 272–73. Burge also notes that this translation aligns with four other instances in the book of John where the Greek *all' hina* precedes the main sentence (1:31; 13:18; 14:31; 15:25). See also Poirier, " 'Day and Night,' " 288–94; Craig R. Koester, *Symbolism in the Fourth Gospel: Meaning, Mystery, Community*, 2nd ed. (Minneapolis: Fortress, 2003), 104–5; Colin G. Kruse, *The Gospel according to John: An Introduction and Commentary*, Tyndale New Testament Commentaries (Grand Rapids, MI: Eerdmans, 2004), 220–21; Barclay M. Newman and Eugene A. Nida, *A Translator's Handbook on the Gospel of John* (New York: United Bible Societies, 1980) 299–300; and Roger Forster and Paul Marston, *God's Strategy in Human History*, vol. 1, *God's Path to Victory*, 3rd ed. (London: PUSH Publishing, 2013), 28–29.

12. Nigel Turner, *Grammatical Insights into the New Testament* (Edinburgh: T and T Clark, 1965), 145–48. See also Gregory A. Boyd, *God at War: The Bible and Spiritual Conflict* (Downers Grove, IL: InterVarsity Press, 1997), 231–34.

13. Poirier argues that shifting the punctuation of John 9:3-4 renders a translation that fits better with the narrative structure of the whole chapter and brings more coherence to Jesus' terminology around *light* and *darkness*; see " 'Day and Night,' " 288–94. Another example of Jesus negating the type of faulty worldview that his disciples demonstrate in John 9:1-2 can be found in Luke 13:1-5. Here Jesus addresses recent Galilean murders and a tower collapse that resulted in multiple deaths. In both cases, Jesus dismisses the notion that those who died were worse sinners than those standing before him. Instead, he changes the conversation's direction and brings the audience's attention to their own standing with God, saying, "But unless you repent, you too will all perish."

14. Koester, *Symbolism in the Fourth Gospel*, 104–5.

15. See Gregory A. Boyd, *God of the Possible: A Biblical Introduction to the Open View of God* (Grand Rapids, MI: Baker Books, 2000). Boyd provides an easily accessible, comprehensive yet concise overview on the concepts presented here; I am grateful to Shelley Boyd for supplying the phrase "God over-knows the future."

16. See Boyd, *God of the Possible*, 40–42.

17. For an examination of texts that supposedly contradict the warfare worldview (Rom 9; Isa 45:7; Lam 3:37-38; etc.), see Boyd, *Is God to Blame?*, chaps. 8–9; and Boyd, *Satan and the Problem of Evil*, 359–66, 394–416.

The Author

*J*essica *Kelley* is a writer, speaker, and survivor of child loss. She has degrees in psychology and counseling and has worked as a school counselor. Born and raised in the South, Jessica now lives with her husband and five-year-old daughter in Saint Paul, Minnesota. She survives the absurdly long winters by going to the gym, dreaming about the beach, and eating copious amounts of chocolate. You can find her processing her faith journey at JessicaKelley.com.